High Expectations Teaching

W9-AJU-752

"You have to erase eight or nine years of low or no expectations,"
Mr. Jenkins said. "You have to make them un-believe what
they've been taught to believe."

—Patricia Leigh Brown

High Expectations Teaching

How We Persuade Students to Believe and Act on "Smart Is Something You Can Get"

Jon Saphier

Foreword by Ronald F. Ferguson

A Joint Publication

FOR INFORMATION:

Corwin

A SAGE Company

2455 Teller Road

Thousand Oaks, California 91320

(800) 233-9936

www.corwin.com

SAGE Publications Ltd.

1 Oliver's Yard

55 City Road

London EC1Y 1SP

United Kingdom

SAGE Publications India Pvt. Ltd.

B 1/I 1 Mohan Cooperative Industrial Area

Mathura Road, New Delhi 110 044

India

SAGE Publications Asia-Pacific Pte. Ltd.

3 Church Street

#10-04 Samsung Hub

Singapore 049483

Program Director: Dan Alpert

Senior Associate Editor: Kimberly Greenberg

Editorial Assistant: Katie Crilley

Production Editor: Cassandra Margaret Seibel

Copy Editor: Sarah J. Duffy

Typesetter: C&M Digitals (P) Ltd.

Proofreader: Caryne Brown

Indexer: Terri Morrissey

Cover Designer: Scott Van Atta

Marketing Manager: Charline Maher

Copyright © 2017 by Corwin

All rights reserved. When forms and sample documents are included, their use is authorized only by educators, local school sites, and/or noncommercial or nonprofit entities that have purchased the book. Except for that usage, no part of this book may be reproduced or utilized in any form or by any means, electronic or mechanical, including photocopying, recording, or by any information storage and retrieval system, without permission in writing from the publisher.

All trademarks depicted within this book, including trademarks appearing as part of a screenshot, figure, or other image, are included solely for the purpose of illustration and are the property of their respective holders. The use of the trademarks in no way indicates any relationship with, or endorsement by, the holders of said trademarks.

"Smart Is Something You Can Get." This statement was originated by Jeff Howard and Verna Ford of the Efficacy Institute and has been a foundation of their work for 35 years.

Printed in the United States of America.

ISBN 978-1-5063-5679-2

This book is printed on acid-free paper.

SUSTAINABLE FORESTRY INITIATIVE
Certified Chain of Custody
Promoting Sustainable Forestry
www.sfiprogram.org
SFI-01268

SFI label applies to text stock

16 17 18 19 20 10 9 8 7 6 5 4 3 2 1

DISCLAIMER: This book may direct you to access third-party content via Web links, QR codes, or other scannable technologies, which are provided for your reference by the author. Corwin makes no guarantee that such third-party content will be available for your use and encourages you to review the terms and conditions of such third-party content. Corwin takes no responsibility and assumes no liability for your use of any third-party content, nor does Corwin approve, sponsor, endorse, verify, or certify such third-party content.

Contents

List of Resources

QR codes and URLs for the following resources appear throughout the book. To read a QR code, you must have a smartphone or tablet with a camera. We recommend that you download a QR code reader app that is made specifically for your phone or tablet brand.

Chapter 1

Video 1.1   A video presentation of the information in Chapter 1.

Chapter 2

Video 2.1   A video presentation of the information in Chapter 2.

Chapter 3

Video 3.1   Richard Rosenthal describes the study that was the basis for *Pygmalion in the Classroom*.

Video 3.2   High school teacher Pierre Gilles gives help in an empowering way.

Video 3.3   Ms. Moore responds to Ricardo (persevere and return).

Video 3.4   Ms. Alcala demonstrates the "My Favorite No" routine.

Video 3.5   Dealing with errors unfolds in Alyssa Ricken's first-grade class.

Video 3.6   Listen for the language of high and positive expectations in the way Zach Herrmann frames the re-teach.

Video 3.7   Michael talks with Yojii the day after the two had a scheduled one-on-one appointment after class and Yojii didn't show up.

Video 3.8   Mr. Herrmann uses positive attributions to frame re-teaching.

Chapter 4

Chapter 5

Chapter 6

Foreword

Every summer for the past five years, I have asked Jon Saphier to teach in the "Closing the Achievement Gap" summer institute that I chair in association with the Harvard Graduate School of Education's Programs in Professional Education. The reason is that no one makes more sense to me when it comes to teaching than Jon Saphier.

I had heard of Jon and his organization Research for Better Teaching before. But I did not appreciate his role in the field until I organized a conference in 2009 on schools that had narrowed gaps while raising overall achievement levels. As I tracked down such schools in Massachusetts and around the nation, I asked the leaders how they knew what to do. In several cases, including then-principal Susan Szachowicz of Brockton High School in Massachusetts and even the whole district of Montgomery County, Maryland, the answer was, "Jon told us how." Indeed, in Montgomery County, they created a department in the system specifically for the purpose of teaching his "the Skillful Teacher" curriculum to the district's educators.

This book, including the videos to which it links by using QR codes, is Jon's crowning achievement. In it, he packs wisdom from four decades during which he has stayed abreast of research on teaching, distilled it into practical implications, and worked with educators to embed those implications into their repertoires. Over the years, Jon has witnessed the types of transformation that are possible when the ideas in this book take hold. He believes that most teachers have unrealized potential just as their students do. He's convinced that the ideas in this book can help them harvest it.

While there are many ways he could have framed the book, Jon chose to focus on the idea that belief in *effort based ability*, better known these days as *growth mindset*, can greatly reduce racial and socioeconomic achievement gaps. He is careful to credit Jeff Howard and Carol Dweck. It was Jeff—Jon calls him "an unsung hero"—who first organized a way of thinking and talking about how "rumors of inferiority" made students of color doubt their ability to learn and then underperform academically. Then and now, Jeff's focus has been on racial disparities and helping children of color achieve to their potential. Carol Dweck has focused on mindsets more generally, producing evidence that a *fixed mindset* undermines persistence and fosters a *performance orientation*, whereas believing that intelligence is malleable—having a *growth mindset*—promotes persistence and supports a *mastery orientation*.

The early work that Jon cites has spawned a rapidly expanding field in which researchers—many of them Carol's students and their students—are documenting ever more ways that mindsets and beliefs can affect performance. There are research networks spanning numerous universities and think tanks. Among the more prominent are the Carnegie Foundation's Networked Improvement Communities and the Mindset Scholar's Network, which brings together both junior and senior scholars from 14 universities in the United States. There is much in this book that scholars in these networks and others could focus on in efforts to disseminate and evaluate effective approaches to teaching.

If you are a teacher, this book provides ideas and examples for things you can do if you truly believe in effort-based ability *and even if you don't*. Twenty-five years ago, I studied the implementation in Oklahoma of an approach to teaching that many teachers resisted when their schools introduced it. The approach had been distilled from the work of Marva Collins, a master teacher in Chicago about whom a movie was made with Cicely Tyson in the starring role. Collins's approach had much in common with ideas this book. I was surprised to find that even among teachers who successfully implemented the approach—teachers who experienced big improvements in student engagement and even standardized test scores—belief was the product of success more than the cause of it. The cause of success was action. Action to implement the approach produced results even before the teachers believed it would make any difference. This is not an uncommon sequence. Effective leaders in such instances are pivotal in providing the reminders, monitoring, supports, and nudges that lead to action before belief.

Jon writes, "to get [students] to believe it, we have to act as if we [their teachers] believe it ourselves in all the daily interactions of class instruction and class business that make up the emotional environment. And we have to create structures and routines that would exist only if we believed our students could be successful at a proficient level." This book is a treasure trove of wisdom on high expectations teaching. Study it carefully because details matter. Apply it relentlessly and watch what happens. Then share your story and help others benefit from Jon's remarkable insights.

Ronald F. Ferguson
Faculty Director of the Achievement Gap Initiative at Harvard
University, Co-Founder of Tripod Education Partners, Inc., and Creator
of Tripod Student and Teacher Surveys

Acknowledgments

In the fall of 2015, my colleague Kathy Spencer realized that for four decades I had been digging into the detailed behavior of how high expectations teachers acted, minute-to-minute, in their verbal interaction with students and other arenas of classroom life. These observations were part of the book *The Skillful Teacher* and part of numerous courses we taught, but not pulled together in any one place. She urged me to do that "pulling together" and put it in a book others could study. So thank you to Kathy for pushing me over the edge to write this book.

In the early 1980s, I attended a course taught by Jeff Howard on what he called the efficacy paradigm. His point, summarized in a graphic in this book on page 34, was that ability could be grown and the bell curve of intelligence was wrong. Jeff not only caused me to challenge long-held beliefs, but set in motion the quest, laid out in this book, to profile in detail how teachers get underperforming, low-confidence students to believe "smart is something you can get." We often strove to work together in school districts where Jeff and his team would precipitate the paradigm shift in educators' beliefs, and we at Research for Better Teaching (RBT) would show how to act in one's teaching behavior from those beliefs.

In that same decade Jeff brought Carol Dweck up from New York (she was at Teachers College at the time) to share her pioneering research on what she called the incrementalist versus the fixed mindset. These two pioneers laid the groundwork for the current explosion of interest in the growth mindset, finally liberated by Dweck's popular book, *Mindset*.

Lauren Resnick picked up the ball from Jeff Howard in the 1990s and brought the belief that ability can be grown to her important program on accountable talk at the Institute for Learning at the University of Pittsburgh.

Lest we forget, Madeline Hunter had also been a strong advocate of working deliberately to get students to attribute their success or failure to the degree of effective effort they had put forth. A decade earlier, Jerome Weiner had correlated success in life with such attributions in his ground-breaking work on attribution theory.

Also let us remember Alfred Bandura's important contributions in the 1960s and 1970s on the importance of self-efficacy beliefs, summarized in *Self-Efficacy: The Exercise of Control*.

Our consultants at RBT have been thought partners with me for decades on High Expectations Teaching. They have all contributed to our collective knowledge and created outstanding training on this material: Marcia Booth, Jan Burres, Laura Cooper, Renee DeWald, Karen Falkenberg, Reena Freedman, MaryAnn Haley-Speca, Elizabeth Imende-Cooney, Nancy Love, Sue McGregor, Deb Reed, Harriet Scarborough, Ruth Sernak, Kathy Spencer, Ann Stern, Aminata Umoja, Jim Warnock, and DeNelle West. Carole Fiorentino, who served RBT so effectively for over two decades, did a final service by making a score of references accurate. Nancy Love especially made key edits in the final weeks of production.

Many thanks are due the teachers and administrators over the decades who have allowed us to make videos of their fine work and share their case studies.

Finally, my wife Margie and four children Genny, Graeme, Greg, and Andrew have each taught me much about the power of persistence and self-efficacy. They have achieved high proficiency at skills for which they had no modeling and no background simply because they wanted to and believed they could. And thank God I never discouraged them.

PUBLISHER'S ACKNOWLEDGMENTS

Corwin would like to gratefully acknowledge the contributions of the following reviewers:

Janice Bradley, PhD
School Improvement Specialist
Utah Education Policy Center, University of Utah
Salt Lake City, UT

Jude A. Huntz
Professor of Philosophy
Penn Valley Community College
Kansas City, MO

Kelly Minick
English Teacher/Instructional Coach
Saluda High School
Saluda, SC

Shanna Peeples
High School English Teacher/English Department Chair
Palo Duro High School
Amarillo, TX

About the Author

Jon Saphier is the founder and president of Research for Better Teaching, Inc., an educational consulting organization in Acton, Massachusetts, that is dedicated to the professionalization of teaching and leadership. Since 1979, he and his RBT colleagues have taught in-depth professional development programs centered on the knowledge base of teaching to educators in more than 200 school districts each year in the United States and other countries.

In 2001, he was appointed a panel member for the National Research Council of the National Academy of Sciences to study the best methods for transferring well-established educational research knowledge to classroom practice. In 2010 RBT's Skillful Teacher model was adopted by the country of Singapore as its national program for training beginning teachers.

He is much in demand for inspirational keynotes and conference presentations across the country. Sloan-Kettering's annual IDEA Institutes voted him "Best of the Best" for their first 25-year history. In recent years he has led large-scale district improvement projects forging working alliances between superintendents, union leaders, and school boards.

Dr. Saphier presents each year at Ron Ferguson's Achievement Gap Initiative Conference at Harvard. In addition to teaching the courses RBT offers and consulting to districts on organizational development, Dr. Saphier has done on-site coaching to more than 1,000 principals on instructional leadership.

Dr. Saphier has a bachelor's degree from Amherst College and a master's degree from the London School of Economics. He was a combat medic in Vietnam. After the war he entered teaching and holds degrees in early childhood from the University of Massachusetts and a doctorate from Boston University. He has been a high school history teacher and has taught fifth grade, second grade, first grade and kindergarten. He has been an administrator and a staff developer in an urban K–8 school.

Dr. Saphier is an author and co-author of eight books, including *The Skillful Teacher* (soon to bring out its seventh edition), *How to Make Supervision and Evaluation Really Work, How to Bring Vision to School Improvement, How to Make Decisions That Stay Made,* and more recently, *On Common Ground* and *John Adams' Promise,* as well as numerous articles. *The Skillful Teacher* has sold over a half million copies and is the bible of teaching in hundreds of districts around the country. It is used as a text in 60 university teacher preparation programs, including Harvard, Yale, Princeton, Columbia, Dartmouth, Brown, Middlebury, and Williams.

Introduction

This book is about getting our students to believe in themselves, to believe that they have able brains, and to believe that effort is the main determinant of their academic success, thus the subtitle "Smart Is Something You Can Get." If they are behind academically, it is not because there is anything wrong with their brains or that their "ability" is deficient.

We will alternately call this belief and knowing how to act from it a belief in *malleable ability, effort-based ability,* and the *growth mindset*: malleable ability meaning ability can be altered, effort-based ability meaning one's ability to do something is based on the effort extended to build it, and growth mindset meaning believing one can grow one's ability.

For students to accept this message, they need to hear that *we* believe in their capacity and they need to be surrounded by an environment that sends these messages at every turn:

- What we're doing is important.
- You can do it.
- And I'm not going to give up on you.

These messages don't get sent by osmosis, cheerleading, or signage. They get sent through everyday behavior—what a teacher says and does. It is not a matter of personality, but it is a matter of behavior.

It will help to share current research with students and teach them about brain plasticity, but that will not be enough for many students. This is because most of them have already accepted the message of the bell curve that ability is fixed . . . ability to do math, to do sports, to do public speaking—anything. This book assembles the evidence that fixed ability is a myth.

All children in all schools, regardless of income or social class, will benefit from the application of the skills in this book. But for children of poverty and children of color, our proficiency with these skills is essential, in many ways life-saving. I am well aware that children of color and children of poverty are in a vortex of many pernicious forces that limit their opportunity to learn and that tell them they are "less than." These forces range from pervasive racism to restrictive housing policies that trap minorities in environments of poverty and low opportunity, to inadequate health care, to public transportation systems that make it hard to get to work from poor neighborhoods, to an unfair criminal justice system. We acknowledge the influence of all these factors on far too many children. But the one thing we can do the most about is the messaging and positive support, both emotionally and instructionally, of the environments we control—the classroom and the school. And the power of that environment has been demonstrated again and again (see schools identified each year on the Education Trust's website).

The point we want to make here is that students who are on the low end of the achievement gap—usually children of color and often also of poverty—have been getting messages about their "ability" all their lives and have experienced being behind academically so long that they have bought the story. How could they not? So if we are to eliminate the achievement gap, we have to change these students' minds about their supposed low ability and persuade them about the benefits of becoming good students. Taking that on will bring us face-to-face with our *own* beliefs about our students' capacity, our own biases, our racial assumptions, and our own inevitable doubt about malleable ability.

If one grows up in the United States, it is impossible to escape the pervasive message that ability is fixed, unchangeable, and unevenly distributed. So as we attempt to inspire our students to believe in themselves, we will need to wrestle with our own histories and conclusions about our own abilities.

There is an embedded concept about the job of teaching here that is particularly important for underperforming, low-confidence students. It goes like this: Our job, especially with students who are behind, is to (1) convince them that they can grow their ability, (2) show them how, and (3) motivate them to want to. To take on this mission we will need to be convinced ourselves that ability can be grown, and we will have to become convinced that learning can be accelerated for students who have experienced systematic disadvantages.

Students are profoundly influenced by the messages they get from the significant people in their lives about their ability. (So are we as adults!) So it is particularly important that we be consistent and authentic in sending the three critical messages—this is important, you can do it, and I'm not going to give up on you—in every way we can, explicitly and implicitly, in our interactions with our students. Each chapter of the book is about specific ways we can do this, ways that encompass deliberate use of language, classroom structures and routines, particular instructional strategies, and school-level policies and procedures.

The task is convincing students that they are not behind because they are deficient learners or lack ability. They can, in fact, grow their ability. They can not only catch up but also achieve proficiency if they learn how to exert effective effort and have sufficient time. Today this is popularly called the *growth mindset*. In previous decades it went by the name of *effort-based ability*.

After decades of advocacy by many educators, the growth mindset has achieved a major presence in educational literature. It has a dynamic and challenging message, especially in the United States, where belief in the bell curve of innate ability is so strong. The growth mindset says that academic ability in any area is not fixed; it can be grown, and performance can be grown to the point of proficiency given sufficient time, good instruction, and, above all, effective effort by the student.

The challenge for us as educators is to

- get our students to believe this,
- teach them how to exert effective effort,
- make them feel known and valued, and
- give them high-quality instruction

all at once! This is especially needed for those students who do not have confidence in their ability and are significantly behind their peers.

Carol Dweck brought us to a turning point in consciousness with her 2007 book *Mindsets*. One of the most important researchers on this topic for some 40 years, she translated her research with great clarity into a readable book aimed at a lay audience. Other writers advocated the same message over the decades (e.g., Jeff Howard, Bernard Weiner), but Dweck's book threw the window open as none before and has thankfully spread like wildfire through the educational community and the popular press. The challenging message out there is that ability is not fixed; ability can be grown if one exerts effective effort. And the evidence is in: Students who proceed from that mindset do much better!

It is important to directly teach students about the difference between a growth mindset and a fixed mindset, as Dweck advocates, and to show that students with growth mindsets do better. It is a great door-opener to share the research that brains are malleable and dendrites and synapses can be grown. But it is yet another thing to convince students that I, your teacher, who know and value you, am convinced that *you* have an able brain and can grow *your* ability in the academic content for which I am your teacher. While teaching students about brain growth and brain malleability certainly has a place in the education of students of color and of poverty, in fact for all students, much more is needed.

Low-confidence, underperforming students have been receiving messages their whole school careers (and out of school too) that they are not smart enough (perhaps not smart overall, but certainly not smart in subject X, which could be math, writing, anything). They don't see the point of putting forth more effort in an area where they are "dumb." Thus they require much more than information about brain malleability. I'd like to focus on the interactive skills that convince them that their teacher believes the growth mindset applies to *them* and that their teacher is committed to and believes in *their* success. This book is about how to do that.

Chapters 1 and 2 are about debunking the idea of the bell curve of ability and intelligence. Chapter 1 traces the history of how fixed intelligence and measureable IQ got established so soundly in the United States. Chapter 2 presents the evidence that ability can be grown and that the bell curve of innate ability is false.

The three key expectations messages—what we're doing is important, you can do it, and I won't give up on you—can be communicated explicitly. But what makes them believable and motivates students to invest in school are the *implicit* messages embedded in the way teachers handle everyday events with them individually.

Say a student asks for help. A teacher communicating belief in a student might respond as follows:

SCRIPT 1

Student: I can't do number 4.

Teacher: What part don't you understand? *["Part" implies there are parts the student does understand.]*

Student: I just can't do it.

Teacher: Well, I know you can do part of it, because you've done the first three problems correctly. *[Explicit expression of confidence.]* The fourth problem is similar but just a little harder. *[Acknowledges difficulty.]* You start out the same, but then you have to do one extra step. *[Gives a cue.]* Review the first three problems, and then start number 4 again and see if you can figure it out. *[Provides a strategy.]* I'll come by your desk in a few minutes to see how you're doing. *[I'll be back and follow through to make sure you succeed.]*

A teacher who doesn't really care, or who does care but doesn't believe the student really "has it," might respond as follows:

SCRIPT 2

Student: I can't do number 4.

Teacher: You can't? Why not? *[A vapid question. If the student knew why he couldn't do it, he wouldn't be stuck.]*

Student: I just can't do it.

Teacher: Don't say you can't do it. We never say we can't do it. *[Perhaps the teacher wants to urge perseverance. But instead he gives the student a moralistic message about having difficulty.]* Did you try hard? *[That's a no-win question. What if he did? Then he must be dumb. What if he didn't? Then he's a slug.]*

Student: Yes, but I can't do it.

Teacher: Well, you did the first three problems. Maybe if you went back and worked a little longer you could do the fourth problem too. *[So working longer and harder with the same old inadequate strategies might somehow magically work?]* Why don't you work at it a little more and see what happens? *[So maybe there will be a miracle. Not likely. I'm out of here.]*

None of the bracketed messages above are communicated explicitly, but they are embedded in the choice of language the teacher employs.

Examining our use of language in arenas of classroom life is the first strand of this work. Similar arenas of classroom life that powerfully communicate embedded belief messages through language are these:

- calling on students
- response to student answers
- giving help
- changing attitudes toward errors
- giving tasks and assignments
- feedback
- positive reframing of re-teaching
- tenacity
- pushback on fixed mindset language

In Chapter 3 we will look in detail at these subtle but powerful ways in which we consistently communicate to our students with choice of language (or not) our own view of their ability. It matters a great deal that our students, *all* our students, get the three crucial messages from us about the importance of what we're doing in school and how persistent we will be in helping them achieve the proficiencies of which their able brains are capable.

That they get these messages from us consistently makes a big difference in their belief in themselves, their investment in school, and their ultimate achievement. And the messages don't get sent by accident; they get sent through deliberate behavior we display in specific arenas of classroom life, that is, things we say and do. Very formal, reserved people and relaxed, outgoing teachers can both succeed in sending these messages. It is not a matter of style, but it is a matter of behavior.

❖❖❖

The second strand of the work is creating classroom routines and structures that help students see their progress and take responsibility (agency) for their learning. These routines give real horsepower and constant reminders to students of their role in doing well academically and embed by their very nature the message that they *can* do well (Chapter 4.) We will introduce these action steps with convincing research that these actions play a significant part in student achievement.

For example, if quizzes are frequent and students have to retake quizzes when they didn't attain proficiency, there is a powerful embedded message: "Nothing short of proficiency will do. You can get there, and I'll make sure you do." Teachers who want to convince their students of the growth mindset provide multiple access channels to learn the content when the students didn't perform well on the quiz. And then the students retake the quiz and get the highest grade they got—not an average. That structure embeds the high, positive expectations message the students need on a daily basis.

Below is a list of other structures we will dig into in this book that embed this message through giving students tools to be active agents in their own learning (known these days as *agency*):

- frequent quizzes and a flow of data to students
- student self-corrections/self-scoring
- student error analysis
- student self-evaluation (e.g., an effort rubric)
- student goal setting
- student feedback to teacher on pace or need for clarification
- regular re-teaching, retakes, and required redos
- grading practices that reward effort
- cooperative learning protocols and explicit teaching of social, group, and language skills for supporting one another
- rewards and recognition for effective effort
- extra help

At this point, for teachers following this path, our verbal behavior and our classroom structures and routines would now be aligned to communicate to students:

Your brainpower is quite competent to do well in this subject and I'm going to show you how. If you are struggling, it's because you have gaps in prior knowledge or don't yet know the best strategies for mastering this content. I'm going to help you find the gaps and fill them and teach you whatever strategies you need.

There would be nothing wrong with saying this explicitly to students, but to get them to believe it, we have to *act* as if *we* believe it ourselves in all the daily interactions of class instruction and class business that make up the emotional environment. And we have to create structures and routines that would exist only if we believed our students could be successful at a proficient level.

The third strand is that certain instructional strategies emerge as vital to convincing students we believe in them and enabling them to succeed (Chapter 5). For example, underperforming students often don't know what our expectations are even though we think our explanations and assignments are perfectly clear. Going out of our way to be sure our students understand exactly what the criteria for success are and take the time to do so with them, perhaps individually, has two implications: First, we wouldn't take the time and effort to do that if we didn't want them to succeed and believe they could. Second, when they actually *do understand* exactly what we want, it is surprising how quickly students rise to the level of expectation.

The fourth strand of work is deliberately and specifically teaching students *how to exert effective effort.* Then we add frequent self-evaluation on how well they have exerted it. Effective effort isn't just working harder and longer, though persistence is an element of it. Effective effort has six specific attributes that can be built into our instruction. We'll take them up in Chapter 6.

Chapter 7 is about student choice: when, where, and how to make students feel legitimately that their voice influences classroom life and their choices exert influence on their learning.

Chapter 8 shows how we can shape school policies and programs that embed by their very nature the tacit assumption that ability can be grown. Examples include the rationale for how teachers are assigned and the reward structures of the school.

All of these approaches together can create a powerful environment of confidence building and achievement for students who otherwise would fail or just slip through the cracks without getting the first-rate academic competencies they could have achieved.

So the intent of this book is to give readers a comprehensive map of personal and institutional responses for fighting the myth of the bell curve of ability. This is a how-to book about getting all of our students, especially our low-confidence, underperforming students, to believe in the growth mindset and acquire the tools to act on it effectively.

While we will focus on the power of in-school approaches to eliminating the gap in this book, we are fully aware of the other factors that surround the problem. Other authors have focused on these factors, such as working with parents, creating comprehensive afterschool programs, encouraging culturally responsive teaching, and changing negative peer culture. Still others who start from a social justice point of view focus on eliminating structural obstacles to equal opportunity, such as tracking, referral and placement procedures, and embedded assumptions for implementing special education services. These are all important approaches to closing the achievement gap. Concerted, coordinated approaches are needed for this deep issue.

But if we can teach students to believe that "smart is something you can get," we can act powerfully in the zone we control—the school—to disable the preschool-to-prison pipeline for students of color and of poverty. It is a personal tragedy for them and their families; it is also a devastating loss and a moral crisis for our country. And it does not have to be. We believe the teaching skills, the classroom structures and routines, and the schoolwide programs and policies described here can surround students with an environment of belief and aspiration that changes their lives.

In 1973 Paul Simon recorded a song titled "50 Ways to Leave Your Lover." Putting that syntax in a more serious title, beginning on page 9 is list of "50 Ways to Get Students to Believe in Themselves" . . . and to act on that.

Each of these 50 ways is a way we would act in our teaching and our schools would organize in their practices if we wanted to press a comprehensive set of levers to get students to believe in themselves. The list is, in effect, the map for a call to action and the outline of this book.

THE BOTTOM LINE OF EFFORT-BASED ABILITY

The ability to do something competently—anything, whether it's mathematics, race-car driving, dancing, or public speaking—is primarily determined by *effective effort* and your belief that you can get proficient at it. "Smart is something you can get." The bell curve of ability is wrong. Even what we call "intelligence" is malleable.

> Thus our work as educators, in fact a major part of it for some students, is
>
> 1. to **convince** them they can grow their ability at academics,
> 2. to **show** them how, and
> 3. to **motivate** them to want to.

50 Ways to Get Students to Believe in Themselves

or

How to Do Attribution Retraining

Verbal behaviors and teacher choice of language in daily interaction:

1. Calling on students

2. Responses to student answers

   - Sticking

   These nine are how we do attribution retraining: "It's effort, not innate ability,"

3. Giving help

4. Changing attitudes toward errors

   - Persevere and return

5. Giving tasks and assignments

6. Feedback according to criteria for success with encouragement and precise diagnostic guidance

7. Positive framing of re-teaching

8. Tenacity when students don't meet expectations: pursuit and continued call for high-level performance

9. Pushback on fixed mindset language and student helplessness

All observable in classrooms

Regular classroom mechanisms for **generating student agency**:

10. Frequent quizzes and a flow of data to students

11. Student self-corrections/self-scoring

12. Student error analysis

13. Regular re-teaching

14. Required retakes and redos with highest grade

15. Cooperative learning protocols and teaching of group skills

16. Student feedback to teacher on pace or need for clarification

17. Reward system for effective effort and gains

18. Extra help

19. Student goal setting

No Secrets teaching **instructional strategies** promoting clarity:

20. Communicating objectives in student-friendly language and unpacking them with students

21. Clear and accessible criteria for success, developed with students

22. Exemplars of products that meet criteria for success

23. Checking for understanding

24. Making students' thinking visible

25. Frequent student summarizing

All observable in classrooms

Explicitly teaching students:

26. Effective effort behaviors

27. Student self-evaluation of effective effort

28. Learning study and other strategies of successful students

29. Attribution theory and brain research

Opportunities for **choice and voice**:

30. Stop my teaching

31. Student-generated questions

32. Negotiating the rules of the classroom game

33. Teaching students the principles of learning

34. Learning style

35. Non-reports and student experts

36. Culturally relevant teaching

37. Student-led parent conferences

Schoolwide **policies and practices** for:

38. Hiring teachers

39. Assignment of teachers

40. Personalizing knowledge of and contact with students

41. Scheduling

42. Grouping

43. Content-focused teams that examine student work in relation to their teaching

44. Reward system for academic effort and gains

45. Push, support, and tight safety net (hierarchy of intervention)

Programs that enable students to value school and form a peer culture that supports academic effort:

46. Quality afterschool programs and extracurricular activities

47. Building identity and pride in belonging to the school

48. Creating a vision of a better life attainable through learning the things school teaches

49. Forming an image of successful people who look like them and value education

50. Building relations with parents through home visits and focus on how to help

It is important to keep in mind that we do not take on any of these 50 items with commitment unless we conceive of our job description in a certain way.

1

The History of "Intelligence"

In the United States we have a belief about intelligence that is

> unique
>
> > dominant
> >
> > > and wrong

Unique because it is stronger here than any other country in the world, though by no means limited to our shores.

Dominant because it is a pervasive organizer of our society.

And wrong because it is simply incorrect, as I hope to demonstrate in this book.

The reason for dealing with this concept of intelligence in a book about high expectations teaching is that it plays a major role in the low achievement of millions of children in this country. We say "all children can learn," but we don't really believe it. And we don't really believe it because of the belief we hold about intelligence.

Beliefs underlie all our actions—our beliefs about teaching and learning, our beliefs about ourselves, our beliefs about institutions. More than any other belief, our belief about children and their capacity to learn influences the messages we send them and the actual learning they attain.

Beliefs are the single most potent anchor of successful teaching behaviors. The belief about ability is beyond technique, but it underlies all motivation for teachers to acquire repertoire. So to the degree that you are influenced by this chapter about our unique (and wrong) concept of intelligence in this country, your teaching will change in significant ways.

Most of this book is about practical strategies, but they are practical strategies in service of a moral imperative: All children deserve a fair chance at a good life, and a good education is big part of how we honor that promise. It is important for readers to understand the history of our national belief in the bell curve of ability so that we can understand how we have created the unequal system we have. And it is also important so that we can act to combat it from a position of belief as well as skill.

In America our concept of intelligence is that it is:

A thing—a tangible entity, something singular and real

Fixed—it is unchangeable; whatever you got is all you'll ever get

Innate—whatever of it you have, you got when you emerged from your mother's womb

Unevenly distributed—unfortunately some of us have more of it than others

Deterministic—it determines how you'll do in school and in life

Measurable—but fortunately we can measure it and create the appropriate educational environment for each student[1]

So therefore intelligence achievement
leads to

This concept of fixed intelligence and achievement lives in each of us to a certain degree. And it isn't our fault. One can't grow up in America without being infected by it. It's like breathing smog in Los Angeles, as Beverly Daniel Tatum used to say of racism. We don't blame the residents of that city for inhaling smog. We are all smog breathers. We all tend to see students' capacity as limited by innate intelligence. But the consequences of that belief for the way we do school and the behaviors we do with children are huge, omnipresent, and tragic. They are life limiting for children. If we can adopt a new and different belief about the nature of intelligence—namely, that intelligence and ability are things that can be developed—and do so with conviction that almost everyone has enough of it to do rigorous academic material at high standards, our schools will become transformed places.

The American concept of intelligence was born out of the convergence of four historical forces at a particular time in our history: 1890–1920. It

---

[1] I first heard a version of this list from Jeff Howard in 1985. He is an unsung hero of this movement to convince students that "smart is something you can get."

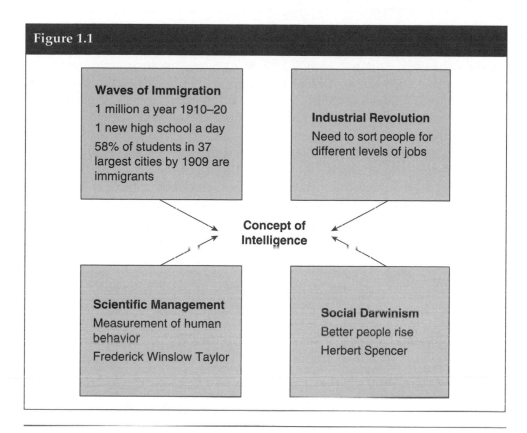

Figure 1.1

Waves of Immigration
1 million a year 1910–20
1 new high school a day
58% of students in 37 largest cities by 1909 are immigrants

Industrial Revolution
Need to sort people for different levels of jobs

Concept of Intelligence

Scientific Management
Measurement of human behavior
Frederick Winslow Taylor

Social Darwinism
Better people rise
Herbert Spencer

Thanks to Greg Ciardi for first thinking this through and putting together this graphic.

didn't exist before then. It was invented here on our shores, and it took form and assumed a dominance in our society with no parallel anywhere in the world.

Between 1890 and 1920, four historical trends intersected that gave the theory of intelligence deep purchase in the American imagination (Figure 1.1). During this period, massive waves of immigration brought new citizens by the millions to our shores. At the same time, the shift from an agrarian to an industrial economy created the needs that industry brings, the need for a stratified workforce: people to sweep the factory floor, people to work the assembly line, foremen to supervise the work, managers to staff and run the operation, capitalists to raise the money and govern the corporation. For the first time in U.S. history, there was a need to sort people for these new jobs, and waves of new people arriving to be sorted.

Coincidentally, the science of measuring human behavior was getting spectacular buy-in across the country as Frederick Winslow Taylor and scores of disciples were hired to study workers with a stopwatch and speed up their performance to make them more efficient. Speed and efficiency became valued commodities, and it became commonly accepted that human behavior of all kinds could be measured. This was an era of science and progress and measurement.

At the same time all of this was happening, from Herbert Spencer in England came the idea of social Darwinism (that "better people" will rise because they are "better," that is, more fit). And in turn-of-the-century America, the country of Benjamin Franklin, individualism, and self-reliance, it was almost inevitable that the notion of survival of the fittest be applied to competition among individual people as well as the evolution of species (Gould, 1981).

It became accepted that those who are at the top of society must therefore be better, and if we could simply figure out who were the more innately fit, we could sort people and invest resources accordingly.

Certain people played central roles in England, France, and the United States in the evolution of the concept of intelligence. The history unfolds logically and deliberately with connections among the key players.

England—1883: Sir Francis Galton (Charles Darwin's nephew) studies men of great reputation and distinction. In 1883 he starts a lab for the physiological measurement of intelligence. In 1886 he conceives of the idea of correlation coefficient. He founded the eugenics movement.

Note three ideas here:

1. A relative of Charles Darwin who has read about "survival of the fittest" seeks to measure whatever it is that great men have that makes them superior. He starts by studying physical reflexes.

2. He conceives of the idea of a mathematical measure of correlation between two phenomena, though he doesn't discover the formula for calculating it.

3. He founds the eugenics movement, which posits that superior people should breed and inferior people should not. That way we will improve the gene pool of the general population.

United States—1893: James McKeen Cattell, a student of Galton, coins the term *mental test* and advocates these tests be given in schools. He begins publishing results. No established "mental test" of intelligence yet exists.

So the idea of mental superiority has come to our shores, but not yet permeated the educational system.

England—1895: Herbert Spencer argues intelligence is inherited and advocates mental testing.

So social Darwinism is now generalized to mental ability, "intelligence," and advanced by Spencer as something that is inherited and should somehow be measured.

England—1901: Karl Pearson, another student of Galton, succeeds in developing *factor analysis* as a statistical technique and also publishes the Pearson product-moment correlation coefficient formula for establishing the relationship between two ideas in relation to chance. Thus it is now possible to take some measured entity (e.g., a test of mental ability) and correlate it with some other entity (e.g., academic success).

United States—1904: Charles Spearman calls the thing being measured by mental ability tests G, standing for general intelligence.

France—1908: Alfred Binet develops a test for identifying learning disabilities.

This test is imported to our shores and used as a test of mental abilities for the first time in a small sample of American schools. A hundred years later this test, now called the Stanford-Binet Intelligence test, still bears the Frenchman's name.

Now read what Binet said about this test that we began using to sort and rank children according to their "natural" ability:

> The scores [on the test] are a practical device; they do not buttress any theory of intellect. They do not define anything innate or permanent. We may not designate what they measure as "intelligence" or any other reified entity.
>
> The scale is a rough, empirical guide for identifying mildly retarded and learning disabled children who need special help. It is not a device for ranking normal children.
>
> Whatever the cause of difficulty in children identified for help, emphasis shall be placed upon improvement through special training. Low scores shall not be used to mark children as innately incapable. (Gould, 1981, p. 155)

> Intelligence is susceptible to development; with practice and training and especially with appropriate methods of teaching, we can augment a children's attention, memory, judgment—helping them literally become more intelligent than they were before. (Binet, 1899, as translated in Wolf, 1973, p. 207)

According to Binet, the supposed father of the IQ test, intelligence was not a fixed amount, or a constant, or some Platonic, bounded essence. Intelligence was educable. Binet advocated "mental orthopedics":

> What they should learn first is not the subjects ordinarily taught, however important they may be; they should be given lessons of will, of attention, of discipline; before exercises in grammar, they need to be exercised in mental orthopedics; in a word they must learn how to learn. (Binet, 1908, in Gould, 1981, p. 154)

So Binet explicitly posits that intelligence is not fixed, is malleable, can be developed, and hinges on will, another way to say effort. Gould (1981, p. 155) comments, "If Binet's principles had been followed . . . we would have been spared a major misuse of science in our century."

In the years leading up to World War I, ideas fell into place that deepened the trend toward IQ testing.

United States—1911: Psychologist Edward L. Thorndike posits that learning is a stimulus-response cycle comparable to natural selection and thus comparable to neurological response times, a "reflex arc." Thus it is measurable.

United States—1911: Charles Davenport, an early leader in the Eugenics movement, publishes *Heredity in Relation to Eugenics*, which becomes standard required reading in college biology courses. Davenport hires Harry Laughlin to propagandize the doctrine of eugenics.

Now we had a pernicious platform in place for measuring intelligence and, as eugenics advocates campaigned for, sterilizing people whose measured IQ showed them to be genetically defective.

United States—1912: Stanley Hall advocated differentiated curriculum for adolescents of differing ability. We shouldn't have the same curriculum for all students. This is the first time we create what will later be called "tracking."

United States—1913: Henry Goddard translates Binet's tests from the French into English and begins using them to screen immigrants at Ellis Island in New York Harbor. He finds that 83% of Jews, 80% of Hungarians, and 79% of Italians are "feebleminded."

The Ellis Island National Museum of Immigration informs us that the test items ask illiterate farm laborers to copy small geometric shapes, which they have trouble doing because of lack of small motor coordination. This leads to many of them being returned to Europe because they are mental defectives.

United States—1916: Lewis Terman popularizes Binet's test and develops it further. He applies statistical techniques to standardize 100 as the mean, and he advocates universal testing across the population.

United States—1917: Robert Yerkes administers the intelligence test to 1.75 million men entering the U.S. Army during World War I. Thus he creates the first norms for the test based on a broad database.

In that same year Yerkes served as chair of the Committee on Inheritance of Mental Traits of the Eugenics Research Associates. He wrote, "The difference between countries is a very wide one.... In general the Scandinavian and English speaking countries stand high in the list while Slavic and Latin countries stand low" (Yerkes, 1921, p. 699).

Readers can see now how the strands were woven together: IQ is measurable, inferior people can be identified, and we should sterilize them to improve the population's gene pool.

Why had Binet's ideas been so turned?

Seymour Sarason wrote about this period and what happened to Binet's ideas:

> The fact is that Binet's "followers," particularly in the United States, were caught up in a confusion between technology and science, between measurement and meaningful rigor, between method and substance. The particular means whereby one studied a problem became so absorbing and complex that it was not long before the original problem became drowned in a sea of measurements. They seized upon the need for measurement and were blind to the complex issues which alone could give significance to their efforts.
>
> Binet had all kinds of qualms about pseudo-precision in regard to his scale, but not in a million years could he be accused of denigrating precise measurement. His qualms stemmed from the strong belief that his scale lacked the substance and scope required by his conception of intelligence in action. How could such a belief withstand the Goddards and the Termans, whose concerns for rigor and precision in measurement were uncluttered by the thoughtfulness of a Binet?
>
> If American psychology celebrated Terman and his achievements, it was because his work had all the apparent trappings of the scientific mind: standardization of procedures, precision in measurement, quantification, replicability, and validity. (Sarason, 1976, p. 583)

Between 1907 and 1928, 21 states passed laws based on eugenics models. Thus the United States became the first nation in the world to permit sterilization as part of an effort to "purify the race"; by the mid-1930s, this practice had been conducted on about 20,000 people.

Americans had been sterilized against their will. Most were residents of state mental hospitals and juvenile detention centers. By 1928, over 75% of the nation's colleges and universities offered one or more courses that included a study of eugenics. Not surprisingly, textbooks reflected that emphasis. Between 1914 and 1949, over 90% of the nation's biology texts contained sections on eugenics.

The movement had an impact on elementary and secondary education. At the urging of Davenport and other eugenics educators, school officials across the nation tried to foster the "development of the intellectual faculties of the few who have outstanding abilities and give limited vocational training to the mediocre" (Hofstadter, 1944, p. 165). To determine which students were best suited to each type of education, they administered IQ tests. Students were then labeled and rigidly tracked. Many children came to believe they were "mediocre" or even "stupid" because of the classes to which they were assigned—a continuing problem a century later.

Few parents questioned testing or tracking. Indeed, many supported the movement after learning about it at exhibits Harry Laughlin (hired by Davenport) and other eugenicists set up at state fairs and museums. Those exhibits featured charts, photos, and graphs that warned against supporting "defectives" at the expense of superior types. They also showcased a variety of techniques designed to protect the nation from an "alien bloodstream." At many of these exhibits, lecturers stressed the importance of positive eugenics—the idea that superior families ought to have lots of children. Eugenicists even sponsored "fitter family" and baby contests at some fairs. The winners were hailed as the kind of "stock America needs more of." These community events helped shape public opinion and win the popular support necessary to translate the principles of eugenics into public policy.

As Oliver Wendell Holmes (*Buck v. Bell*, 1927) is quoted as saying, "Three generations of imbeciles are enough!"

Alan L. Stoskopf (1995), in "Confronting the Forgotten History of the American Eugenics Movement," summed up the situation this way:

> Perhaps at another time Galton's ideas would have been relegated to the dustbin of history. But in the late 1800s and early 1900s, his ideas captured the imagination of many people around the world. Eugenics found a particularly receptive audience in the United States. There Galton's supporters were not night riders for the Ku Klux Klan or individuals on the fringes of society. They were well-respected educators who enlisted the support of some of the nation's most prominent scientists, philanthropists, social workers, and politicians.
>
> The Eugenics movement was particularly attractive to native-born, white Americans with some education. It addressed many of their anxieties and fears. It also offered them a "a rational" way of dealing with those anxieties and fears. Many of these Americans were troubled by the rapid changes that were taking place in the United States in the early 1900s.
>
> Charles Davenport, an early leader in the movement, had been an instructor at Harvard and an assistant professor of zoology at the University of Chicago before founding the Station for Experimental Evolution (SEE) at Cold Springs Harbor in 1904. . . . [He] conducted experiments on plants and animals. He also ran a summer institute for teachers and field workers.

Davenport was eager to extend his research to humans, but lacked the funds to do so. That year Mary Harriman, the widow of the deceased railroad magnate, agreed to fund that research. In subsequent years, the Carnegie Foundation, which had long bankrolled SEE, also supported Davenport's work on humans.

Laughlin lobbied intensively for restrictions on immigration. At congressional hearings he plastered the wall with charts warning against unrestricted immigration. Over an exhibit of photographs showing "defectives" seeking to enter the nation, he hung a banner labeling those individuals as "Carriers of the Germ Plasma of the future American Population."

The lurid evidence and the testimony of Laughlin's "experts" amplified the fears of many in Congress. They were repeatedly warned that the nation was headed for disaster unless they placed draconian restrictions on immigration. That testimony provided a pseudo-scientific rationale for the Immigration Restriction Acts of 1921, 24, and 27. It was a rationale that even the President of the United States supported. In signing the 1924 bill, Calvin Coolidge declared, "America must be kept American. Biological laws show . . . that Nordics deteriorate when mixed with other races." Eugenic ideas had reached the highest levels of government. The combination of the need to sort people for the needs of the economy and the unease with the influx of foreigners lent strength to the growing Eugenics Movement. (p. 3)

The public statements of prominent figures in these years show the depth of the prejudice and stereotyping of peoples of non-Nordic origin in striking terms.

United States—1885: A member of the Boston School Committee said, "Many of these children come from homes of vice and crime. In their blood are generations of iniquity. . . . They hate restraint or obedience to law. They know nothing of the feelings which are inherited by those who were born on our shores."

United States—1916: In *The Measurement of Intelligence* Lewis Terman wrote:

Border-line intelligence is very common among Spanish-Indian and Mexican families of the Southwest and also among Negroes. Their dullness seems to be racial, or at least inherent in the family stocks from which they come. . . . The whole question of racial differences in mental traits will have to be taken up anew and by experimental methods. The writer predicts that when this is done there will be discovered enormously significant differences in general intelligence, differences which cannot be wiped out by any scheme of mental culture.

> Children of this group should be segregated in special classes. . . . They cannot master abstractions, but they can be made efficient workers. . . . There is no possibility at present of convincing society that they should not be allowed to reproduce, although from a eugenic point of view they constitute a grave problem because of their unusually prolific breeding. (Terman, 1916, as cited in Baca and Cervantes, 1989, p. 147)

These views do not seem significantly different from those represented by prominent figures more recently. In 1994 Herrnstein and Murray wrote, "For many people, there is nothing they can learn that will repay the cost of teaching" (p. 520). And later, "In short, by custodial state we have in mind a high tech and more lavish version of the Indian reservation for some substantial minority of the nation's population, while the rest of America tried to go about its business" (p. 526).

Stanley Fish (1993) wrote in "Reverse Racism, or How the Pot Got to Call the Kettle Black":

> In 1923 Carl Campbell Brigham published a book called *A Study of American Intelligence* in which, as Owen notes, he declared among other things that we face in America "a possibility of racial admixture infinitely worse than that faced by any European country today, for we are incorporating the Negro into our racial stock, while all Europe is comparatively free of this taint."
>
> Brigham had earlier analyzed the Army Mental Tests using classifications drawn from another racist text, Madison Grant's The Passing of the Great Race, which divided American society into four distinct racial strains, with Nordic, blue-eyed, blond people at the pinnacle and the American Negro at the bottom.
>
> Brigham discovered that differences among test scores of immigrant groups reduced with length of time in the country, and in fact, disappeared after 20 years. Yet he wrote: "The hypothesis of intelligence increasing with length of residency may be identified with the hypothesis of an error in the method of measuring intelligence. . . . We must assume that we are measuring native, inborn intelligence."
>
> Nevertheless, in 1925 Brigham became director of testing for the College Board, and developed the SAT. So here is the great SAT test, devised by a racist in order to confirm racist assumptions, measuring not native ability but cultural advantage, an uncertain indicator of performance, an indicator of very little except what money and social privilege can buy. (p. 209)

Not everyone at the time believed these ideas about fixed intelligence. Gould tells us that in 1892 Charles Eliot, president of Harvard University, wrote:

It is a curious fact that we Americans habitually underestimate the capacity of pupils at almost every state of education from the primary school through the university. . . . It seems to me probable that the proportion of grammar school children incapable of pursuing geometry, algebra, and a foreign language would turn out to be much smaller than we now imagine.

We hope that people will refuse to believe that the American public intends to have its children sorted before their teens into clerks, watchmakers, lithographers, telegraph operators, masons, teamsters, farm laborers and so forth and treated differently in their schools according to the prophecies of their appropriate life careers. Who are we to make these prophecies?

Almost 30 years later opponents still spoke out. Walter Lippmann debated Terman in the pages of the *New Republic* magazine and wrote, "We will breed generations of students and educators who don't believe that those who begin weak can ever become strong" (reprinted in Block and Dworkin, 1976, p. 4). Nevertheless, advocates of IQ tests and eugenics carried the day.

A video presentation of the information in this chapter is available at http://rbteach.com/products-resources/video/history-intelligence-1-myth-bell-curve.

Video 1.1

REFERENCES AND RESOURCES

Baca, L., & Cervantes, H. (Eds.). (1989). *The bilingual special education interface.* (2nd ed.). Columbus: Merrill.

Block, N. J., & Dworkin, G. (Eds.). (1976). *The IQ controversy.* New York: Pantheon Books.

Brigham, C. (1923). *A study of American intelligence.* London: Oxford University Press.

Buck v. Bell, 274 U.S. 200 (1927).

Davenport, C. (1911). *Heredity in relation to eugenics.* New York, NY: Henry Holt.

Fish, S. (1993, November). Reverse racism, or how the pot got to call the kettle black. *Atlantic Monthly.*

Gould, S. J. (1981). *The mismeasure of man.* New York, NY: W. W. Norton.

Herrnstein, R. J., & Murray. (1994). *The bell curve.* New York, NY: Free Press.

Hofstadter, R. (1944). *Social Darwinism in American thought*. Boston: Beacon Press.

Houts, P. D. (Ed.). (1977). *Myth of measurability*. New York, NY: Hart.

Hunt, J. McV. (1961). *Intelligence and experience*. New York: Ronald Press Company.

Sarason, S. B. (1976). "The unfortunate fate of Alfred Binet and school psychology." *Teachers College Record, 77*, 579–592.

Stoskopf, A. L. (1995, Winter). Confronting the forgotten history of the American eugenics movement. *Facing History and Ourselves News, 3*.

Terman, L. (1916). *The measurement of intelligence*. Boston: Houghton Mifflin.

Wolf, T. H. (1973). *Alfred Binet*. Chicago: University Press of Chicago.

Yerkes, R. M. (1921). *Psychological examining in the United States Army*. Washington, DC: U.S. Government Printing Office.

2

Malleable Intelligence: The Evidence

Attribution Retraining and the Growth Mindset

"Beliefs about intelligence are important predictors of student behavior in school. . . . Teachers should know that students are more motivated if they believe that intelligence and ability can be improved through hard work."

Daniel Willingham and Paul Bruno (2015, p. 7)

"Students beliefs or perceptions about intelligence and ability affect their cognitive functioning and learning."

American Psychological Association (2015, p. 1)

Students know exactly what we think of their abilities by the way we handle daily business and respond to them in regularly recurring arenas of classroom life. The next chapter, Chapter 3, will lay out how we convey belief or nonbelief in our students' ability through our verbal behavior. Before we get into those skills, however, we want to lay out the evidence that "smart is actually something you can get" and that ability is malleable. When we budge on that continuum, we can expect to act with energy on the skills and structures we are urging in this book.

The previous chapter chronicled how the belief in the bell curve of intelligence got such a strong hold on the American psyche and on the way we do school. Now let's look at the data that challenge that belief. The chapter will end with an injunction to suspend disbelief about those whom we may still think are "low-ability" students and act as if we believe they have what it takes, that "smart is something they can get." We can act our way to new beliefs.

DATA CHALLENGING THE INNATE ABILITY THEORY

The notion of innate ability as fixed and deterministic is not an easy or comfortable one to challenge. Our everyday experience seems to confirm over and over again that all children are not formed with equal ability. Teachers see daily how quickly some learn and how slowly others do. So if one accepts the presumption of the bell curve (unequal distribution of intelligence), differences in observable learning rate or ability to perform skills are seen and explained as a function of natural brightness or gifts or aptitude for learning academic material. The accompanying belief goes something like this: "All children can learn, but they can't all learn as much. All children can learn, but many have limits of how rigorous the material can be. They can all learn more than they know now, but they can't all reach proficiency with high-level literacy and numeracy skills. That's just the way the world is. Why fight it?"

We should fight it because it isn't true; however, not only do most educators believe it at some level, so do students and their parents. Thus, the stereotypes children form of their own ability early in their lives serve as a self-limiting regulator on their expectations, their confidence, and their willingness to work harder or learn to work smarter. Each of us can surely remember a time when something happened or someone said something that convinced us we were inept, unable, or untalented in a certain area of performance. This conclusion, often formed at a young age, led to negative self-image in this area, to avoidance, and to self-perpetuating low performance. If one reaches such a conclusion about dancing or singing, it has some social effects. But if one reaches such a conclusion about academic ability, it can have profound and life-altering consequences.

Consider the following information that challenges this model of innate and fixed ability. First, the correlation of measured intelligence with academic grades can be made to account for only 25% of variability in performance. "IQ may matter, but it does not matter overwhelmingly—statistically, a correlation coefficient of .5 only accounts for 25 percent of the range of variation in [academic] performance, leaving 75 percent to be explained by other factors" (Perkins, 1995, p. 61). That figure includes children with borderline cognitive disabilities and children classified as gifted and talented. "If we were to reduce the spread to the normal range in a typical class, we would probably be able to account for only 5% to 10% of the variability" (Jim Pelligrino, personal communication, June 2002). Hence, 90% to 95% of the variation in performance is probably attributable to factors other than measured IQ.

Second, what goes for intelligence can actually be increased. What goes for innate ability is actually the capacity to do certain discrete tasks that intelligence tests measure, and those capacities can be increased. Sustained increases in IQ points that endure long after the training is over result from the best of the 20th century programs aimed at increasing cognitive abilities, such as Edward DeBono's Five Hats and Reuven Feuerstein's Instrumental Enrichment.

Other examples include Perkins's Project Intelligence (two- to seven-point increase) and the Carolina Abecedarian Project (cited in Neisser et al., 1996), an early childhood intervention program where the enrichment group scored higher than the control group at age 2 and were still five points higher at age 12.

In Currie's (2000) review of the research on early childhood intervention programs, she cites the Milwaukee Project, which showed that participants in the program not only raised their IQ scores but maintained their advantage over the control group through the eighth grade. On measures of scholastic success, however, participants scored similarly to the control group. What does this tell us about IQ and achievement? As Currie puts it: "The Milwaukee Project suggests that an exclusive focus on IQ is unwarranted because other factors also contribute to children's success at school and in life" (p. 11).

Measured IQs in the United States have risen nine points per generation since 1932 (Flynn, 1994). The Wechsler and the Stanford-Binet tests are renormed every 10 years, so this increase does not show up in publicly reported results. This suggests that if our grandparents (as children) were given the current IQ tests, they would almost surely have scored in the cognitive disability range based on today's scoring guides!

Does this steady advance in IQ scores mean we are actually getting smarter as a nation? What accounts for this rise? Could it be that ever more people go to school for more years and in school they develop skills (like vocabulary) that intelligence tests measure? Whatever accounts for it, one thing is sure: What the tests measure is susceptible to external influences that have led our population to be steadily more proficient at whatever it is the tests are measuring (Berliner & Biddle, 1995).

Third, there is a correlation between school achievement and measured intelligence, but it is the inverse of what the entity (bell curve) theory suggests. In short, considerable evidence suggests that schooling modifies intelligence.

A study conducted in 1989 by Israeli researcher-psychologists, Sorel Cahan and Nora Cohen, asked if as you grow from year to year, does your measured intelligence determine your achievement in school, or does what you achieve in school determine your measured intelligence. In other words, do children have to be intelligent to profit from schooling (as is widely believed in America), or do they have to have schooling to become intelligent? Although Cahan and Cohen used complex statistical methods, their findings were straightforward. They found that school achievement was a major factor in the prediction of intelligence test performance. In contrast, measured intelligence was only a weak predictor of school achievement. Thus, measured intelligence is strongly influenced by the opportunity to learn in school. Over the past 50 years, high-quality public education has been offered to larger and larger numbers of students in the industrialized world, and this fact explains why the average person today is measurably smarter than the average person was in the past. In 1910, only 10% of American children even entered high school, and half of that percentage graduated. Today almost all enter (though nationwide about 80% graduate).

Other evidence supports the relationship between school experience and measured IQ. Torsten Husen and Albert Tuijnman (1991), distinguished educational researchers from Sweden and Holland, respectively, examined data from a study originally conducted in Malmo, Sweden, that looked at the IQs of 671 Swedish males over a 10-year period, from childhood to adulthood. Using complex statistical techniques unavailable at the time of the original study, the authors examined whether changes in measured IQ had occurred and, if so, what might explain these changes. Their conclusion was unequivocal: Measured IQs had changed for many of the persons studied, and those who had experienced more schooling had also grown more in measured intelligence.

Thus, the characteristic that we call intelligence is not only dependent on inheritance and home background, but also influenced by schooling. Intelligence during the educative years is not a static and immutable characteristic. It appears to be quite dynamic and continues to be affected by environmental factors, particularly by access to high-quality schooling. Husen and Tuijnman (1991) concluded,

> Schools not only confer knowledge and instrumental qualifications but also train and develop students' intellectual capacity. The results [of this study] suggest . . . that IQ as measured by group intelligence tests is not stable but changes significantly between 10 and 20 years of age. . . . [Apparently] schooling co-varies with and produces positive changes in adult IQ. (p. 22)

American psychologist Stephen Ceci (1991) reported similar findings. As a result of his research, Ceci concluded that the specific skills measured on intelligence tests and the processes underlying intelligence test performance are taught and learned in school. Ceci also estimated that these influences are substantial. A child could lose as many as six IQ

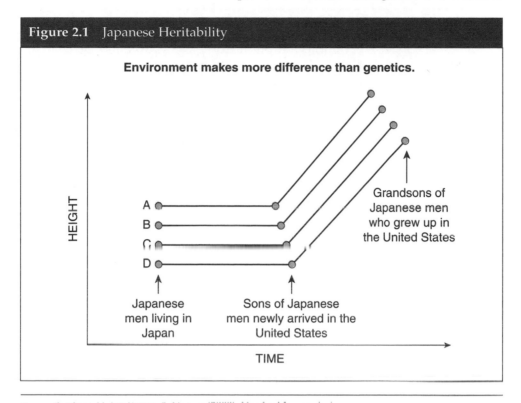

Figure 2.1 Japanese Heritability

Source: Saphier, Haley-Speca, & Gower (2008). Used with permission.

points for each year in which he or she misses high-quality education from birth onward.

In brief, schooling matters. Genes and home environment are not the only contributors to intelligence. "A society that chooses to nurture and develop high levels of intelligence among its youth must also provide high-quality education for them. Poor schools, like poor home environments, have negative lasting consequences" (Berliner & Biddle, 1995, p. 49).

Fourth, regarding the popular belief in the heritability of intelligence: "Heritability" is a statistical measure of the relation between a given trait and the presence of that same trait in a parent. Ceci (2001) noted in a personal communication:

> You can have high heritability [between parents and children, yet] large differences between children. An example from my 1996 book *On Intelligence: A Bioecological Treatise on Intellectual Development* is that the male sons of Japanese immigrants to the United States during the first part of the twentieth century grew, on average, five inches taller than their fathers despite heritability remaining approximately at .9! So heritability says nothing about *malleability*. [see Figure 2.1]

This means that even heritability was far outclassed by environmental influences. Ceci continued:

All this renders heritability a very tricky and not very useful or practical concept. A famous adoption study by Capron and Duyme (1989) shows evidence of children's IQs going nearly 22 points higher than those of their biological mothers. Nevertheless, the heritability estimate was quite high [between the children and their biological mothers].

Another interesting finding that challenges the belief that most intelligence is inherited is a finding that the heritability of intelligence between young children and their parents is .45. But when studies are done of the same children grown into adults and their parents, the heritability correlation is much higher: .70. Intelligence does change when measured over time, and as we get older, measured intelligence gets closer to what our parents scored. Here is one interpretation of how these numbers play out. "Smart" children (who had high IQ scores) born to low-IQ parents get dumber the older they get. Their IQ scores get closer to those of their parents. Therefore, the environment provided by lower-IQ parents drags their children's IQ down. But low-IQ children (who had low IQ scores as youngsters) born to smart parents get smarter the longer they live. Their IQ scores get closer to those of their parents. Therefore, the environment that higher-IQ parents provide pulls the children's IQ up.

Nature Versus Nurture: Who Is Winning Here?

Fifth, in people regarded as genius, a consistent characteristic is a huge investment of time and effort devoted to their area of interest and expertise. "Genius is 1% inspiration and 99% perspiration," said Thomas Edison. Studies of people of genius performed by Benjamin Bloom (1985) and later by Howard Gardner (2001) and by Michael Howe (2001) have all found that geniuses are people who spent incredible amounts of time studying and practicing, literally immersing themselves in their area of expertise. In sports, music, scholarship, and research, this is the story one finds again and again: It's perspiration, not inspiration. These world-class performers were often undistinguished students in their school careers, and their performance in their chosen fields was often judged unpromising by their mentors. But they persevered. In Malcolm Gladwell's (2011) *Outliers*, each chapter is a case study in 10,000 hours' worth of effort and what it produces in "geniuses."

Sixth, children who believe that ability can be increased do significantly better in school. Carol Dweck has shown this conclusively and repeatedly over decades of research. She called it the *incremental* view of intelligence before she came up with the current term *growth mindset*, meaning a belief that intelligence can be increased in increments by working hard and working smart.

What all of this evidence suggests is that the variables that appear to have the most significant impact on a person's development and achievement extend well beyond—and are most likely far more significant than—any attempted measurement, perception, or comparison of a person's innate ability. These variables appear to include the quantity and quality of schooling one experiences, the amount and kind of effort one invests, and the belief one holds in the individual's capacity to grow ability itself!

We propose an alternative way of explaining differences in human performance and achievement and will refer to this as the effort-based ability or incrementalist theory, now popularly known as the growth mindset.

Jeff Howard has made the case repeatedly (Howard, 1995; Howard & Hammond, 1985) that the deeply ingrained American paradigm that intelligence equals achievement is simultaneously wrong and the governing principle behind the design of our schools. Lauren Resnick (1995, pp. 55–57) agrees:

> What is the relationship between aptitude and effort? Early in the [20th] century we built an education system around the assumption that aptitude is paramount in learning and that it is largely hereditary. The system was oriented toward selection, distinguishing the naturally able from the less able and providing students with programs thought suitable to their talents. In other periods, most notably during the Great Society reforms, we worked on the compensatory principle, arguing that special effort, by an individual or an institution, could make up for low aptitude. The third possibility—that effort actually creates ability, that people can become smart by working hard at the right kinds of learning tasks—has never been taken seriously in America or indeed in any European society, although it is the guiding assumption of education in societies with a Confucian tradition.
>
> [In such an ability-bound view] students do not try to break through the barrier of low expectations because they, like their teachers and parents, accept the judgment that aptitude matters most and that they do not have the right kinds of aptitude. Not surprisingly, their performance remains low. Children who have not been taught a demanding, challenging, thinking curriculum do not do well on tests of reasoning or problem solving, confirming our original suspicions that they did not have the talent for that kind of thinking. The system is a self-sustaining one in which hidden assumptions are continually reinforced by the inevitable results of practices that are based on those assumptions.
>
> It is not necessary to continue this way. Aptitude is not the only possible basis for organizing schools. Educational institutions could be built around the alternative assumption that effort actually creates ability. Our education system could be designed primarily to foster effort.

The notion of effort-based intelligence and effort-based ability turns this idea on its head, and in many ways effort-based intelligence is a much better fit with the democratic promise of a free society where education is meant to be the equalizer and schooling is supposed to give every child a chance to make something of himself or herself.

In the United States we still don't have a guaranteed right to health care; we don't even have a guaranteed right to clean water. But Americans have a legally guaranteed right to education, no matter what their background. Schools can't fulfill that right equally for all children if they don't bring effort-based ability to personal interactions with children and parents, to teaching, and to an examination of our schoolwide practices.

Now let's look at the alternative theory of action to the bell curve for how we "do school."

ATTRIBUTION RETRAINING

The theory and research of the last 35 years has urged a reconsideration of the belief in the bell curve of intelligence and of academic ability. The research is quite convincing that belief in the bell curve as innate and unchangeable is wrong.

Consider the following juxtaposed terms:

- malleable ability vs. innate ability
- growth mindset vs. fixed mindset
- incrementalist theory vs. fixed-ability theory
- learning goal orientation vs. performance goal orientation
- effective effort and attribution theory
- attribution retraining and student agency

Underperforming, low-confidence students, however, have generally accepted this erroneous belief, as has the society around them. They attribute their failure when it occurs to their lack of ability in the subject and to the difficulty of the task. "It was too hard!" Conversely, when they succeed, they attribute that to good luck or easy work. We ask readers now to consider the following exploration of innate ability theories and the literature on attribution theory (Weiner, 1972) as well as our beliefs about our own students.

Here are two theories about innate ability and its relationship to performance and achievement. As you read, consider which theory dominated the environment in which you spent your formative years and how each of these theories plays out in your teaching.

Innate Ability Theory

The innate ability theory of achievement and development is best represented by the bell curve (Figure 2.2), representing in this instance an uneven distribution of intellectual ability in human beings. We described this in detail in Chapter 1.

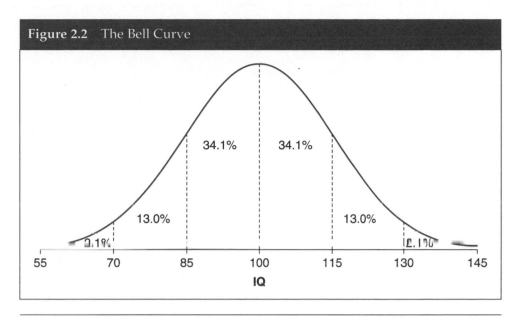

Figure 2.2 The Bell Curve

34.1%   34.1%

13.0%   13.0%

0.1%   0.1%

55   70   85   100   115   130   145

IQ

Source: Saphier, Haley-Speca, & Gower (2008). Used with permission.

Most of us were raised in an environment that reinforced this theory and set of assumptions, and we bought into those assumptions as if they were fact. This is not a statement of blame. It's a statement about the air we breathe in a society where this belief is played out more strongly than anywhere else in the world. These are undiscussed assumptions that dominated our country and our schools throughout the 20th century and still have equally pervasive influence now. Our contention is that these assumptions are flat-out wrong.

The Effort-Based Ability or Incrementalist Theory

The effort-based theory posits that all children are born with sufficient innate ability to achieve anything asked of them in school and that this ability (in fact, intelligence itself) is malleable through application of effective effort (Figure 2.3). Whether a student achieves and develops (gets smarter) is not a matter of having the raw material or ability to work with, but rather believing he or she has what it takes (confidence) and investing effort effectively (working hard and acquiring knowledge and strategies for working smart). Another way of summarizing this theory is that "smart is not something you *are*; smart is something you *get* (incrementally) by working hard and working smart" (Jeff Howard and Verna Ford, Efficacy Institute maxim).

Indeed, all teachers see differences in children every day in their classrooms, sometimes big differences: differences in readiness to learn, in speed of learning, in motivation, and clearly in current academic performance. Some students are way behind the others. But unlike an entity theorist, who would explain away the differences as a matter of how much

Figure 2.3   Jeff Howard Diagram

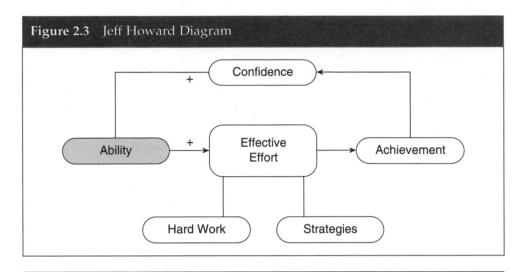

Source: Adapted from Efficacy Institute, Lexington, Massachusetts.

intelligence or innate ability one is endowed with, an incrementalist believes that all children have the intellectual capacity to eventually meet proficiency standards; it is not a deficient brain that is holding them back but any number of other variables, all of which can potentially be modified, accommodated, or influenced in some way.

Those who hold to this theory, when confronted with differences in children's development or performance, interpret the disparity as a function of disadvantages in their past that have created obstacles to their development and learning: gaps in knowledge, limited experiences and vocabulary, mismatch in learning-teaching style, and myriad other possible causes, none of which is internally hardwired in a person, and all of which may be subject to change under the right circumstances. This not to say that there are no differences in learners that are part of their birthright, and students clearly bring different inclination or disposition to topics. But they all have *enough* god-given brainpower to attain proficiency in literacy and numeracy at rigorous standards.

Two assumptions are embedded in this theory:

- There is no way of telling from children's attitudes, speech, cleanliness, clothing, record of past performance, and current performance what they are capable of learning and achieving if given time, motivation, and instruction that reaches out to meet their needs.
- Differences of color and culture have nothing to do with the capacities of children's brains.

Whereas the entity theory is deterministic, the incrementalist theory is optimistic. Those who espouse the incrementalist theory engage in an ongoing quest to discover what will enable students to turn on and take off.

Both explanations for achievement and development have been explored historically as part of a body of research referred to as *attribution theory* (Dweck, 1999, 2002; Nicholls & Burton, 1982; Weiner, 1972) and now as the *growth mindset*. Attribution theory is concerned with the explanations we give ourselves when we succeed for why we succeeded, and when we fail, for why we have failed. The research associated with it suggests that the explanations we give ourselves of the causes of our successes and failures (attributions) are based on our perceptions, and those perceptions and explanations ultimately influence our self-concept. They also influence our expectations for future situations, feelings of power and efficacy, and subsequent motivation to put forth effort. Weiner (1972, 1974) found four basic reasons to which individuals might attribute their success or lack thereof: ability, task difficulty, luck, and effort. Weiner arranges them in the grid shown in Figure 2.4.

According to Weiner, successful, confident people attribute their success to internal factors (having the ability and exerting effort) and lack of success to the internal factor they control and can most readily influence (effort). Unsuccessful, low-confidence people tend to attribute success to external factors (e.g., task difficulty: "Must have been an easy test"; luck: "I guess I just luckily studied the right chapters!") and lack of success to external factors (again, luck or task difficulty, those over which they have no control) with a secret inner fear that they really just don't have enough ability.

Figure 2.4   Attribution Theory

	Internal	External
Constant (Stable)	Ability	Task Difficulty
Variable (Unstable)	Effort	Luck

Source: Weiner (1972, 1974). Used with permission.

Young children believe success comes from effort; in fact, effort and ability are synonymous to them (Nicholls & Burton, 1982). But as they get older, some children start attributing academic success more and more to innate ability rather than effort. This creates a bind, because the only possible conclusion for such a child who is not doing well is that he or she must be dumb. Thus, many underperforming students opt out of school and quit trying by middle school because it's better to be considered lazy than dumb.

Dweck (1999) found that children (and adults) tend to be either entity theorists about intelligence and achievement or incrementalists. Entity theorists believe that intelligence is a thing, an entity that is fixed and responsible for any success; conversely, having low intelligence results in poor academic performance. Entity theorists take every assignment, every test, every task as an evaluation of their innate ability in a direct, causative way. These students form what Dweck calls a "performance goal orientation" toward academic work. Low performance (errors) indicates low ability. High performance indicates high ability. "I only like to do the things I already do well," says a girl who is an entity theorist.

Incrementalists believe that ability is built incrementally through effort and use of feedback from the environment. They form a "learning goal orientation," according to Dweck, where their goal is to learn something new rather than to prove themselves able, as is the goal of an entity theorist.

The consequences of these two internal theories of intelligence and the goal orientations that go with them are huge. Imagine the pressure felt by a student who is constantly on trial, who experiences every academic challenge as a measure of self on a dimension so highly prized in our society: intelligence.

Not all students (or adults) are at the poles of the entity versus incrementalist continuum, but large numbers are. The closer students are to the entity pole, the harder it is to mobilize energy and strategies when experiencing difficulty. Instead they tend to interpret difficulty as a measure of limited ability and frequently give up. The closer a student is to the incrementalist pole, the more likely he or she is to treat difficulty and errors as data saying that working harder or working smarter (different strategies) is what is needed in order to overcome the difficulty.

This brings us around to why an examination of standards and expectations is so central to the work of teachers. The standards of performance teachers set and the beliefs they hold about a child's capacity to meet those standards play a vital role in the messages sent to students and ultimately in what students are likely to achieve. Do we really have high expectations for student who are behind and appear discouraged?

Let us suspend disbelief for a time about what is possible and act as if we did. Let us undertake a detailed examination of what we would do every day if we really believed that all children could learn and wanted them to believe it too.

A video presentation of the information in this chapter is available at http://rbteach.com/products-resources/video/history-intelligence-2-myth-bell-curve

Video 2.1

REFERENCES AND RESOURCES

American Psychological Association. (2015). *The top 20 principles from psychology for PreK–12 teaching and learning.* Washington, DC: Author.

Berliner, D. C., & Biddle, B. J. (1995). *The manufactured crisis: Myths, fraud, and the attack on America's public schools.* Reading, MA: Addison-Wesley.

Black, P., Harrison, C., Lee, C., Marshall, B., & Wiliam, D. (2003). *Assessment for learning.* New York, NY: Open University Press.

Bloom, B. (1985). *Developing talent in young people.* New York, NY: Ballantine.

Cahan, S., & Cohen, N. (1989). Age versus schooling effects on intelligence development. *Child Development, 60,* 1239–1249.

Capron, C., & Duyme, M. (1989). Assessment of effects of socioeconomic status on IQ in full cross-fostering design. *Nature, 340,* 552–553.

Capron, C., & Duyme, M. (1996). Effect of socioeconomic status of biological and adoptive parents on WISC-R subtest scores of their French adopted children. *Intelligence, 22,* 259–275.

Ceci, S. (1991). How much does schooling influence general intelligence and its cognitive components? *Developmental Psychology, 27,* 703–722.

Ceci, S. (1996). *On intelligence: A bioecological treatise on intellectual development.* Cambridge, MA: Harvard University Press.

Currie, J. (2000). *Early childhood intervention programs: What do we know?* Washington, DC: Brookings Institution.

Dweck, C. S. (1975). The role of expectations and attributions in the alleviation of learned helplessness. *Journal of Personality and Social Psychology, 31,* 674–685.

Dweck, C. S. (1991). Self-theories and goals: Their role in motivation, personality, and development. In R. Dienstbier (Ed.), *Nebraska Symposium on Motivation.* Lincoln: University of Nebraska Press.

Dweck, C. S. (1999). Caution: Praise can be dangerous. *American Educator, 23,* 4–9.

Dweck, C. S. (1999). *Self-theories: Their role in motivation, personality, and development.* Philadelphia, PA: Taylor and Francis/Psychology Press.

Dweck, C. S. (2002). Messages that motivate: How praise molds students' beliefs, motivation, and performance (in surprising ways). In J. Aronson (Ed.), *Improving academic achievement* (pp. 38–60). Orlando, FL: Academic Press.

Flynn, J. R. (1994). IQ gains over time. In R. J. Sternberg (Ed.), *Encyclopedia of human intelligence* (pp. 617–623). New York, NY: Macmillan.

Gamoran, A. (1992). *Alternative uses of ability grouping: Can we bring high-quality instruction to low-ability classes?* Madison, WI: Center on Organization and Restructuring of Schools.

Gardner, H. (2011). *Frames of mind: The theory of multiple intelligences.* New York, NY: Basic Books.

Gladwell, M. (2011). *Outliers.* New York, NY: Routledge.

Gould, S. J. (1981). *The mismeasure of man.* New York: W. W. Norton.

Howard, J. (1995). You can't get there from here: The need for a new logic in education reform. *Daedelus, 124*(4), 85–92.

Howard, J., & Hammond, R. (1985, September 9). Rumors of inferiority. *New Republic,* pp. 17–21.

Howe, M. (2001). *Genius explained.* New York, NY: Cambridge University Press.

Husen, T., & Tuijnman, A. (1991). The contribution of formal schooling to the increase in intellectual capital. *Educational Researcher, 20*(7), 17–25.

Marzano, R. J., Pickering, D. J., & Pollock, J. E. (2001). *Classroom instruction that works.* Alexandria, VA: Association for Supervision and Curriculum Development.

Neisser, U. (1997). *The rising curve: Long-term gains in IQ and related measures.* Washington, DC: American Psychological Association.

Neisser, U., Boodoo, G., Bouchard, T. J., Jr., Boykin, A. W., Brody, N., Ceci, S. J. . . . Urbina, S. (1996). Intelligence: Knowns and unknowns. *American Psychologist, 51*(2), 77–101.

Nicholls, J. G., & Burton, J. T. (1982). Motivation and equality. *Elementary School Journal, 82,* 367–378.

Perkins, D. (1995). *Outsmarting IQ.* New York, NY: Free Press.

Plomin, R. (1996). *Genetics and experience: The interplay between nature and nurture.* Thousand Oaks, CA: SAGE.

Resnick, L. B. (1995). From aptitude to effort: A new foundation for our schools. *Daedalus, 124*(4), 55–62.

Sternberg, R. J., Grigorenko, E. L., & Bundy, D. (2001). The predictive value of IQ. *Merrill Palmer Quarterly, 47,* 1–41.

Streufert, S., & Nogami, G. Y. (1989). Cognitive style and complexity: Implications for I/O psychology. In C. L. Cooper & I. Robinson (Eds.), *International review of industrial and organizational psychology* (pp. 93–143). London, UK: Wiley.

Terman, L. (1916). *The measurement of intelligence.* Boston, MA: Houghton Mifflin.

Weiner, B. (1972). *Theories of motivation: From mechanism to cognition.* Chicago, IL: Markham.

Weiner, B. (1974). *Achievement motivation and attribution theory.* Morristown, NJ: General Learning Press.

Weiner, B. (1985). An attributional theory of achievement motivation and emotion. *Psychological Review, 92,* 548–573.

Weiner, B. (1996). *Human motivation: Metaphors, theories, and research.* Thousand Oaks, CA: SAGE.

Willingham, D., & Bruno, P. (2015). *The science of learning.* Austin, TX: Deans for Impact.

3

Verbal Behavior in Nine Arenas of Classroom Life

"My students hear every message I send—whether overt or implied—about their capacity to learn and succeed."

Carol Ann Tomlinson (2015, p. 76)

The numbers in the list below are keyed to the section in the Introduction called "50 Ways to Get Students to Believe in Themselves."

1. Calling on students
2. Responses to student answers
   - Sticking
3. Giving help
4. Changing attitudes toward errors
   - Persevere and return
5. Giving tasks and assignments
6. Feedback according to criteria for success with encouragement and precise diagnostic guidance
7. Positive framing of re-teaching
8. Tenacity when students don't meet expectations: pursuit and continued call for high-level performance
9. Pushback on fixed mindset language and student helplessness

It is through daily interactions in everyday classroom life that we

- convince students that "smart is something they can get,"
- show them how, and
- get them to want to.

Let us begin to show the specifics of how one does that, illustrated with video examples of teachers committed to this path.

There are a number of arenas of classroom life in which we communicate these three critical messages. An "arena" is a regularly recurring event, scene, or setting—like what we do when a student answers a question. The arenas in the following section are all ones in which we operate verbally.

1. CALLING ON STUDENTS

Pygmalion in the Classroom—Eliminate Unconscious Bias

If you observe me teaching, what are the patterns you might observe in how I call on students and interact with them?

The notion that teachers communicate their impressions to students about their academic ability through subtle and indirect messages is not new. Many years ago, based on a landmark study, researchers Rosenthal and Jacobson (1968) wrote the famous *Pygmalion in the Classroom*. It caused quite a stir. They even were invited to make an appearance on the *Today* show to share their findings.

Their study called attention to ways in which teacher perceptions of student ability result in differential treatment of students and have a positive or negative impact on their inclusion in classroom discourse and ultimately their performance in academics. Teachers were given falsified records of students' IQ scores: High-performing students might be represented as having high, average, or low IQs, and low performers as having high, average, or low IQs. And that information, rather than the students' actual IQs, influenced how teachers dealt with their students and how the students actually achieved.

Watch Richard Rosenthal describing the study.

https://www.youtube.com/watch?v=hTghEXKNj7g

Video 3.1

Cooper (1979) later organized these differential teacher communication behaviors into five categories:

1. *Climate.* "It was found that teachers who believed they were interacting with bright students smiled and nodded their heads more often than teachers interacting with slow students. Teachers also leaned towards bright students and looked brights in the eyes more frequently" (p. 393).

2. *Demands.* "Students labeled as slow have been found to have fewer opportunities to learn new material than students labeled as bright" (p. 393).

3. *Persistence.* "Teachers tend to stay with the highs longer after they have failed to answer a question. This persistence following failure takes the form of more clue giving, more repetition, and/or more rephrasing. Teachers have been found to pay closer attention to responses of students described as gifted. Teachers allowed bright students longer to respond before redirecting unanswered questions" (p. 394).

4. *Frequency of interaction.* "Teachers more often engage in academic contact with the high- than low-expectation students" (p. 394).

5. *Feedback.* "Teachers tend to praise high-expectation students more and proportionately more per correct response, while lows are criticized more and proportionately more per incorrect response" (p. 395).

There are 12 distinct behavioral items in these five categories, and they provide empirical evidence that teacher perceptions of a student's ability can lead to classifying students as "brights" and "slows" and to acting differently toward them, thus creating self-fulfilling prophecies. Here is a list of related questions you might investigate as you examine and reflect on your practice:

- Do I smile and nod more toward "highs"?
- Do I lean more toward "brights"?
- Do I look "brights" more in the eyes?
- Do I give "slows" fewer opportunities to learn new material?
- Do I stay with "highs" longer after they have failed to answer a question?
- Do I give "highs" more clues when they fail to get an answer—more repetition or more rephrasing?
- Do I pay closer attention to the responses of the "gifted"?
- Do I allow "brights" longer to respond?
- Do I have more frequent academic contact with "highs"?
- Do I give "highs" more praise per correct response?
- Do I give "lows" more criticism per incorrect response?
- Do I do any of the above more or less with white than with African, Asian, Hispanic, or Native American students? With English language learners? With special education students? With boys? With girls?

In the 1970s, Sam Kerman developed a professional development program called Teacher Expectations and Student Achievement (TESA; Kerman, Kimball, & Martin, 1980) in which teachers visited each other's classrooms and gave objective feedback to each other on the bulleted list above. The results were eye-opening. See the box for a report a teacher in one of our courses gave about her results from TESA-style peer observation.

One Teacher's Analysis of TESA Data on Her Teaching

Pygmalion Effects: A Teacher's Experiment

I have always been aware that my expectations for the children in my lowest performing reading group were different than my expectations for the children in the middle and high reading groups. I never stopped to think if this was "right" or "wrong." I never thought I sent different body messages to these lower performing children during our reading group sessions. I asked my graduate student teacher to log my smiles, positive remarks/gestures, the response time (in seconds) I allowed each student, and the number of clues I provided.

Much to my surprise and embarrassment, I found the results of this informal survey showed that I not only smiled, gave more pats on the back and easier clues to the children in my high and middle reading groups than those in the low group, but also I was only allowing the children in the lower performing group an average of 2–3 seconds to respond before I provided another hint. In fact, I was leaning backward in my chair while I taught these lower performing children and while they responded. In addition, I tended to sigh and look puzzled that they didn't know the answer. How could this be? After all my training thus far in this course, I found these facts hard to accept. I shared these results with my partner teacher. (I tried to blame my ear problems of this week, but my partner teacher said she's noticed a difference in the way I talk "in a general way" about the children in my lowest reading group.) I felt so terrible and asked for her help and advice.

To begin with, my partner teacher suggested having Mike be a "visitor" in the middle performing reading group in addition to his attending the low performing group. In this way I will be making a small "dent" in my attempt to treat all the children in my class the same regardless of their ability. I will be heightening my expectations for Mike as he attends the middle group and I will make a real effort to treat him the same while he is in the low group. I felt this was a realistic place to start, but truly felt this past week had been my unhappiest in my 12 years of teaching—with my earache and the realization that I was treating children of different levels of achievement differently.

Cooper's (1979) list of 12 behaviors gives specificity to ways in which we inadvertently may be differentiating our patterns of calling on students in synch with unconscious bias. So let's eliminate that differentiation—"reduce variation" to use a modern research term—and clear the decks for confidence-building messages to students.

2. RESPONSES TO STUDENT ANSWERS

Sticking

Here is another arena of classroom life that occurs, in this case, hundreds of times a day. We ask a question; a student answers; we do something. The "something" may be a nod, a word, a sentence or a question, or simply moving on to another question, but for sure we do something. It's a repetitive triadic cycle.

What is the range of those "somethings" we do in response to students' answers (including a student being silent and not answering at all)?

Exhibit 3.1 shows that range, laid out in a repertoire and divided into three types of teacher move.

Wait Time: A Purposeful Pause of 3–5 Seconds or More

Effects

1. There is a 300%–700% increase in the length of student responses.
2. The number of unsolicited but appropriate student responses increases.
3. Failures to respond decrease.
4. Confidence increases—there are fewer inflected responses.
5. Speculative responses increase.
6. Teacher-centered show-and-tell decreases, and student-student interaction increases.
7. Teacher questions change in number and kind:
   - The number of divergent questions increases.
   - Teachers ask higher level questions (Bloom's taxonomy).
   - There is more probing for clarification.
8. Students make inferences and support inferences with data.
9. Students ask more questions.
10. Contributions by "slow" students increase.
11. Disciplinary moves decrease, and more students are on task.
12. Achievement on logic tests improves.

Source: Adapted from Rowe (1987).

Teachers who stick with students—especially if their initial response is seemingly incorrect—send messages that they have confidence in their

Exhibit 3.1   Teacher Responses to Student Answers

Ways of Moving on to Another Student	• Criticize. "Come on. That answer shows no thought at all." "No," and redirect to another student. • "No," then give the correct answer. • "No," with the reason, which may serve as a cue. • Cue, but move on to another student. • Move to another student if the first student doesn't answer. • Redirect to another student to add, build, or extend. "Would you add anything to that, Zach?" • Student authorized to call on another student to answer in his or her place.
Ways of Sticking With a Student	• Supply the question for which the answer is right, cue, and hold the student accountable. • "No, but it's good you brought it up because others probably thought that too." "Try again." • Validate what is right or good about an answer and then cue, sticking with the student. • Ignore the answer, and cue the student. • Wait time. • Follow up with an expression of confidence or encouragement: "I think you know." • Follow up with an expression of confidence or extend. • Ask the student to elaborate. • Call for a self-evaluation of the answer. • Follow-up question to clarify: "Are you saying that . . . ?"
Ways of Acknowledging, Affirming	• Acknowledge, "Um-hmmm." • Repeat the student's answer. • Restate the answer in fuller or more precise language. • "Right." • "Right," with the reason. • Praise or praise and extend.

Source: Saphier, Haley-Speca, & Gower (2008). Used with permission.

students' ability to think through to an appropriate response. Giving a student a cue and lingering sends quite a different message than saying no and immediately calling on another student. Cuing the student but then immediately calling on another says the teacher doesn't really think the student has the capacity (or sufficient speed) to use the cue.

Whereas any response from this continuum might be effective in a given situation, the main point of this section is that teachers who convey positive expectations and build confidence and risk-taking in students use moves mainly from the middle of the continuum. And most of the time a student response is followed by the teacher asking a follow-up question such as "What makes you think that?" (See Making Students' Thinking Visible in Chapter 5.)

Sometimes teachers in our workshops wonder aloud how instructors have enough time to do such sticking and cuing with students and still get through all the material they wish to. The fact is that it takes hardly any more time at all to do so—seconds more at most. Sticking with a student does not need to slow the rate of coverage (though for other reasons, such slowing down might be a very good idea). But consider the cost of not sticking with a student who doesn't answer or answers incorrectly the first time: The student can easily feel inept at a moment like this—and consequently shut down cognitively. Also, by not sticking with the student, the teacher forfeits the chance to support the student's thinking and explicitly build confidence in his or her capacity to perform with academic material. Every long wait or period of silence when a student feels intimidated or unsure about a question is an opportunity to build confidence and capacity. Finally, it is not only the single response to an individual student that matters, but the pattern of responses over time that signals what the teacher thinks is important.

There are other responses to student answers as well. A *follow-up question* to double-check or extend (called a probe in research literature) is a way of checking to see if the student really understands the meaning of an answer or is just parroting. For example, a student might be able to recite "pi r^2" without knowing that r stands for the radius of the circle. So a follow-up question might be, "And the r stands for . . . ?"

Asking students to elaborate on their responses helps the teacher know what they really meant: "Could you explain that further?" "I'm not sure what you meant by that, Cho. Can you say a little more?" "You need to be more specific, Destiny. How far exactly are you saying the fulcrum has to be from this end?"

Acknowledging a student's answer nonjudgmentally leaves the door open for further comment from other students or for adding to the original answer by the same student. "So one possible explanation is. . . . Thank you. What might be some others?"

Restating in fuller language is a move a teacher might do for the benefit of the other students—to make sure they understood what the answer meant. Teacher asks, "Why do you suppose we celebrate Lincoln's birthday but not all presidents' birthdays?" Student says, "He freed the slaves." Teacher says, "So you are thinking that he did something really important and that's how we decide whose birthdays to celebrate?"

Praise can be an effective response to a student answer, but only if used well (Dweck, 2002; Henderlong & Lepper, 2002). Brophy's (1981) definitive review of the research on praise summarized how to praise well. To be effective, teacher praise must meet the following criteria:

- *Specific.* It specifies exactly what is praiseworthy about the student's performance: "John, I'm impressed with the variety of verbs and sentence patterns you used in this composition. This is your best work so far."
- *Contingent.* The praise is dependent on successful student performance and not given randomly or for encouragement. Noncontingent praise (given randomly and sometimes for incorrect answers) is frequent and found "most often among teachers who have low expectations for student learning. Within any given class, it is most likely to be directed toward the lowest achievers. No doubt such praise is given in an attempt to encourage the student. However, it seems likely that to the extent that the students recognize what the teacher is doing, the result will be embarrassment, discouragement, and other undesirable outcomes" (Brophy, 1981, p. 13).
- *Genuine.* The teacher means it. The praise is not manipulative, or given to reinforce (that is, engineer) a specific behavior, but reflects real appreciation on the teacher's part.
- *Congruent.* Gesture, tone of voice, stance, and posture send the same message as the words. If the teacher leans back, looks away, and says in a bored tone of voice, "I can see you really worked hard on these problems, Jorge," Jorge is not likely to be convinced.
- *Appropriate.* The choice of words, setting, and style is matched to the particular student. Public praise to individual middle school students can embarrass them. Public praise for certain behaviors can make them want to crawl under the table: "Oh, John, your handwriting is so tidy and neat" (said to a macho eighth grader).

Brophy (1981) also points out that effective praise

- uses students' own prior accomplishments as the context for describing present accomplishments,
- is given in recognition of noteworthy effort or success at difficult (for this student) tasks,

- attributes success to effort and ability, implying similar successes can be expected in the future ("You tried three different strategies until you came up with a winner!"),
- fosters endogenous attributions (students believe that they expend effort on the task because they enjoy the task and/or want to develop task-relevant skills).

Each of the behaviors just described—wait time, supplying the question for which the answer is right, cuing, holding the student accountable, follow-up questions, asking students to elaborate, acknowledgment, restating in fuller language, and praise—has research to support it as an effective teacher behavior (Costa, 1985; Dunkin & Biddle, 1974). There is similar support for redirecting in the literature and even a case for the appropriateness of criticism with certain students as long as the criticism is not a put-down (Graham & Barker, 1990). These findings have been reinforced by subsequent research (Dweck, 2002; Henderlong & Lepper, 2002).

Since many of these response techniques are inherently worthwhile in and of themselves for stimulating thinking and attaining clarity, they are worth adding to all teachers' repertoires. And it is a good bet that among the list cited, there are several new ones for any teacher. (Least frequently seen, in our observations, are wait time, asking students to elaborate, and effective praise.) But beyond incorporating them into one's repertoire is the issue of matching.

Are the response techniques being used appropriately in the right situation and with the right students? Wait time, for example, is less appropriate when asking low-level questions or doing drill. Giving students time to think and process is most effective when higher level thinking is called for. Redirecting prematurely can deny a student the opportunity to think through an answer or refine one already given. Restating in fuller language can aid the understanding of the rest of the class, but if done unnecessarily or to excess can teach students not to listen to one another. The bottom line here, as elsewhere in the quest to understand teaching, is to work first to expand repertoires to respond more appropriately to more students in different situations, then improve the effectiveness of matching.

And finally, the main point of this section: Focus responses *to the middle part of the repertoire* so as to take every opportunity to build confidence and capacity in students.

When Students Don't Answer at All

Sometimes students are called on and don't answer or don't have a ready answer, and there is that loaded second or two in which we must make a decision: Do we get embarrassed for the student and want to get the spotlight off that child? Do we stick with the student, giving cues? Do we ask the question over again? Do we redirect the question to another student?

There is a progressive continuum of responses we might employ to keep students open and thinking when they don't answer:

- Use wait time.
- Repeat the question.
- Cue.
- Ask a simpler question.
- Ask a fact-only question.
- Give choices for the answer.
- Ask for a yes or no response.
- Ask the student to repeat or imitate an answer.
- Ask for a nonverbal response (shaking the head or pointing).
- Instruct the student to say, "I need more time to think" or "I don't know yet. Please come back to me."

The benefits of wait time were described earlier. Simply enduring a little silence while Isabella grimaces may give her the time she needs to come up with the answer. Modeling this behavior—taking time to think after a student has posed a question—can have a powerful influence too.

I once attended a session where David Perkins, co-director of Project Zero at Harvard University, was asked a question. (Project Zero's mission is to understand and enhance learning, thinking, and creativity in the arts, as well as humanistic and scientific disciplines, at the individual and institutional levels.) He turned his head, looked sideways, then up at the ceiling, and continued in silence for a full 10 seconds. By this time I was getting nervous for David as a presenter and looking for something to say, some way to jump in and rescue him from what seemed like a paralytic attack. But just at that moment, David looked the questioner calmly in the eye and delivered a brilliant reply, paragraphs long, with no wasted words. He didn't appear in the least ruffled. He had simply been comfortably thinking out his answer. It was I who had been uncomfortable with the pause, not Perkins.

Several other times in that session, similar pauses for reflection followed complicated questions from the audience. After the first time, I was not worried about David anymore and spent the time thinking about the question too. In fact, David's modeling of wait time for himself to think through an answer had an immediate effect on the class. The whole discussion became more reflective and thoughtful. And by having our instructor model his willingness to think before he spoke, we became more comfortable doing so. The result was to elevate the level of the entire discussion.

Turning to the other behaviors on the continuum, we see a progression where less and less is required of the student, until finally only imitation or headshaking is requested. This continuum was adapted from Good and Brophy (2000) for nonresponsive students. Their point is that students should not be allowed to practice nonresponsiveness but instead should be expected to participate.

As long as they appear to be trying to answer the question, the teacher should wait them out. If they begin to look anxious, as if worrying about being in the spotlight instead of thinking about the question, the teacher should intervene by repeating the question or giving a clue. He or she should not call on another student or allow others to call out the answer. (Good & Brophy, 2000, pp. 192–193)

Vocabulary Changes

Our very vocabulary begins to change as we work to transform student attributions. The word *ability* hardly passes our lips anymore. We refer to *performance groups* when talking to peers, not *ability groups*. We can't say anymore "C'mon, this is easy" to encourage students to try; if it's easy, what's the thrill in accomplishing it? And if they experience difficulty, what's the obvious conclusion of their inability to complete something that's supposed to be "easy"?

We don't say, "Good luck on the test." It's not luck they need, it's good study and preparation beforehand.

To use feedback and praise as a vehicle for attribution retraining, we need to intentionally embed specific effort and ability attributions in our responses: "You've proven in your work all week that you have the brainpower to do some very challenging problems. There must be some strategy you aren't using yet that would be the breakthrough on these. Let's look at how you are approaching them and do some brainstorming." "You really concentrated on organizing your ideas and taking time to plan before you wrote your final piece. Nice job!" "You stuck with the task—you never gave up—and now look at what you've accomplished." "When you saw that your first strategy wasn't working, you took another approach, and now look at the progress you've made on this."

3. GIVING HELP

Convey a New View of Making Mistakes; Embed Useful Cues and Messages of Belief

If we could follow teachers around while they are circulating among individual students and groups at work, we would hear numerous exchanges where students ask for help. How teachers respond at such moments—the words they actually say—contains explicit and implicit messages about their belief in the students' ability. This is an arena of classroom life where we can deliberately monitor our language and make sure we are communicating the three essential messages that frame this book.

Chapter 1 demonstrated how choice of language in these situations reveals our beliefs not only to an observer but clearly to students as well. This finding encourages a third ear that listens to us as we speak and becomes a self-governing alert system for how we respond in all these arenas.

Watch high school teacher Pierre Gilles give help in an empowering way.

http://rbteach.com/products-resources/video/feedback-and-building-confidence-mistakes-are-normal

Video 3.2

Pierre Gilles, an algebra teacher at Brockton High School, is a high-gain teacher, meaning his students achieve more than a single year's worth of academic progress in an academic year. Look at accompanying video with the script below, and see if you can identify language in this "Giving Help" situation that embeds messages for his students.

Script	Comments
JS: You make comments to kids in the context of explaining things to them that create a classroom climate where the kids are really willing to struggle even if they don't get it the first time. So I am going to show you this clip and then I am going to ask you what are other things that you do that are in your head about how to create this climate.	

Clip 1

Script	Comments
PG: I hope you guys realize that learning is messy, so . . . it's gonna be. . . . It is OK to make some mistakes, so there is nothing wrong with that. So let's see what we have. . . . Now, I do have one issue in here with number 12. What is the formula to find axis of symmetry? Student: All right, see, we have to fix that.	Normalizing error.

Script	Comments
PG: You have to use that always. Why don't you write that down, Louie? If I was you before I start looking for the axis of symmetry, write down the rule for that. How do we find the axis of symmetry? What's the rule we have to use? It is right here—number one.	Advice. Pressing for specifics.
Student: X = –b	
PG: Right, write it down. And look at number 12 and tell me what's wrong in number 12.	Asking for self-evaluation.
Student: B is 8 . . . 8 divided by 2 is 4.	
PG: Look at the axis of symmetry again—read it out. X = –b, minus b, negative b.	Cueing.
Student: Oh, it is supposed to be negative . . .	
PG: All right, if I was you when I was doing it . . . because if you don't have the right axis of symmetry, most likely the graph will be wrong. So use the axis . . . write it down. Do it as practice, before you start looking for it just always write it down.	Advice.

Conference

Script	Comments
JS: And the essence is that first time, "I hope you guys realize that learning is messy. . . . Yeah, it's all right, don't worry about it when you make mistakes. . . ."	
PG: Here is what I was thinking about—the kid gets so uptight when they make a mistake that the teacher will start yelling at them. The philosophy is if you know what you are doing, you aren't supposed to be here. . . . It is because you don't know it and therefore by trying it is OK to make mistakes. So that's the reason I told them, learning is messy, so you're not going to be able to get it the first time you try, you have to keep trying over and over until you get it.	
JS: There's another one coming up here; I think you may have still been with these boys. I saw this as part of the climate too—the way you responded. This has to do with the way you correct errors when something is wrong or incomplete.	

Clip 2

Script	Comments
Student: That's 13.	
PG: That's 13, opens down. Let me look at the example. OK, guys, let's pick up the pace, please.	
Student: It's y equals negative x to the second plus 4x plus 3.	
PG: Now we know it is going down, very good. So that would be 2 for the axis of symmetry. Do you have –2? I am looking at –2 here.	Identifying the error.
Student: But it's 2.	
PG: All right, so you need to change that on that, all right, so that's 2. Plug it in. Very good. Do you have –4 or 4?	Checking for understanding.
Student: –4.	
PG: Beautiful. But you need to show me . . . that is the perfect, I am impressed with that, but you need to show me how you get –4. Whenever you're doing substitution you need to use parentheses. That is the right answer, but if I were in your shoes doing that, all right, I would do . . . you got the right answer, there is nothing wrong with that, but there is just something I would like to share with you. That is –1 times what is the value of x?	Acknowledgment. Criteria: show your thinking.
Student: 2.	
PG: 2 to the second power plus 4 times 2 plus 3. So that would be 2 to the second power, which is 4, 4 times –1 is –4. That's what. It is like when I am checking your work, that is what I am looking for . . . even if you got it wrong or right it really doesn't matter to me, I need to see that step. All right? And if there is any mistake if you do that step, I am going to be able to help you out. . . . OK, very good . . . so let's finish that up, that's –4. That's 4 plus 3, that's 7, why –7?	Sending the message—the reason to show your work is so I can help you if something went wrong. Mistakes are OK, I am here to help you fix them, and you CAN!
Student: No, it's 7. I erased something over it.	
PG: It's 7, OK. All right, –1, plug it in. That will be –1, –4. –3 plus 2. Check that again when you do the substitution. Show the work for the –1 you are using.	Calling for self-evaluation, specific guidance.

Conference

Script	Comments
JS: Now, that's very respectful language.	
PG: Thank you.	
JS: Um, something I would like to share with you. That is a very different way of saying, "Let me show you how to avoid screwing this up again!" So there is the acknowledgment that there is an error—actually there is the acknowledgment that he's done a lot of things right. "Beautiful, but you need to show your work . . ." and then you explain—which is another part of what I saw as respect in here, Pierre—you explain the reason why you want them to show the work and it comes back to them, if you don't get the right answer, I will know how to help you.	
PG: This kid, he is a special kid. He's really smart. I mean, the first 2 months of the year, it was a struggle because I was trying to build up that confidence. But now the issue is that he is overconfident.	
JS: Ah, overconfident.	
PG: He is overconfident so he is trying to solve everything in his brain, without showing the work at all. So . . .	
JS: Aha, I see. What else do you do to build confidence?	
PG: It is really simple. I just let them know I am here to help them out and I set the bar so high, the expectation; I told them since day one when they walk in, you guys in this classroom, in this setup you have no excuses at all to get an F. The least you're supposed to be able to can get is a B–. And since then I have been pushing them so hard. I told them we have 66 minutes and we are going to be working for 66 minutes. You stop working when the bell rings. We set that at the beginning of the year, and now it's working. It's working.	

"Learning Is Messy" Analysis

Feedback

When asked for help, Mr. Gilles gives responses to students that are specific and helpful. At different times, the responses display the following aspects of quality interaction:

1. Gives guidance with specifics. (The guidance is often the minimal amount to lead the student to action or discovery. Does not do the thinking for the student.)

2. Limits corrective information to the amount of advice that the student can act on.

3. Presses the student for specifics.

4. Presses the student to generate ideas and asks the student to make choices.

5. Affirms, encourages, and reassures.

6. Asks the student to add or extend.

7. Asks the student to self-evaluate according to clear criteria.

8. Catches and prevents an error in a way that allows the student to identify and correct it.

In addition, Mr. Gilles's interactions with the students communicate high expectations and mutual respect.

Confidence and Risk-Taking

An important element of classroom climate is present, too. In our previous book, *The Skillful Teacher* (Saphier, Haley-Speca, & Gower, 2008), we defined classroom climate as "the feelings and beliefs students have and the cumulative patterns of behavior that result from those feelings and beliefs regarding community and mutual support, *risk taking and confidence,* and influence and control" (p. 330, italics added). Mr. Gilles makes moves that are particularly targeted at confidence and risk-taking. These are moves that say "mistakes are OK" and even emphasize that it is important to show how a mistake is made so that he can help get the student back on track.

Making mistakes and getting help are expected activities in his class, and he communicates this message with respect. The responses of his students demonstrate their level of trust and confidence. Mr. Gilles even reports that he thought that one student's confidence had actually built up too high—remarkable for a student who had previously been failing. To rectify the situation, Mr. Gilles tells him to back up and make sure to show his work, and again he does so in a very respectful, supportive manner.

Yet another aspect to note here is that, while Mr. Gilles's classroom climate is a positive and supportive one, he still holds students to a high academic standard. He very clearly teaches his students that putting in extra effort will result in increased achievement.

Commentary on Unsolicited Help

Graham and Barker (1990) and Zimmerman and Marinez-Pons (1990) found that when teachers give unsolicited help, students often conclude that their teachers think the students are not able and need support. And some will then begin acting as if to confirm this belief. Another side effect of premature unsolicited help is that students learn not to struggle, that struggle is bad, that struggle means they are unable— which is exactly the way entity theorists plunge deeper into a subtractive belief system.

This is tricky, because teachers want to be available to the students who need the most support; we want, in fact, to arrange our time and other resources to deploy them efficiently in support of students who do need extra help. So how do we do that without inadvertently sending debilitating expectation messages? We think the answer lies in the subtleties of word choice and body language, as in these three separate examples:

- Instead of going right over to Brian on the first problem and saying, "Need help, Brian?" Mr. Flood works with another child near him and watches how Brian is doing. He is able to pick up early whether Brian is struggling.
- "Trouble?" he says off-handedly while catching Brian's eye. "No," says the student. "Okay, a good scholar knows when to ask for help. So struggle is good. But be strategic, and ask me or someone else if you hit a wall."
- "Trouble?" Mr. Flood says off-handedly as he catches Brian's eye. "Yeah," says the student. "Okay. So what part has you hung up?" "The whole thing." "Okay, now you can do this with a little coaching. What's the first step?"

Another recommendation is to make asking for help a rewarded behavior, used by "good students" or "scholars" in the culture of the classroom, when they have used their own resources first. That way you won't have to give much unsolicited help. You can establish such a culture by teaching, practicing, and rewarding such behavior explicitly. It becomes part of the curriculum.

4. CHANGING ATTITUDES TOWARD ERRORS

Persevere and Return

In the following video we go into Ms. Moore's middle school science class and see Ricardo answer a question half-correctly—a common event in any class. How do we handle half-right or incorrect responses?

Following the guidelines of the previous arena of "Responses to Student Answers," we would stick with the student, giving cues and wait time and also expressing confidence. But if students cannot think their way through, we often bring other students into the conversation to produce the information and the thinking required. "Persevere and Return" means that at the end of such an episode, we come back to the first student (in Ms. Moore's case, Ricardo) and ask him to "put it all together."

The fact that we come back to this student shows we want him to succeed, we care about his learning, and we believe in his capacity to "put it all together." He gets to emerge as the synthesizer and be a winner, not the student who needed to be helped out by others who are more able ("smarter").

Watch Ms. Moore respond to Ricardo.

http://rbteach.com/products-resources/video/persevere-and-return-natural-resources

Video 3.3

There are mental guidelines that start to creep inevitably into our way of being when we take on this mission of convincing students to believe in themselves. Whatever the situation, we ask ourselves how to frame a response that is confidence building and linked to a belief that ability can be grown. This mental filter eventually takes over, and I don't have to remind myself, "Oh, I should persevere and return to Ricardo!"

"Persevere and Return" and the other forms of verbal behavior in this chapter may require breaking old habits. One can't be coverage driven and still send the three critical messages to students.

Errors Are Normal and Useful

Mathematics teacher Dale Leibforth once put a strip of cash register paper along the top of his whiteboard that read: "Failure, Failure, Failure, Success, Failure, Failure, Success, Failure, Success, Success, Success." Students finally asked what it meant after the first week of the semester. "What do you think?" he responded.

The ensuing discussion surfaced all ideas he wanted them to consider—namely that errors are to be expected, they are normative and useful in the learning process. Failure is an opportunity for learning and not to be avoided or considered a disgrace. Failure to do something correctly is an invitation to find out why, fill the knowledge gap, identify the misconception, learn the missing step in the process, fix the faulty logic. The point is "You may not be able to do it yet, but you will as soon as you know what the gap is. There's nothing wrong with your ability." This message is sent tacitly (or not) every time we respond to a student's error.

A teacher named Ms. Alcala gives a "Do Now" mathematics problem on an index card as part of the opening class routine. She collects the index cards and quickly sorts them into those that are correct and those where there is an error. She is looking for the *best* mistake, "My Favorite No," meaning a mistake from which we can all learn. With this message embedded in her language, she then puts the student's work (without identifying the student) under the document camera and explores the error with the class. Her students are thus getting practice doing error analysis.

Check out Ms. Alcala's "My Favorite No" routine.

https://www.teachingchannel.org/videos/class-warm-up-routine

Video 3.4

Some years ago a fifth-grade teacher in Fairbanks, Alaska, told me he gave a "Great Misteak" (spelling deliberate) award every week to highlight this new attitude toward errors.

The word *yet* often comes up when a high expectation teacher has exchanges with individual students. "Oh, well, you haven't got it yet, but you will. Let's see if we can find what went wrong."

Another approach to student errors is inviting the students to talk through their own thinking out loud. Peers can be asked to react or question the student. The intention is to give the students thinking time and input that allow them to correct their own error.

Watch how dealing with errors unfolds in Alyssa Ricken's first-grade class.

http://rbteach.com/products-resources/video/mstv-first-grade-ella-fixes-her-error

Video 3.5

This arena of classroom life, dealing with error, becomes a pivotal one for classroom climate building and making it safe for students to take risks—risks to answer when they are not sure, risks to share their work with peers because no one will make fun of them, risks to try again and try harder when they encounter struggle. It is one of the most powerful ways to cultivate the growth mindset and convince students that "smart is something you can get."

5. GIVING TASKS AND ASSIGNMENTS

It's easy to conjure how one could send negative expectation messages to a student when giving assignments. If the set of ten problems gets progressively harder, the teacher says, "Bo, just do the first five problems. That will be enough."

A high expectations teacher might say, "Bo, there is a step with common denominators that you have to learn in order to do problems six through ten, so I want you to ask Jayla how to do that and then come and show me what you've learned before we go home." The point is, the teacher is not going to excuse Bo from the level of expectation the curriculum calls for; the teacher is going to provide the scaffolding he needs to meet those expectations.

When difficulty presents itself, the teacher's language will acknowledge that difficulty and express confidence in students' ability and perseverance. "Number ten is a real stinker, but I know you'll all get there even if it stumps you at first."

6. FEEDBACK ACCORDING TO CRITERIA FOR SUCCESS WITH ENCOURAGEMENT AND PRECISE DIAGNOSTIC GUIDANCE

"Praise will keep you in the game, but it's feedback that makes you better."

There are many ways one might respond to students' work, whether it is products they create or some type of skill-based performance. Among these are feedback, encouragement, suggestions or advice, praise, and questions. "Good" feedback on student work is known to improve student learning. In fact, summaries of research on teaching skills show it to be one of the highest leverage skills for a teacher to master (Black, Harrison, Lee, Marshall, & Wiliam, 2003; Marzano, Pickering, & Pollock, 2001). "The most powerful single modification that enhances achievement is feedback. The simplest prescription for improving education must be 'dollops of feedback'" (Hattie, quoted in Marzano et al., 2001, p. 96).

True feedback contains no judgment. It is objective information about which elements of the student performance meet the criteria for success. In an early video on feedback, the late Grant Wiggins tells his young son Justin, who is learning to write his name, that "the N looks more like a Z." That's all. Justin erases the lopsided ⇄ and rewrites it with the correct verticality: N. The information from Grant enabled Justin to self-adjust/self-correct his performance.

Skillful feedback enables that kind of student self-adjustment and self-correction. For example: "The author's point of view is correctly stated, but the reasons he has it are missing."

Threaded within a teacher's reactions or responses are tacit expressions of confidence (or no confidence), and embedded in the language we use are messages about how capable we think students are. First, if feedback is specific, detailed, frequent, and useful, the implied message is that we want the students to master the material and are giving them every support to do so. Otherwise we wouldn't take the trouble to give all the feedback.

Second, while "pure" feedback is nonjudgmental and simply identifies what students have or haven't accomplished in light of a set of established criteria or standards, the responses we make to student work often do and should include more than pure feedback: encouragement, appropriate leads and suggestions for how to improve it, and so on. This is especially true when responding to students' writing, both fiction and nonfiction. So it is important not only to give students a high volume of specific, useful feedback, but also to pay attention to the embedded belief messages that surround the feedback:

> "You listed your findings in the lab report but never addressed the next two questions about the conclusions you draw from the findings and new questions this has raised. This isn't up to your best work." (Implied message: You are capable of good work.)

> "So these are the parts you have to improve to have a first-class essay." (Implied message: You can, indeed, make this first-class. There are some parts of it to address and then you'll be there.)

> "What help do you need to meet this standard?" (Implied message: If you identify the help you need, the resources are here and you can meet the standard.)

"Now the only thing you have to do is get a really potent lead." (Implied message: You've done a good job and have met most of the criteria. If you get a potent lead, you will have a complete and high-quality product.)

Feedback sometimes needs to be married to advice, cues, or guidance for the student, because the student can't spot the error or figure out how to access the missing part:

"Look back at the previous problem and see what you did with the decimal there when you multiplied by 100."

"You have to go back to the way he started the speech to see why he ended here. Do that and then tell me how you think they tie together."

When studying feedback, we occasionally have participants mourn the absence of enthusiasm and warmth from what they interpret as cold information. Not so. Feedback is information, all right, but it can certainly be delivered with warmth and enthusiasm, and even explicit statement of confidence and encouragement:

"So if you do that missing step in the science experiment, I know you're going have your eyes opened to this amazing process, and you'll write a great lab report!"

Our point here has been that the moment of responding, the actual event in which it is delivered, either verbal or written, is one of those moments when we need heightened awareness of our choice of words, body language, and tone of voice so as to send a positive expectation message.

Students are so used to response behaviors from teachers that convey judgment rather than objective information and expressions of confidence! This is why so much recent research on praise has focused on its potentially negative impact. Praise is especially harmful if it connects your performance with your ability. "Oh, you're so smart to have figured out that way to do it" versus "Oh boy, I can see that you have worked really hard on applying the new strategy to figure this one out." Attributing success explicitly to effort and strategies is what high expectations teachers do, and it is a strong force to moving students' own attributions of success or failure to internal factors other than "ability."

Connected to this arena are two other regularly recurring situations that call for reaction from us to students: when students don't meet the expectations we set and when there is a significant change in performance. Each of these situations represents an opportunity to reinforce effort as the cause of the results a student has produced (attribution training), and it is through these reactions that students get the message about how important something is and whether we believe they are capable of achieving the performance targets.

Praising Low-Quality Work

Praising low quality work communicates low expectations. This practice has a particularly damaging effect on students of color and students of poverty who may receive praise and approval for work that does not meet the standards expected of white students or advantaged students (Mandara & Murray, 2007). The consequence is to communicate low expectations to already underachieving students and not push them to meet standards they could actually reach. The alternative effect, even more damaging, is to convince students of color that you don't think they can really do as well as the white students. And the worst outcome of all is that they accept this inference!

This particular syndrome can come from a desire to be positive to students of color, to be encouraging and supportive, to be nice. Teachers want them to feel good. But what students of color need from their teachers is press, push, help, confidence, and strategies to do better, not an easy pass that lets them "get over" without truly meeting standards. Such teachers embody the descriptor *warm demanders* (Kleinfeld, 1975).

Reacting When Students Do Well

When students do well, it is important that the praise given to them attributes their success specifically to effort (and perhaps secondarily, by implication, to their having sufficient ability): "You came in for extra help, studied before the test, and took your time checking your answers before handing it in. And it really paid off!"

Reacting to a Change in Performance

A significant change in performance, either dramatically better or worse, is another opportunity for sending expectation messages and attribution retraining: "This is nowhere near the standard you're capable of. We need to figure out what is happening and what you can do to get back on track." A remark like that from a respected teacher can be a powerful spur to a flagging student. But what about the reverse?

Suppose a student with a D average gets an 83 on a test. The teacher stops the student on the way out the door and says, "You did really well on this test. Why do you think you did so well?" The student pauses, looks down, and mumbles, "Must have been an easy test." (Note the connection to external attribution—luck or task difficulty.) The teacher replies, "Easy test! I don't give easy tests; everybody knows that. And you got number 14 right. That was the hardest one. Now come on, what do you think you did to accomplish that?"

This teacher is trying to get the student to consider that not only does he have the ability to do well, but there is something he has done to bring about this result (effort attribution). But if the student doesn't see himself as having that ability, he will more than likely be silent at this point in the dialogue. The suggestion behind the teacher's question can be threatening in several ways: "What if I am capable of good work? Will she expect it of me all the time? What if I tried and couldn't do this well again?" Another student may want to keep expectations low just to avoid working hard.

Still another possibility is that by challenging the student to think about why he succeeded, the teacher may be throwing him into social jeopardy. Segments of peer culture in schools are built around not doing academic work and dumping on school. To become a student and be seen as trying hard could be interpreted as a rejection of one's peer group. This syndrome may occur in certain environments for students of color, where striving in school settings gets interpreted as "acting white" (Fordham & Ogbu, 1986). A teacher who seizes opportunities like the student doing unexpectedly well on a test needs to be ready to support the student through the thinking and the possible perceived risks: "Well, you think about it, and when you come in tomorrow, I'm going to ask you again why you think you did so well." Whether or not the student has a response tomorrow, the hope is that he will start thinking about the possibility that he is capable of higher performance than he'd imagined and weighing the risks and rewards of trying hard. It is also a time for the teacher to devise strategies for how to work with him to provide support and scaffolds while he proves to himself that he has what it takes.

7. POSITIVE FRAMING OF RE-TEACHING

The very fact that we organize for in-class re-teaching of small groups of students who didn't get it the first time around is an expression of high expectations teaching. We wouldn't go to the trouble if we didn't want the kids in the group to master the concept or the skill. But what we say when we call up the group can embed that message of our positive desire and our faith in them, or the opposite.

Watch Zach Herrmann and listen for the language of high and positive expectations in the way he frames the re-teach.

http://rbteach.com/products-resources/video/differentiation-my-favorite-part

Video 3.6

The choice of language embeds so many messages implicitly.

"This is my favorite part . . . where we actually get what we need."

"Favorite part" signals his desire and his pleasure in making sure every student understands and can do the problems. "Get what we need" implies that there's a gap somewhere that is going to be filled now."

"If you have an E, then you're ready for the extension for that type of problem."

"Ready" conveys that the student is ready for the next step in their learning and that they will, in fact, be getting just what they need.

"If you have an S, that means that you're ready for the support session. We talk about it; we make sure we get it."

Again, "ready" for the support session. It's just the right place for the student to be. And the purpose of the session is (note expression of intent and confidence) to make sure the student gets it.

"That's the whole point. That we all leave here making sure we all know how to do every single one of these problems."

That's why he's doing this, because he wants to make sure they do get it.

"In the past I've been confident that when we leave here we really do get how to do these things."

And they've proven that they can before. So he's confident they will today too.

"The answers to the extensions are back here."

So after students do them, they can check how they did against this model of the problem worked out correctly. Then they can correct errors if they made any.

"I'm going to hand these out to everybody."

Everyone will have a chance to do the hard ones, not just some.

"And that's our goal—that everyone leaves here understanding. . . ."

A concrete expression of his positive goal for ALL of them.

This examination of language when calling up groups for re-teaching assumes that one is *doing* re-teaching. Because that is a different though related issue, we have treated it separately below in #13 in Chapter 4, about routines and structures that embed the growth mindset and the critical messages.

8. TENACITY WHEN STUDENTS DON'T MEET EXPECTATIONS

When students do poor work, it is important they hear about it in a way that conveys our belief that they can do better, and that we are looking for investment of their effort because we believe it will pay off. Students may display reluctance or resistance when we react in a direct (and sometimes high-energy) way.

But students also can easily interpret low affect or a neutral or noncommittal response to low-quality work as an expression of our lack of interest or belief in them. It often is. And in the absence of a reaction, a large segment of students will not believe sufficiently in themselves to work hard or do well. This danger is particularly present for students who believe it's their innate ability that either enables or disables them to perform (Dweck, 2002). When students who hold this belief find something to be challenging or do poorly at something they attempt, they interpret it as confirmation of not having enough ability. These same students, according to attribution theory (Weiner, 1996), believe that when they do poorly, it is because of task difficulty—and underneath that belief, the damning suspicion that they are not bright enough. Thus, when students do poorly, going after them with high energy and affect becomes an implicit statement of belief in their ability and a call for more effort—an opportunity to retrain their attributions about what causes their success and failure.

Here's where the phrase *warm demander* gets defined. Students may not praise you for it at the time, but later they often say about their favorite and most effective teachers, "I could run but I couldn't hide!" You come after them in your own style, which can vary widely, but you keep coming.

The very fact that you do so says you care. You wouldn't take the time and exert the effort to make sure they meet standards if you didn't think they were worth it. That's the bottom-line embedded message, intuited rather than clear in words by students: "She thinks I'm worth her effort."

What does tenacity look like? If you're reading this book with a group, stop here and generate a list of behaviors you think you would see a tenacious teacher doing with underperforming students. When you finish, go to the next page to see my examples.

Making Appointments

Stephanie stands by the door as the class exits and taps four students to join her right after lunch and before the fifth-period class starts. "I want to see you right here at 12:20 to finish these problems, capiche?" (Italian slang for "understand"?)

Michael makes an appointment for a one to one after class with Yojii and he doesn't show up. Watch as, at the end of class the next day, he approaches him at his desk and has the following conversation. (Watch from 11:53 to 14:35.)

http://rbteach.com/products-resources/video/teaching-effective-effort-motivational-structures

Video 3.7

Charlotte has escorted her class to the bus as usual and calls to Irma, who is waving from the window as the bus pulls out: "Have you got your biology book? Fixing number 7, right?"

Positive Attributions

A positive attribution is an explicit or embedded statement that a student has the capacity to do something. Mr. Herrmann uses this approach with Kelyn. She's been asked to speak for her group in explaining why "3N – 30" is the correct translation rather than 30 – 3N for the word problem "If three times a number minus 30 is 45, what is the number?" Note how the girl to her right picks up at the end with asking Kelyn to explain her thinking.

Watch Mr. Herrmann use the positive attributions approach.

http://rbteach.com/products-resources/video/stimulating-effective-effort

Video 3.8

Here's another version of positive attribution: Donal says to a student, "This isn't nearly what you are capable of, Brandon. I want to see a rewrite of this tomorrow with all the evidence supporting your main points."

Another example is a written note atop Brenda's paper: "This isn't up to your usual standard. Come see me right after class so we can list the edits that will earn you an A."

Pursuit

Ronda goes into the cafeteria and has a private conversation with Sophia about the exit ticket she failed to leave after class. Sophia says, "I didn't know how to do it." Ronda responds, "Then you can write *that* on the ticket if you have to, but I need to know where you and all the other students stand whenever we introduce new material so I can help you close gaps if you have them. Everyone gets confused at times. Now come in before class tomorrow and we'll plug this hole. 7:45 sharp!"

9. PUSHBACK ON FIXED MINDSET LANGUAGE AND STUDENT HELPLESSNESS

Discouraged students often speak from a stance of disability or helplessness.

- "This is too hard."
- "I can't do this."
- "No matter how hard I work, I never seem to do well."
- "I'm just stupid at figuring out problems like this."
- "I never was very good at writing."
- "These are just too hard."
- "Only smart kids can do work like this."

These are all opportunities for us to push back directly on negative attributions with strong statements of belief.

Student: "My father wasn't any good at math either."

Teacher: "Well, he would have been if he'd had me for a teacher! And you will be too. There was nothing wrong with your dad's math brain and there's nothing wrong with yours. You just have some gaps in background math knowledge. Now sit right down with me; we're going to find out where they are and fill them in."

These pushback statements have to be delivered with strength and confidence. Student beliefs that their ability is low and fixed in an academic area are strong and stubborn. Palliative assurance or feel-better messages of hope are insufficient. Students need to hear from us in no uncertain terms that we do not accept their negative self-assessment and will not allow them to give up on themselves.

The statements above make a useful practice field for gearing ourselves up to push against and gradually change students' negative attributions. (See Teacher Case Study 4 in Appendix A.) Try this: Get with a partner and divide up the statements at the top of this page. Pretend a student said one to you. What would your pushback statement be to that student? Taking turns this way, invent a retort for each statement above. Give you partner feedback on the strength of the pushback statement and the conviction you hear in his or her voice!

REFERENCES AND RESOURCES

Black, P., Harrison, C., Lee, C., Marshall, B., & Wiliam, D. (2003). *Assessment for learning*. New York, NY: Open University Press.

Brophy, J. (1981). Teacher praise: A functional analysis. *Review of Education Research, 5*, 5–32.

Cooper, H. M. (1979). Pygmalion grows up: A model for teacher expectations, communication and performance influence. *Review of Educational Research, 49*, 389–410.

Costa, A. L. (1985). *Developing minds*. Alexandria, VA: Association for Supervision and Curriculum Development.

DuFour, R., Eaker, R., Karhanek, G., & DuFour, R. (2004). *Whatever it takes.* Bloomington, IN: National Educational Services.

Dunkin, M. J., & Biddle, B. J. (1974). *The study of teaching.* New York, NY: Holt.

Dweck, C. S. (2002). Messages that motivate: How praise molds students' beliefs, motivation, and performance (in surprising ways). In J. Aronson (Ed.), *Improving academic achievement* (pp. 38–60). Orlando, FL: Academic Press.

Fordham, S., & Ogbu, J. U. (1986). Black students' school success: Coping with the burden of "acting white." *Urban Review, 18,* 176–206.

Gladwell, M. (2011). *Outliers.* New York, NY: Routledge.

Good, T. L., & Brophy, J. E. (2000). *Looking in classrooms* (8th ed.). Reading, MA: Addison-Wesley.

Graham, S., & Barker, G. (1990). The down side of help: An attributional-development analysis of helping behavior as a low-ability cue. *Journal of Educational Psychology, 82*(1), 7–14.

Henderlong, J., & Lepper, M. (2002). The effects of praise on children's intrinsic motivation: A review and synthesis. *Psychological Bulletin, 128,* 774–795.

Kerman, S., Kimball, T., & Martin, M. (1980). *Teacher expectations and student achievement: Coordinator manual.* Bloomington, IN: Phi Delta Kappa.

Kleinfeld, J. (1975). Effective teachers of Eskimo and Indian students. *School Review, 83,* 301–344.

Mandara, J., & Murray, C. B. (2007). How African American families can facilitate the academic achievement of their children: Implications for family-based interventions. In *Strengthening the African American educational pipeline* pp. 165–186). Albany: State University of New York Press.

Marzano, R. J., Pickering, D. J., & Pollock, J. E. (2001). *Classroom instruction that works: Research-based strategies for increasing student achievement.* Alexandria, VA: Association for Supervision and Curriculum Development.

Rosenthal, R., & Jacobson, L. (1968). *Pygmalion in the classroom.* New York, NY: Holt.

Rowe, M. B. (1987). Wait time: Slowing down may be a way of speeding up. *American Educator, 11*(1), 38–43, 47.

Saphier, J., Haley-Speca, M. A., & Gower, R. (2008). *The skillful teacher* (6th ed.). Acton, MA: Research for Better Teaching.

Tomlinson, C. A. (2015). Being human in the classroom. *Educational Leadership, 73*(2), 74–77.

Weiner, B. (1996). *Human motivation: Metaphors, theories, and research.* Thousand Oaks, CA: SAGE.

Zimmerman, B. J., & Marinez-Pons, M. (1990). Student differences in self-regulated learning: Relating grade, sex, and giftedness to self-efficacy and strategy use. *Journal of Educational Psychology, 82,* 51–59.

4

Regular Classroom Mechanisms for Generating Student Agency

"It's not magic, it's not mental telepathy. . . . It's very likely these thousands of different ways of treating people in small ways every day."

Richard Rosenthal, author of *Pygmalion in the Classroom* (quoted in Siegel, 2012)

The numbers in the list below are keyed to the section in the Introduction called "50 Ways to Get Students to Believe in Themselves."

10. Frequent quizzes and a flow of data to students

11. Student self-corrections/self-scoring

12. Student error analysis

13. Regular re-teaching

14. Required retakes and redos with highest grade

15. Cooperative learning protocols and teaching of group skills

(Continued)

(Continued)

16. Student feedback to teacher on pace or need for clarification

17. Reward system for effective effort and gains

18. Extra help

19. Student goal setting

Items 10 through 14 complement one another and together bring students directly into contact with a flow of information about how they are doing. The structures also press students into taking responsibility for their learning. The term used for this idea these days is *student agency*.

While research on frequency of quizzing is mixed, it is anything but mixed on frequent quizzing used for formative assessment purpose (Wiliam, 2013). This is because quizzes of this nature are intended to provide information that both students and teachers can use for improving learning.

Mr. VanKrey, a foreign language teacher in Evanston, Illinois, combines weekly quizzes with student self-correction and then a requirement that students retake the quiz if they scored below 80%. He also asks students what kind of errors they made.

Watch Mr. VanKrey's students self-correct the weekly quiz and then identify what kinds of errors each made so they can use the errors as opportunities for learning. (Watch from beginning of video to 11:53.)

http://rbteach.com/products-resources/video/
teaching-effective-effort-motivational-structures

Video 4.1

10. FREQUENT QUIZZES AND A FLOW OF DATA TO STUDENTS

11. STUDENT SELF-CORRECTIONS/ SELF-SCORING

12. STUDENT ERROR ANALYSIS

Frequent quizzes give teachers a great deal of information on what students understand and don't understand. Thus they can do something about a lack of understanding the following week. But it is also true that frequent quizzes create a data flow to *students* because they correct the quizzes themselves and record their scores in a notebook. Thus they always have information about how they're doing. Remember the shock and surprise at the end of a semester that we've seen some students register when they see how poorly they've been doing? That doesn't happen when teachers use these practices.

These agency structures make it incumbent on the teacher to offer re-teaching opportunities.

It is a common event for a class to end with several students who don't understand the material yet. What, if anything, is going to happen so they have another chance? This is another of the regularly recurring situations where we can seize opportunities to build student confidence (or miss opportunities and inadvertently signal to some students that there is no hope for them).

If we assume that some students won't or can't ever get it really, or will get it only partially, we feel obligated to move on to new material and drop their gap in understanding by the wayside. "After all, they get what they can get. I can give them slightly different assignments [translation: less demanding] so they can feel success [what they really feel is shame]. I have to move on with the curriculum. After all, I have to get the other kids ready for the Regents/APs/finals! I can't hold the others back!" The belief behind this statement is that the slower students couldn't really ever get the material anyway and that getting all students to pass would require slowing down the whole class and dumbing down the standards.

But what if we really believe that all students can reach a high standard given hard work, effective effort, and adequate prior knowledge? What instructional practices would we be considering? We would provide time and structure to re-teach for students who don't "get it" the first time around. In addition, we would employ all of the best practices in differentiating instruction and take the initiative to design courses, units of study, and lessons accordingly: pre-assessing readiness levels, analyzing the data we collect, and designing learning experiences that are geared to a common objective and high standard of performance while incorporating options as to how students will arrive there. The options might include variety in how students take in information, how they process or practice what is to be learned, and how they are expected to demonstrate understanding and achievement of the objectives. The degree and kind of support are variables that would be differentiated as well.

One possibility for differentiating support is setting up what some call a re-teaching loop, or a *scholar's loop,* as a regular classroom practice.

13. REGULAR RE-TEACHING

The use of the term *scholar's loop* is deliberate. It signals that good students, "scholars," seek out what they need and take advantage of opportunities

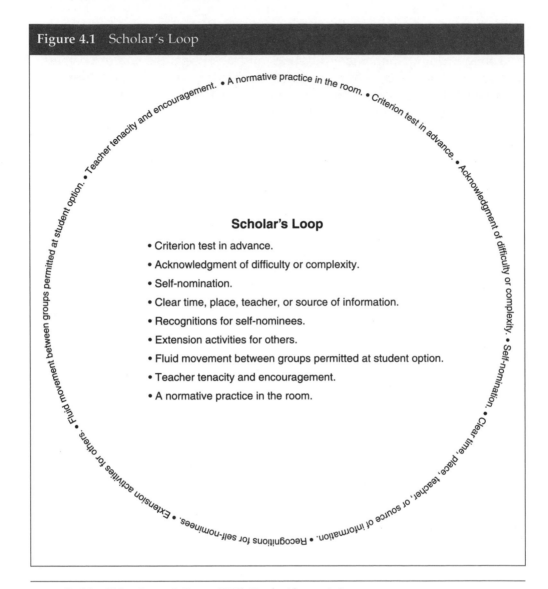

Figure 4.1 Scholar's Loop

Scholar's Loop

- Criterion test in advance.
- Acknowledgment of difficulty or complexity.
- Self-nomination.
- Clear time, place, teacher, or source of information.
- Recognitions for self-nominees.
- Extension activities for others.
- Fluid movement between groups permitted at student option.
- Teacher tenacity and encouragement.
- A normative practice in the room.

Source: Saphier, Haley-Speca, & Gower (2008). Used with permission.

to learn what they didn't get the first time around. And it removes stigma from not getting it the first time around.

A scholar's loop may or may not be teacher led. Other students or other adults may lead it. Self-directed learning experiences or computer simulations may be in the loop. But something happens for students who didn't get it the first time around to ensure they do get it, and at the original level of rigor and at the original standard, not a watered-down one.

Ideally, re-teaching loops would be a norm and have a number of these components:

1. Students would be asked to self-select for the re-teaching loop. To do so means they have to self-evaluate: "Do I really get this?"

2. Students would have the clarity and aid of a criterion quiz or task given in advance so they could accurately self-assess. The learning target or the performance they are shooting for would be no secret.

3. The teacher would create and continually reinforce a psychological climate of safety and esteem for students who nominate themselves for the scholar's loop by doing the following:

   - Explaining to students when the process is introduced—and regularly reinforcing—that scholars are people who desire to understand something at a very deep level.
   - Explicitly acknowledging the difficulty of the material: "This is really quite difficult because you have to get used to thinking about two things at once: identifying the relevant information and the relevant operation."
   - Praising the thoughtfulness of self-evaluation and the risk it takes to say one doesn't know something: "Good going, Kristina. You looked hard at your writing and decided to get a boost in this skill before moving on. You're going to know it very thoroughly when you're through, and probably incorporate this skill into your writing for life."

4. The teacher would encourage students who have entered re-teaching while they're there. "Keep struggling—you've almost got it. I know you're going to get there. Try to put it in your own words now."

5. The teacher would acknowledge difficulty and make the re-teaching loop a team effort: "Katrina, I must not be saying it right. Manuel, can you take a crack at putting it in your own words and explaining it to Katrina?"

The most important part of the re-teaching loop is the tenacity and expressed confidence of the teacher to each student that sticking with it will bring success. That means frequent assessments and follow-up with the students until they succeed.

Creating re-teaching loops often requires breaking the class into groups and giving the other members of the class an enrichment or extension activity to apply their knowledge in new contexts. It takes extra time and effort to come up with those activities. There is no doubt that carrying out the belief that all children can learn to a high level calls for more work from teachers than if they allow those who don't get it first and fast to settle to the bottom of the tank. Sorting students has always been easier than teaching them.

One way to make the workload more reasonable in managing re-teaching loops is to team teach. Two teachers with a double-size class can divide up the preparation when they decide they need to have re-teaching and extension activities.

14. REQUIRED RETAKES AND REDOS WITH HIGHEST GRADE

Though there may be some ostensible irritation, motivation goes up for students when they are required to retake a quiz on which they scored below a criterion level.

Watch Mr. VanKrey's students describe what it means to them that they *have* to retake any quiz on which they score below 80. (Watch from 14:35 to 18:46.)

http://rbteach.com/products-resources/video/teaching-effective-effort-motivational-structures

Video 4.2

In addition, these two videos by Rick Wormeli make the case for teachers and parents that retakes are a necessary feature of a high expectations classroom.

https://www.youtube.com/watch?v=TM-3PFflfvl

Video 4.3

https://www.youtube.com/watch?v=wgxvzEc0rvs

Video 4.4

15. COOPERATIVE LEARNING PROTOCOLS AND TEACHING OF GROUP SKILLS

Older readers will remember the 1970s and 1980s, when cooperative learning was a mainstream topic for professional development. The research was clear and consistent that cooperative learning models improved student learning. It still is. Cooperative learning stands high today in the pantheon of teaching practices that increase student learning reviewed in John Hattie's (2009) *Visible Learning*. An essential attribute of those cooperative learning models that resulted in strong student achievement gains was explicit instruction and feedback to students on the interactive skills of effective group members. (For the defining attributes of any true cooperative learning model and the teaching of social skills, see Johnson, Johnson, & Holubec, 2008.)

A novel approach to teaching group interaction skills is used by Mr. Herrmann, whom we've seen before, as he uses feedback to groups on helpful comments to highlight what productive groups do for each other when they are working effectively.

Watch Mr. Herrmann use his tablet to give students feedback on how their dialogue helps or hinders the group.

http://rbteach.com/products-resources/video/teaching-group-skills-highlighting-things-i-heard

Video 4.5

After this short episode, whenever he gets near a student group, they look at the screen and try to interact with the verbal forms he has highlighted on the tablet. Without any direct instruction (though there's nothing wrong with direct instruction and practice of social skills), he's used immediate highlighting of helpful group behavior to teach group skills.

The other aspect of cooperative learning that builds student agency is the reward structure where, though students still get individual grades based on their own performance, the group achieves recognition and rewards based on the group total. Thus students generate a stake in each other's success.

16. STUDENT FEEDBACK TO TEACHER ON PACE OR NEED FOR CLARIFICATION

Lillian Katz (1992), a distinguished educator and professor at New York University in the 1980s, told a wonderful vignette about her son in his first year of teaching. Her point was that we must teach children to stop us when they are confused, signal us not to proceed when the pace or the content has left them behind. What powerful form of student agency that is! And what a clear message that we *want* them all to understand.

One of the things you always want to do as a teacher . . . teaching children old or young, doesn't matter who, you always want to teach the children to say to you things like: "Hold it; I'm lost." "Can you go over this one more time?" "Is this what you mean?" "Can you show me again?" "Have I got it right?" We want lots of ways in which you empower the learner to keep you posted on where they need help. If the children are very young you just say, "Pull my sleeve," whatever, as long as the child has the strategy to say to you "I don't get it." "I'm lost." "You're going too fast." "Hold it" and so on. (Katz, 1992)

The more students feel empowered, the more they will send us such signals even when we don't ask for them to do so. Charlotte Thompson, a sterling biology teacher at Newton North High School in Massachusetts, began using the thumbs up, thumbs down, thumbs to the side signals with her students some years ago as a system for checking for understanding. She soon found they started sending her thumbs down signals unbidden when they wanted her to slow down or re-explain something. That's a tribute to the climate she'd built, not the power of that particular thumb-oriented signal. It is, however, a marker for us in terms of what true student agency looks like when it is vital.

17. REWARD SYSTEM FOR EFFECTIVE EFFORT AND GAINS

We don't want effective effort to supplant achievement as a goal, but we do want to recognize students who are actually mastering the elements of effective effort and encourage them to continue. "You really reached out to the resources of your peers on that one, Ananda, so I bet you're right on the edge of putting it all together now. What do you think might be missing?"

The other element of the classroom reward system that supports student agency and effort is recognizing and rewarding gains. Students may still be behind their peers in reading, but if they gain a grade level in six months, that's worth a party! The celebration (or the more low-key recognition) must be associated with the effective effort the student put in and connected to the promise of future gains and ultimate proficiency.

18. EXTRA HELP

Students sometimes don't take advantage of the extra help we offer. What could account for that?

- They don't think we mean it.
- They don't want to be seen as needing it.

- They think they will fail despite the extra help, so what's the point of exposing themselves to another negative experience.
- They can't stay after school because they work or care for siblings (or don't want to miss a team practice).

Let's think about this in a different way. Let's say our task is to set up an extra help system that may not be dependent on us delivering it. For example, peer tutoring, homework buddies, fifth-grade lab period (a period each week where students post topics or skills they need help with and are matched with another student willing and able to give that help), or high school English lab period. The ethos around these mechanisms needs to be repeated often, embedded in our daily language: that everyone can and will get it if they take advantage of the resources that are available to them.

19. STUDENT GOAL SETTING

The power of student goal setting has been amply demonstrated over many decades. It's about the most direct form of student agency we could imagine. But our students need direct instruction and coaching on how to do it well—both the goal setting and the plans of action to achieve the goals.

When students get involved in goal setting for their own learning, they learn more. In addition to being common sense, this conclusion is strongly supported by a continuous line of research started by Schunk and Gaa (1981). When students take ownership for goals (either self-set, teacher set, or jointly negotiated), their motivation to accomplish them and their ability to self-evaluate (and self-regulate) increase.

Student goal setting will not happen by itself except with very motivated students. Teachers have to do something to facilitate the process—perhaps take a few minutes of class time for students to write their goal for the period (or the unit) on a piece of paper or hold periodic goal-setting conferences with individual students at timely intervals (like at the beginning of new units or projects). These conferences can be quite short, but the goals chosen should be recorded, and students should be asked later to evaluate how they did.

Student goal setting does not automatically lead to increased student performance. Certain properties of effective goals need to be present; they need to be specific, challenging but attainable, and able to be accomplished soon. Specific goals contain items that can be measured, counted, or perceived directly as criteria for accomplishment. "Try my best" doesn't fit this mold. "Master the 20 spelling demons" does. SMART goal criteria for those who are familiar with them are appropriate here. These are goal statements that are **S**pecific, **M**easureable, **A**chievable (meaning stretching and challenging targets for students, but that they can reach), **R**ealistic, and **Time-bound** (meaning a finishing date is specified and there are appropriate deadlines for steps in the plan to meet the goal).

The more difficult the goal is, the more effort the student will expend, provided the goal is viewed as attainable. In guiding students to set goals, teachers have to help them walk the tightrope between what is achievable and what is unrealistically difficult.

Finally, goals that can be accomplished in the short term work better than long-term goals. This does not mean long-term goals should not be set, only that long-term goals need to be broken down into short-term goals or subgoals with their own plans of action, if one is to be maximally effective in reaching them. Learning goals or work accomplishment goals for students seem to work best around specified skills and products and for time spans of one period to several days rather than over several weeks or months.

A common misinterpretation of this principle is that it means students are picking what they will study (that is, the content). This is not the case. Much more often (and usually more productively), they are setting goals about speed, quantity, or quality. Here is an example of a speed goal: The student makes a commitment to how fast he will do some amount of work:

Teacher: Anthony, how many of these do you think you'll get done in the next half-hour?

Anthony: I think this whole page.

Teacher: Really? Do you really think that's a reasonable amount?

Anthony: Yes, I'll do it.

Teacher: Okay. Show them to me when you're done.

And here is a quantity goal:

Teacher: How many references will you use in researching that, Kayla?

Kayla: About six.

Teacher: Okay. If you think that's enough, put it down in your outline sheet.

There is no particular rate at which the researching must be done (except ultimately to meet the deadline of the paper). It is a commitment Kayla makes to do a specified amount. The same kind of goal applies to how many books students will read for free reading, for example, or how many extra credit or supplementary exercises they'll do.

Quality goals are particularly interesting. In these goals, students make a commitment to how well they'll do something. This can take the form of targeting what aspect of their work they'll focus on improving. Teachers can give them the assignment to explain what they're working to improve (and maybe even ask for it in writing):

Teacher: So, Jamie, what's your quality goal going to be on this paper?

Jamie: I'm going to work on improving spelling and punctuation.

Teacher: How about you, Tara?

Tara: My goal's going to be to use fewer tired words.

By getting students to set goals, teachers do not relinquish their ability to make assignments; they enlist the students in making personal commitments to speed, quantity, or quality.

It is possible to have students choose content in some cases. "I want to learn everything I can about frogs," says Hai. There are places where it will fit in with curriculum requirements and time available to help Hai do so (especially if one of the teacher's goals is to stimulate and support an inquiring attitude). But it may be equally powerful to get students to set quality goals, thus involving them inevitably in self-evaluation to come up with a target for improvement.

Setting a worthy goal is half the story. The other half is making a plan of action that is likely to achieve it.

Teacher: What are you going to do, Jameyl, to be better at the comprehension questions?

Jameyl: Work harder.

Teacher: That's a good intention. Let's look at the "work smarter" part of it.

Jameyl: What do you mean?

Teacher: Well, we have to pick what *kind* of comprehension questions you're getting stuck on.

Jameyl: All of them.

Teacher: I don't think so. You got the first half of them correct on the last quiz. What's the difference between this one (points to number 4) and this one (points to number 9)?

Jameyl: The first one's a *what* question. The second one's a *why* question.

Teacher: Aha, so it's the *why* questions that are the stumbling block.

Jameyl: I guess.

Teacher: Like this one: "Why did Percy want to leave the camp even though he would be safe there?"

Jameyl: I don't know.

Teacher: OK, try this. Reread a few pages and see if there are any clues about what makes him eager to get out there on a quest.

In our experience, student goal setting is one of the least practiced principles of learning in education. If we devoted just a little time and energy to it, we might see big payoffs in student performance and in students' learning directly about self-regulation and self-evaluation.

See Appendix D for teacher reports on their experiments with goal setting with their students.

REFERENCES AND RESOURCES

DuFour, R., DuFour, R., Eaker, R., & Karhanek, G. (2004). *Whatever it takes.* Bloomington, IL: National Educational Service.

Hattie, J. (2008). *Visible learning.* New York, NY: Routledge.

Johnson, D. W., Johnson, R. T., & Holubec, E. J. (2008). *Cooperation in the classroom.* Edina, MN: Interaction.

Katz, L. (1992). *Five keys to successful implementation of the whole.* Presentation to the annual meeting of the Association for Supervision and Curriculum Development, New Orleans, LA.

Schunk, D. H., & Gaa, J. P. (1981). Goal-setting influence on learning and self-evaluation. *Journal of Classroom Interaction, 16,* 38–44.

Spiegel, A. (2012, September 17). Teachers' expectations can influence how students perform. *NPR.* Retrieved from http://www.npr.org

Wiliam, D. (2013). Feedback and instructional correctives. In J. H. McMillan (Ed.), *SAGE handbook of research on classroom assessment* (pp. 197–214). Thousand Oaks, CA: SAGE.

5

No Secrets Instructional Strategies That Support Student Agency

The numbers in the list below are keyed to the section in the Introduction called "50 Ways to Get Students to Believe in Themselves."

20. Communicating objectives in student-friendly language and unpacking them with students

21. Clear and accessible criteria for success, developed with students

22. Exemplars of products that meet criteria for success

23. Checking for understanding

24. Making students' thinking visible

25. Frequent student summarizing

The instructional strategies listed above are productive for all students, but they are *essential* for underperforming, low-confidence students. These students can't mobilize effective effort if they don't know exactly what they're supposed to learn and be able to do. They can't focus on improving if they don't know (and we don't know) exactly where the gaps are in their learning. "No secrets teaching" aims at making this information crystal clear. Our underperforming students quickly conclude that the extra effort we exert to make sure they understand the objectives and criteria for success represents our genuine desire for them to succeed and our belief in their ability to do so.

20. COMMUNICATING OBJECTIVES

Communicating objectives to focus student effort and attention involves far more than just saying objectives or writing them on the board. The objectives have to be put in student-friendly language, free of jargon and full of common sense. And at that point we need to spend a minute or two unpacking them with the students, asking them what we think they mean, what their "understandings and their wonderings" are. These additional steps also produce useful information for us on what vocabulary terms we assume they know, but they don't!

Watch a class unpack learning objectives.

http://eleducation.org/resources/students-unpack-a-learning-target

Video 5.1

Table 5.1 presents the larger picture of communicating objectives.

Table 5.1   Communicating Learning Targets
1. Identify the most worthwhile learning target for these students at this time by analyzing the materials you've picked or that the curriculum presents.
2. Determine whether the students have adequate prior knowledge for the target you have in mind. This is especially important for low-confidence, underperforming students who can get overwhelmed and tune out if this isn't considered.
3. Compose the learning target in mastery language so you yourself know what student performance ("will be able to do") you would take as evidence of mastery.
4. Communicate the learning target to the students in student-friendly language.
5. Check for a minute or two to be sure the students understand the learning target (i.e., unpack it).

6. Be sure the learning target is posted somewhere in the room so students can refer back to it.
7. Tell the students the series of steps they'll be going through to meet the learning target.
8. Get the students to understand why the learning target is something worth learning (i.e., the reason it is important).
9. Establish the criteria for success for performances or products the students will be producing.
10. Have the students self-evaluate according to the criteria for success.
11. Return to what the learning target is, at least once during the lesson and again at the end.
12. Be sure to distinguish in your planning between thinking skill objectives and mastery objectives in the academic disciplines.

21. CRITERIA FOR SUCCESS

The criteria for success are usually a bulleted list that says what a student product will include if it meets the standards of the objective. These criteria, in essence, define what the objective means in performance. For example:

Your learning log

- summarizes the major events in the chapter
- identifies the central conflict and progress toward its resolution
- includes your own reflections on the decision that the protagonist is making in her attempt to deal with and solve her problem

The lab report

- lists all the steps for the process of titration
- explains your observations
- explains your conclusions about the relationship between _____ and _____
- Uses technical terms correctly

Watch Ms. Nichols in her second grade class make the criteria crystal clear, have students self-evaluate according to the criteria, and then give them feedback.

http://rbteach.com/products-resources/video/framing-learning-criteria-success

Video 5.2

It is quite common that underperforming students don't actually know what we're looking for in a quality product. The clarity of the criteria plus the implicit message of valuing when we take the time to go through criteria personally with them can have a big impact. In case studies our participants have done with students in the past, this action has stood out as having surprising results.

22. EXEMPLARS

Showing students exemplars of quality work, perhaps saved from previous classes, accomplishes the same clarity as sharing criteria for success, with this addition: Exemplars are models. They show what it actually looks or sounds like to have a good performance. And exemplars can be analyzed in detail to identify where each criterion is represented.

23. CHECKING FOR UNDERSTANDING

High expectations teachers don't want any students going out the door with the teachers not knowing where the kids stand on today's content. So checking for understanding (or doing formative assessment) becomes a dedicated and passionate commitment in every lesson. Checking questions, over-the-shoulder looks at student work, exit tickets, listening in to partner talk—these and many other moves can be seen to permeate the classes of high expectations teachers. Otherwise they have no way of deciding who is going to be in a support group for that skill in the next class.

Watch Mr. DeCraene use strategies for ongoing checking for understanding in his high school mathematics class.

http://rbteach.com/products-resources/video/checking-understanding-ii-one-question-quiz

Video 5.3

Watch a variety of ways that elementary teachers check for understanding.

http://rbteach.com/products-resources/video/checking-understanding

Video 5.4

24. MAKING STUDENTS' THINKING VISIBLE

This arena is a constellation of 24 teaching principles that create robust student dialogue where students talk more than teachers, at a high level of thinking, and simultaneously develop a safe and supporting climate for making errors and risk-taking. These skills are important in high expectations teaching for several reasons. First of all, the perseverance we often display to get students to speak their thinking is a sign of respect. So is the use of wait time. Second, we get a great deal of information about what students do and don't understand (misconceptions, gaps in knowledge). We can use this directly with our low-confidence students to accelerate their learning. Third, these moves are surrounded by a judgment-free environment that embeds a new and constructive view of error (it's normal and useful) and encourages student risk-taking in a safe environment that focuses on thinking rather than winning the competition to be first, fast, and right all the time.

Cultivating Classroom Discourse to Make Students' Thinking Visible

When you lead classroom discussions, follow the principles below to create a talk environment of robust student-to-student discourse. This will shift the dynamic from the teacher listening to and interacting with just one student at a time to everyone listening to each other and contributing to each other's thinking.

Table 5.2 24 Operating Principles and the Verbal Behaviors That Go With Them	
Getting the conversation started	
1. **Engage student thinking**	**Begin the dialogue with a planned question or statement designed to engage student thinking.**
	"Why do you suppose Fitzgerald always has Gatsby comment on the Eckleburg sign between East and West Egg?"
	"What is the difference between an ionic and molecular compound?"
	"How can you tell if two fractions are equivalent if their denominators are different?"
	"What do you think Papa really wants when he says that to the children?"

(Continued)

(Continued)

Laying the foundations by creating a safe and inclusive environment for discourse	
2. **Call on all**	**Call on all students over time in large groups whether hands are raised or not.** Engage all students when it is a small group. This sets the expectation for everyone to participate in the learning.
3. **Pause, use wait time**	**After posing a question or hearing a student's response, allow a brief silence.** Give all students time to process a question or a student comment by pausing for a minimum of 3–5 seconds after posing a question and before calling a student or before calling on another student to answer.
4. **Avoid judgment**	**Respond to students without judgment.** Replace the language of praise (or blame) with specific feedback, naming what the student did. "You expressed an idea and gave an example that helps us understand your thinking." This affirms effort and reinforces visible thinking behaviors.
5. **Validate confusion**	**Validate students who acknowledge confusion and give encouragement, expressing confidence in their ability.** "Strong students say when they are confused like you just did, Jasmine. Let's start by going back over what we know so far. I know you'll get it."
Getting started on making students' thinking visible	
6. **Explain**	**Get students to explain or elaborate.** When a student responds to a question, *stay with the student for several exchanges*, whether his or her response is right or wrong. This shifts the dynamic from short answers to developing students' stamina to engage in complex conversations. "Tell us why." "How did you arrive at that; what is your thinking?" (Student responds.) "So then what was different about his wife's motivation?"
7. **Restate**	**Get another student to paraphrase or restate what has been said to highlight an important idea (or to check listening).**

	"Marie, how would you restate what Josh just said?" This sends the message that everyone's voice has weight and sets the expectations that students need to listen to one another's ideas, not just the teacher's voice.
8. **Turn and talk**	**Use turn and talk often in large-group settings.** "So what are the five criteria for a good pictograph? Turn and talk to a neighbor and see if you can come up with them all." "How was Scout's opinion of Boo changing? Turn to a partner and talk about what you think the change was and why." This gets more active participation more of the time and promotes speaking and sharing openly and frequently. It also gives reticent students the opportunity to rehearse their ideas prior to speaking to the whole group.
Helping students who are wrestling with concepts and problems	
9. **Establish norms**	**Make norms of interaction explicit between students in groups.** "Today please be sure to say 'because . . .' after you say that you agree or disagree." "In your groups remember to make sure you check each person's understanding before going on to the next problem."
10. **Listen actively**	**Paraphrase and use careful active listening to unpack student thinking, especially for a wrong or incomplete argument, until there is mutual understanding of what the student actually intended to say.** "You seem to be saying that Antigone really spurns her sister, has no respect for her at all. Is that right?" "I think what you are saying is . . . am I understanding you?"
11. **Revoice**	**When students are grappling with an idea, or their explanations are vague, occasionally revoice (paraphrase or extend) an answer, infusing academic language when appropriate.** "So, Mike, you're saying that the combination of rising prices—inflation—and wages staying the same—wage stagnation—was hurting the middle class."
12. **Scaffold**	**When students experience difficulty explaining their response, scaffold their thinking by asking questions**

(Continued)

(Continued)

	that allow the pieces they *do* know to surface and then nudge them to build on it. S: It's a multiplication *and* a division problem! T: How did you figure that out? S: Ummm . . . I just know. T: Uh huh. So let's see. . . . How many boxes of notebooks did the school buy, Damian?" S: Eight. T: How did you know that? S: 'Cause the delivery man could only carry two in each of the four trips. T: And how many classes needed notebooks? S: (Silence) T: If it's not in the words, maybe it's somewhere else. S: Oh, the map of the school! T: And books in each box? S: 100. T: So then what was your reasoning? S: Oh, well, first you had to . . .
13. **Persevere and return**	**Return to a student whose answer was initially incomplete or incorrect. Ask him or her to put together the points that were produced in subsequent class discussion by others.** "So now, Ricardo, put it all together for us. What are natural resources?"
Relinquishing old habits	
14. **Adjust speed for coverage**	**Slow down the conversation to get repetitions and restatements of answers.** People need to hear things more than once and have the opportunity to put ideas into their own words in order to understand them.
15. **Save students**	**Allow students to struggle, and stick with them, dwelling on their thinking.** Attend and listen without commenting as they talk through their ideas.
16. **Answer yourself**	**When a student asks you a question, see if another student can answer it rather than answering it yourself.** "Who would like to try answering Jason's question?" "Elaine, how would you answer that?" "Jamil, what do you think would be the next step?" when Jason has asked for the next step.

| 17. **Do the thinking for students** | **Leave a student with a puzzle to ponder and come back later to see what he came up with.** |
| | "Keep thinking about it. I think you are onto something we will be talking about later. So see if you can make a connection." |

Getting students to interact with one another

18. **Agree or disagree**	**Invite students to agree or disagree with an idea someone shares, and require them to explain their thinking or reason why.**
	"What do you think, Jane? Agree? Disagree? Why?"
	"Who agrees . . . who disagrees? Tell us why."
	"Show me a sign: Agree? Disagree? Why?"
19. **Add on**	**Ask a student to comment on or add to another's thinking.**
	"Let's comment on what Mike said. Leo, what do you think about Mike's interpretation?"
	"Who has something to add on to what Tiffany is saying?"
20. **Compare thinking**	**Have students comment on the similarity or difference between two students' ways of thinking or approaches.**
	"You seem to be thinking about this with economic motives whereas Wanda was thinking more about people's emotions driving them. Which helps us more at this point?"
	"So Anthony made his rectangle 3 across and 4 down. Erika made hers 4 across and 3 down. Is one more correct than the other? Would either work? Why?"
21. **Surface discrepancies**	**Ask questions to surface discrepancies.**
	"How can that be if. . . . What do you think is going on there?"
22. **Revisit previous thinking**	**When, after reflection or struggle, a student changes his or her opinion or answer, ask the student to compare the two lines of thought that led to a different answer.**
	"So what was different on this second try from the first way you did it?"

Teaching and reinforcing academic vocabulary

| 23. **Infuse academic vocabulary** | **Seize opportunities to infuse academic vocabulary and the language of thinking into dialogue and, ultimately, into the culture of the classroom.** |

(Continued)

(Continued)

	"Yes, and what you just did, Brendan, is an example of *analysis*." "I see your point. That's a *generalization*, and we'll be looking for more of them later in the period."
24. **Record academic vocabulary**	**Record and keep the emerging academic vocabulary visible so students have access to it when writing and speaking.** On the board in the corner is this vertical list: proposition, thesis, antithesis, argument, evidence, contrary evidence.

Communicate "This is important, you can do it, and I won't give up on you."

Space prevents a full exposition of these skills here. Readers can go to http://rbteach.com for a thorough online course with dozens of videos of the skills in action across many grade levels and subjects.

A teacher uses making students' thinking visible in a small group.

http://rbteach.com/products-resources/video/making-thinking-visible-small-groups

Video 5.5

A teacher uses making students' thinking visible with a total class discussion.

http://rbteach.com/products-resources/video/making-thinking-visible-and-classroom-climate

Video 5.6

25. FREQUENT STUDENT SUMMARIZING

Active summarizing strategies not only get students cognitively active in recasting their learning but also give the teacher information about what students know and any errors or gaps. Summarizing can be a twofer: summarizing and checking. Learning logs, 3-2-1 summarizers (3 things I learned, 2 things I wonder about, and 1 thing I'm confused about or didn't understand), and many other devices serve this purpose.

6

Teaching Effective Effort

26. EFFECTIVE EFFORT BEHAVIORS

Effective effort means a lot more than working hard. Let's take the following as a definition, building on a set of elements laid out by Jeff Howard many years ago. Effective effort consists of six elements:

TIME	FOCUS	USE OF FEEDBACK
A willingness to spend the hours needed to finish the job well	Concentrating only on the work; no TV or other distractions	Looking carefully at responses to my work so I know exactly what to fix
RESOURCEFULNESS	COMMITMENT	PERSISTENCE
Knowing where to go and whom to ask for help when I'm really stuck	Being determined to finish and do my very best work	If one strategy isn't working, trying different ones until I find one that works

How does one teach a student about effective effort? For each of the six elements we need to (1) explain the concept, (2) give examples with modeling, and then (3) have students practice it.

Time

On leaving middle school, two of my four children didn't really have a concept of (or ask themselves) how long a given task should take. Therefore during freshman year they would spend 10 minutes revising compositions and think that was what it took. It wasn't!

They weren't shirking deliberately; they were merely acting from an unconscious assumption about the scope of revising and how long a thorough job of it should take. So part of our job with some students is to find out how long they spend on various tasks and, without blame or accusation, give them realistic time budgets for the tasks we assign.

"Well, Jason, given the conversation we've had about your first draft (or first translation, first experiment design, etc.), it should take about a half-hour to get it to the next stage.

Use of Feedback

"I look carefully at responses to my work so I know exactly what to fix."

It is obvious but necessary to be sure that we are giving students good feedback before we try to direct their attention to using it well. This is easier said than done.

Elsewhere we have defined pure feedback as the late Grant Wiggins did: specific and objective information about which criteria for success have been met, or about what gaps there are between the current performance and proficient performance.

"You have a thesis statement and three supporting pieces of data, but you don't have a connection yet to the overall theme."

Often, good feedback should be paired with some specific guidance or suggestions.

Middle School English

"Mark is a very interesting character. He has a job and plays chess. But it would give the story a better flow if we understood why he was so angry."

Second-Grade Math

"Lining up the columns of numbers so they're right under one another would prevent most of these adding errors."

11th-Grade Chemistry

"If you count the number of hydrogen atoms on both sides and they're not the same, then you know there's a mistake somewhere."

The issue here is getting students to look at and then think about the feedback and, finally, use it! That may not seem such a hard task, except for the habit some students bring to us of looking only at a grade and not at all the comments we have taken time to write on their work. For students with this habit, simply saying "Please examine my feedback to you and use it" will not suffice. We have to show them what doing so would look and sound like with a real work sample, visually displayed. Modeling thinking aloud is an ideal instructional strategy for doing this.

"Let's see, my teacher said I hadn't connected my examples to the conclusion of the author. So the author's conclusion . . . what was it again? Let's see, at the end of his essay he said . . ."

Following this direct instruction, we can have students practice using feedback the next time we give it to them and go around and ask individuals to explain how they are using the feedback.

Focus

I used to think a student couldn't work effectively while listening to music, because I never could. But I got a reality check on that while carefully watching my children do homework when they were teenagers. Watching television, however, or playing video games or talking on the phone are another matter.

Effective effort indicates that we teach our students to name distractors and then to take action to sidestep them. This is a demanding topic to teach, because distractors are usually found at home, outside of our watchful support. So we must ask our students to plan their response to these distractors, explicitly say what they will do to avoid them, and then report through self-evaluation how they did.

For some students, their entire home environment is a distractor because there are no quiet corners. The apartment may be chaotic, loud, and filled with demands. So as high expectations teachers we may talk a student through or do a guided imagery visualization of finding a private space, or a library, or, for older students, a coffee shop on the way home where they can study. For students with responsibilities for taking care of younger siblings, this option may not exist. Then other possibilities must be explored, like coming to school early. That, in turn, may require a high level of commitment.

Watch this video on the incredible power of focus and of concentration.

http://www.flixxy.com/the-incredible-power-of-concentration-miyoko-shida.htm#.UYwp74UVxno

Video 6.1

Commitment

A commitment is a promise. For underperforming, low-confidence students, it is first a promise to oneself, but equally important, a promise to us, their teachers. If we have a relationship of regard and respect with students, they will care about keeping a commitment to us, and they will know that we will be looking to see if they honor it.

Therefore it is useful to have students record their commitments. Making commitments is the part of the student goal setting process where students make plans of action (see #19, Student Goal Setting). But on a daily basis in verbal discourse, we can call for commitments and follow up the next day by having students tell us what they did.

Watch as Mr. VanKrey has students write down every day what they did between the last class and now to further their learning.

http://rbteach.com/products-resources/video/teaching-effective-effort-motivational-structures

Video 6.2

Another part of teaching students about commitment is asking them to self-evaluate their work according to the criteria for success; after all, the commitment is to doing their very best work and not settling for less.

Persistence

Students with a fixed mindset experience struggle as confirmation of their low ability. Students who believe their effort can grow their ability (the growth mindset) see struggle as evidence of a knowledge gap or a missing strategy, not inferiority. Thus they don't give up; they persist. To bring students' attention to persistence, we can share stories of well-known people who exhibited it (Gladwell, 2011). We can also have students self-evaluate upon the completion of complex tasks.

This slide show, created by a team of teachers in Webster, Massachusetts, in 2008, provides running inspirational messages to accompany our work with faculty and with students.

Visit http://www.rbteach.com/products-resources/downloads/all and select Effective Effort Quotes: PowerPoint Presentation.

Resource 6.1

Watch these same teachers and their students and parents describe the amazing transformations possible when an entire group of faculty members takes on the challenge of getting students to believe that "smart is something you can get."

http://rbteach.com/products-resources/video/high-expectations-teaching

Video 6.3

Resourcefulness

When you're stuck, do you know where to go to get reliable help? Many students not only don't know where to go, they don't think they have a right to ask. Phillip Michael Treisman (1985) surfaced this in his ground-breaking study of African American students in the engineering program at the University of California, Berkeley. When they broke out of a tacit belief system that they had to do it alone and formed study groups as the Asian students did, the achievement gap disappeared. Therefore we should have our students form study buddy pairs or study groups like college students do to help one another out. This will usually mean teaching them protocols for dialogue and for helping one another with academic work.

Another form of teaching students how to act resourcefully is telling them about websites like Khan Academy (www.khanacademy.org) and resource books that are helpful in clearing up misunderstandings or getting clarity on difficult ideas.

27. STUDENT SELF-EVALUATION OF EFFECTIVE EFFORT

Following are various instruments teachers can use to have students self-assess after completion of tasks or after benchmark assessments or projects.

STUDENT SELF-EVALUATION OF EFFECTIVE EFFORT

Time: I am willing to spend the hours needed to finish the job well.

Not true   Somewhat true   True   Very true

Focus: When I work, I stay very focused. I concentrate only on work and am not distracted by TV or anything else.

Not true   Somewhat true   True   Very true

Resourcefulness: I am resourceful. When I am really stuck, I know where to go and whom to ask.

Not true   Somewhat true   True   Very true

Use of feedback: I make good use of feedback. I look carefully at responses to my work so I know exactly what to fix.

Not true   Somewhat true   True   Very true

Commitment: I am committed to doing good work. I am determined to complete my assignment and to do my very best.

Not true   Somewhat true   True   Very true

Persistence: If one strategy isn't working, I keep trying different ones until I find one that works.

Not true   Somewhat true   True   Very true

EXAMPLE OF AN EFFORT SELF-EVALUATION: MATH CLASS

_____ I am prepared for class. I have done my homework and know what questions I have. I bring my book, homework, notebook, and pencil.

_____ I am responsible for my knowledge. I separate what I know from what I don't understand, then plan when I will ask questions to improve in these areas.

_____ I take notes in class. My notes and papers are organized, as is my written math work.

_____ I complete all homework assignments. I work through assignments carefully and thoroughly. I pass them in on time, never late.

_____ I show all my work. I write out every step. I use all the steps when solving word problems.

_____ I turn projects in on time. I turn them in early sometimes!

_____ I read the chapter section that we are working on before that section begins. I write notes and questions I have and include the steps for each example.

_____ If I don't know how to do a homework problem, I look it up in my notebook and in the book.

_____ If I can't figure out a homework problem after trying, I ask for help in class. I write these questions and problems on my homework paper.

_____ I don't repeat the same mistakes on homework and then on a quiz or test. I ask for help instead before the test or quiz. I understand that I can't get help during the test.

_____ I study for tests and quizzes by practicing problems and by reviewing my notes, the book, past quizzes, and past homework assignments.

_____ Following failure (or a much lower grade than I expected), I create a plan for improving my understanding and grades, and share the plan with my teacher.

_____ I ask for help before or after school when needed.

_____ I listen to other students and use their advice or comments to improve my understanding.

_____ I try to act respectfully in class at all times. I care about my classmates' education.

_____ I communicate with my teacher about what I am learning and how I am doing in class.

Source: Kerri Murphy, Easton High School, Massachusetts. Used with permission.

Frequent student self-assessment according to effective effort makes students own their investment in learning. It also allows us, when needed, to have some data for coaching them on whatever aspect of effective effort that they see as a weak area for themselves.

28. LEARNING STUDY AND OTHER STRATEGIES OF SUCCESSFUL STUDENTS

High expectations teachers explicitly teach study strategies. While some students might learn or deduce these strategies on their own, teaching them to all students helps to level the playing field.

In the 1960s, a surprising study (Garner, Hare, Alexander, Haynes, & Vinograd, 1984) surfaced the gain in reading scores when fifth-grade students were taught the "look-back" strategy. Almost shocking about the study is what would seem the obvious nature of the strategy. Here it is:

If students are asked a comprehension question they can't answer about a reading passage, they could look back into the text to find the place where the information exists to provide the answer. What do students do who don't have the look-back strategy when they can't answer a comprehension question? Nothing. They go on to the next question either because they don't think they're allowed to look back or it doesn't occur to them to do so; they just conclude, "I don't know that one." And they take no agency for rectifying that situation. While the strategy seems simple, not all students have this in their repertoire.

Complete research traditions and associated how-to texts are devoted to study strategies, literacy strategies, and problem-solving strategies that have positive effects on student achievement if they are taught explicitly (Lockett, 2006; Santa, Havens, & Valdes, 2004). Most of them are more complex than the look back. Strategies for solving mathematical word problems, for example, involve many steps like reading the whole thing through, identifying the central question, differentiating relevant from irrelevant information, breaking down solutions into logical steps, and so on. Our point here is that high expectations teachers consider it part of their job to teach strategies as well as content. Some of the strategies are content related, like outlining a persuasive essay. Some are generic, like Cornell note-taking (see Figure 6.1 on page 101). Part of my job as a teacher is to isolate the important strategies my students should have and identify the students to whom I need to teach these directly because they don't walk through the door with them already in their repertoires.

Along with the direct teaching and practice of these strategies is the opportunity for positive framing of *why* we're teaching the strategy. "So that's one more tool, Mason, for getting the success you're so capable of!"

Steps to Teaching Learning Strategies

Teaching learning strategies means explicitly teaching students the learning strategies that link effort to achievement. To do this, the teacher does the following:

1. Name the learning strategy.

2. Explain why the learning strategy is useful (i.e., the contexts in which it will be useful).

3. Demonstrate the learning strategy, model it, and think aloud to show what it looks like when used.

4. Teach the related vocabulary of the learning strategy.

5. Give students multiple opportunities to practice the learning strategy.

6. Provide feedback on the use of the learning strategy to improve performance.

7. Celebrate with students when they use the learning strategy.

Four excellent and large comprehensive compilations of study strategies for direct instruction are listed in the reference section at the end of this chapter. The following is a list of classic strategies to teach to students.

Learning Strategies That Help
Students Make Their Efforts Effective

Reading strategies that students use to be successful in my class:

- text-to-self connections
- text-to-text connections
- text-to-world connections
- before reading

    ○ use pictures to predict
    ○ skim for textual aids
    ○ activate background knowledge
    ○ chapter tour

- during reading

    ○ self-monitor
    ○ determine meaning of words in context
    ○ visualize

    ○ confirm predictions
    ○ question self

- after reading

    ○ identify main idea and details
    ○ draw conclusions
    ○ make inferences
    ○ distinguish important from interesting
    ○ summarize
    ○ identify story structure

- SQRW (survey, question, read, write)
- use textual aids to aid comprehension

- compare and contrast
- pose questions (to self and author)
- use RAFT (role of the writer, intended audience, format, topic) when writing

Math strategies that students use to be successful in my math class:

- problem-solving strategies
  - draw a picture
  - look for a pattern
  - work backward
  - guess and check
  - logical reasoning
  - make a list
  - make the problem simpler
- use the structure of text

Learning strategies that students use to remember ideas:

- create mnemonics
- read-talk-write
- read-draw-talk-revise
- construct concept maps
- procedural talk

Study strategies that students use to be successful in school:

- note-taking
- participation in discussions
- time management
- goal setting
- participation in a study group
- practice
- flash cards (and the principle of learning: sequence)
- graphic organizers
- positive self-talk

Wall Chart: Figuring Out Unfamiliar Words

- Ask: What would make sense there?
- Look for context clues before and after the word.
- See if there are parts of the word you already know:
  - word family
  - root
  - prefix/suffix
- Look at the pictures for clues.
- Ask someone the meaning of the word.
- Look up the meaning of the word.

Wall Chart: Learning New Information

- Copy daily objectives (so I know what's important).
- Copy key questions for the day.
- Write a summary of class notes.
- Read the questions at the end of the chapter and take notes on those questions.
- Read actively (highlight, underline, take notes).
- Make flash cards with definitions of important terms.
- Practice terms and vocabulary with a friend.
- Write sample questions based on the objectives.

Source: The above lists represent research-based and observed strategies that Research for Better Teaching consultants have recorded from their work with teachers. The lists were organized by Judy Duffield and Sue McGregor, consultants at Research for Better Teaching.

A Note-Taking Method

Figure 6.1   Variant of Cornell Method of Note Taking

Left-hand side of notebook   *Right-hand side of notebook*

Top 2/3		Topic: _____ Date: _____
• outline	Key Terms	Class Notes
• graphic organizer		• lecture
• response to a prompt or question		• on chalkboard, whiteboard
		• video
		• demonstration
Bottom 1/3		• Summary of Notes
• personal connections and reflections		

Source: Adapted from work developed by Walter Pauk (1975).

In addition to subject-specific study strategies, there are principles of learning that are a century old and produced by psychological laboratory studies that are venerable and as valid today as when they were established. A number of these principles should be explicitly taught to our students. Letting them in on some of this "secret, inside teacher knowledge" will make them empowered students. The following principles are especially useful. We will describe them in more detail in Chapter 7 because they are vehicles for empowering student agency.

- sequence
- say-do
- mnemonics
- cumulative review
- close confusers
- breaking complex tasks
- practice

Study habits are not quite the same as the study strategies we explicitly teach, but they are another route to getting students to own how they approach academic work. What follow are some useful instruments for students to self-assess their study habits. They give us a menu of items we can take on for direct instruction and support, just as we described above with self-assessment of effective effort.

Name _____   Grade and subject _____

STUDY HABITS CHECKLIST

	Almost always	More than half the time	About half the time	Less than half the time	Almost never
1. Do you keep up-to-date in your assignments?*					
2. Do you keep a written study schedule on which you show the time you plan to set aside each day for studying?					
3. Do you divide your study time among the various subjects to be studied?					

Physical Setting

4. Is the space on your study table or desk large enough?*					
5. Is your study desk or table kept neat, that is, free of distracting objects?*					
6. Do you study in a quiet place that is free from noisy disturbances?					
7. Is the lighting and ventilation good?					

8. When you sit down to study, do you have the equipment and materials you need?					

Preview

9. When you sit down to study, do you get settled quickly?					
10. Do you look the chapter over before reading it in detail?					
11. Before reading an assignment in detail, do you make use of any of the clues in the book, such as heading, heavy print, pictures, and so on?					

Reading

12. As you read an assignment, do you have in mind questions that you are trying to answer?					
13. Can you find the main ideas in what you read?*					
14. Do you try to get the meaning of important new words?*					
15. Are you able to read without saying each word to yourself?					

(Continued)

(Continued)

Note-Taking

	Almost always	More than half the time	About half the time	Less than half the time	Almost never
16. As you read, do you make notes?					
17. Do you review class notes as soon as possible after class?					

Remembering

	Almost always	More than half the time	About half the time	Less than half the time	Almost never
18. Do you try to find a genuine purpose and goal for yourself as you study?*					
19. Do you find a genuine interest in the subjects that you study?					
20. Do you try to understand thoroughly all material to be remembered?*					
21. When studying material to be remembered, do you try to summarize it yourself?					
22. Do you distribute the study of a lengthy assignment over several study sessions?					
23. Do you try to relate what you are learning in one subject to what you are learning in other subjects?					

Tests and Quizzes

24. In addition to reading the book, do you read other materials for the course?					
25. When you have questions about your work, do you try to arrange to talk them over with your instructor?					
26. Do you discuss the content of the studies with others outside of class?					
27. Do you make specific preparations for tests and quizzes?					
28. In studying for a test or quiz, do you distribute your time over at least two sessions?					
29. Do you combine important notes from your textbook and from class into a new master outline in studying for a major examination?					
30. In preparing for an exam, do you review the important facts and principles?*					

(Continued)

(Continued)

	Almost always	More than half the time	About half the time	Less than half the time	Almost never
31. In studying for a test or quiz, do you attempt to predict exam questions?					
32. On the night before a test or quiz, do you go to bed about your usual time?					

Which questions did you answer *almost always* or *more than half the time*? They represent your strong points as a student. Write down their numbers.

Which ones did you mark *less than half the time* or *almost never*? These are your weak points. Write down their numbers.

Now look back at each of the questions represented by these numbers on the checklist and decide which you consider to be your three strongest points and your three weakest points. Name them briefly.

Strong Points   Weak Points

_____   _____

_____   _____

_____   _____

Now look at those questions in the checklist that have an asterisk (1, 4, 5, 13, 14, 18, 20, 30). These questions are about practices that the best students in three colleges think are especially important. How many of these eight questions did you answer *almost always* or *more than half the time*?

Now give yourself 4 points for each mark in column 1 (*almost always*), 3 points for each mark in column 2 (*more than half the time*), 2 points for each mark in column 3 (*about half the time*), 1 point for each mark in column 4 (*less than half the time*), and no points for the marks in the last column (*almost never*).

Add these points and list your total score: _____. Compare your score with the average scores of the following:

	Boys	Girls
Senior high school students	74	82
College freshmen	86	94

Now for the most important task. Go through the questions and note the ones dealing with the study habits in which you are the weakest. Try to strengthen these habits.

Source: Sandrine Colson-Leary, Wayland High School, Massachusetts.

29. ATTRIBUTION THEORY AND BRAIN RESEARCH

Carol Dweck recommends teaching students directly the scientific research that brains are malleable and that ability can be grown. A 2007 study demonstrated that students who were taught about the malleability of the human brain were more perseverant and did better at academic tasks (Blackwell, Trzesniewski, & Dweck, 2007).

Her company's program, Brainology, makes this happen by teaching students how the brain functions, learns, and remembers, and how it changes in a physical way when we exercise it.

Similarly, teaching students directly about attribution theory (Weiner, 1996) provides students with information and an operating theory of action for why good students do well and how to change their own internal attributions (explanations) for their success when they succeed and failures when they fail.

The following are good resources for keeping the conversation going and deepening students' understanding of the growth mindset:

Videos and Websites

Mindset Works (which offers Brainology)
http://www.mindsetworks.com

"Growth Mindset for Students" (animated films)
https://youtu.be/2zrtHt3bBmQ

"You Can Learn Anything" (Khan Academy)
https://youtu.be/JC82Il2cjqA?list=PL4111402B45D10AFC

"Neurons and What They Do: An Animated Guide"
https://youtu.be/vyNkAuX29OU

"Growth Mindset Video"
https://youtu.be/ElVUqv0v1EE?list=PL4111402B45D10AFC

"The Skating Lesson"
https://youtu.be/xIxGbFK9UH4

"The Power of Yet" (Sesame Street)
https://youtu.be/XLeUvZvuvAs

"Share Strategies With Posters"
https://www.teachingchannel.org/videos/classroom-posters-educate

"Practicing Perseverance With 'Lifelines'"
https://www.teachingchannel.org/videos/teaching-technique-group-work

"Neuroplasticity"
https://www.khanacademy.org/science/health-and-medicine/nervous-system-and-sensory-infor/neural-cells-and-neurotransmitters/v/neuro plasticity

"Are Your Brains Tired?"
https://www.teachingchannel.org/videos/praising-student-effort

"Growth Mindset Lesson Plan"
https://www.mindsetkit.org/static/files/YCLA_LessonPlan_v10.pdf

Children's Books

Deak, J. (2010). *Your fantastic elastic brain: Stretch it, shape it.* Belvedere, Canada: Little Pickle Press.
Keats, E. J. (1998). *Whistle for Willie.* New York, NY: Viking Press.
Piper, W., & Hauman, G. (2001). *The little engine that could.* New York, NY: Platt and Munk.
Reiley, C. E., & Pastrana, J. (2015). *Making a splash: A growth mindset children's book.* San Francisco, CA: Go Brain!
Saltzberg, B. (2010). *Beautiful oops book.* New York, NY: Workman.

In addition, signage and posters of inspirational quotes around the room can be useful, as can two-column charts that contrast the growth and fixed mindset (see Figure 6.2).

It is never too early to begin instilling the habits of effective effort in children or the belief that they can grow their ability. Appendix E is a log of a prekindergarten/kindergarten teacher's weekly activities and successes in building these beliefs in her students. Kristin Allison is explicit with her students about what she is teaching them and comes at it from many of the angles profiled in this book.

Figure 6.2   Two-Column Chart That Contrasts the Growth and Fixed Mindset

Growth Mindset:
Ability
Can Be Developed

Leads to a desire
to learn and
therefore tending to:

Fixed Mindset:
Ability Is Stable

Leads to a desire to
look smart
and therefore tending to:

Growth Mindset		Fixed Mindset
Welcome challenges	CHALLENGE	Avoid challenges
Persist in the face of setbacks	OBSTACLES	Give up easily
See effort as the path to mastery	EFFORT	See effort as fruitless or worse
Learn from criticism	CRITICISM	Ignore useful negative feedback
Find lessons and inspiration in the success of others	SUCCESS OF OTHERS	Feel threatened by success of others

Results in:

Higher
achievement

Plateau early and
achieve less

REFERENCES AND RESOURCES

Blackwell, L. S., Trzesniewski, K. H., & Dweck, C. C. (2007). Implicit theories of intelligence predict achievement across an adolescent transition: A longitudinal study and an intervention. *Child Development, 78*(1), 246–263.

Garner, R., Hare, V. C., Alexander, P., Haynes, J., & Vinograd, P. (1984). Inducing use of a text lookback strategy among unsuccessful readers. *American Educational Research Journal, 21,* 789–798.

Gladwell, M. (2011). *Outliers.* New York, NY: Routledge.

Pauk, W. (1975). *How to study in college*. Boston: Houghton Mifflin.

Treisman, P. M. (1985). *A study of the mathematics performance of black students at the University of California, Berkeley* (Doctoral dissertation). University of California, Berkeley.

Weiner, B. (1996). *Human motivation: Metaphors, theories and research*. Thousand Oaks, CA: SAGE.

Four Study Strategy Compendiums

Buehl, D. (2009). *Classroom strategies for interactive learning* (3rd ed.). Newark, DE: International Reading Association.

Lockett, S. M. (2006). *Study skills* (4th ed.). Laguna Niguel, CA: Educational Innovations.

Moses, L. (2010). *Content area learning strategies*. Eugene, OR: School District 4J.

Santa, C. M., Havens, L. T., & Valdes, B. J. (2004). *Project CRISS*. Dubuque, IA: Kendall/Hunt Publishers.

directly at that. A third main highway to student agency is choices that we invite them to make, as usual, always framed with the language of positive expectations.

"Effective teachers know that to become engaged, students must have some feelings of ownership—of the class or the task—and personal power—a belief that what they do will make a difference" (Dodd, 1995, p. 65). This belief is echoed in two bodies of literature of the 1980s and 1990s. First, many frameworks for understanding thinking and personality style (Harrison & Bramson, 1982; Myers & McCaulley, 1985) find large percentages of people who have the need to be in charge or in control of at least certain aspects of their environment in order to function well. Second, the literature on constructivist learning and teaching posits that learning for true understanding requires students to construct their own meaning (Brooks & Brooks, 1993). This involves owning their own questions and pursuing their own lines of inquiry with teacher guidance. These two bodies of literature support the same proposition: Successful teachers find ways for students to have some ownership of and influence over the flow of events and the intellectual life of the classroom.

There are many ways to offer students choice and influence over their lives in school. One pertains to the social system of the classroom—the rules of the classroom game as opposed to the rules for interpersonal behavior one often sees posted on classroom walls. The rules of the classroom game pertain to social norms and procedures for conducting class discourse. They are often undiscussed and unwritten, though that is something we recommend changing. The teacher asks a question, the student responds, and the teacher evaluates is a typical cycle of discourse reflecting the "rule" that the teacher will control the talk in the room. Without losing control of the class or the curriculum, a teacher can permit students to participate in shaping and operating these procedural systems for discourse and business.

The sections that follow might be thought of as levels of depth and sophistication in a strategic approach to giving students authentic influence in classroom life. Whereas you could work on them in any order or even simultaneously, it is useful to understand which ones are more complex and why. Then you can choose them appropriately. You need not address the eight issues sequentially and wait for a certain level of development before beginning practices aimed at another level. For example, there is no need to wait until students are stopping a class to ask for clarification before teaching students about their own learning style and how to use that knowledge to influence assignments. But it might be worth bearing in mind that the eight approaches described do increase progressively in complexity. Therefore, if you are interested in developing student ownership and influence, you might start with the simpler and then move slowly to the more complex forms of student ownership.

30. STOP MY TEACHING

"Stop my teaching" refers to empowering the students to use signals to tell a teacher when the instruction is leaving them behind. Teachers who take this information seriously develop signal systems whereby students can indicate on their own initiative that they are lost and want the teacher to stop and explain again. Hand signals like thumbs down held tight against one's chest could be such a signal. Or students could put red, yellow, or green cards on the corner of their desks like traffic light signals. Thus, teachers could get a quick visual read on how well students understand a discussion.

When the idea of stopping the teaching becomes part of classroom culture, other symbols or phrases come to represent the practice. One teacher told her class the story of a family vacation where she and her husband and six children stopped at McDonald's for lunch. Loading up hurriedly in the tightly packed van after their quick meal, they didn't do a head count and were four miles down the road before she said, "Where's Bobby?!" Bobby was back at McDonald's.

The teacher now uses that phrase frequently in class as a coded signal: "Have I left you at McDonald's?" and the children also use the code to signal when they're getting lost. "Ms. Swift, I think I'm back at McDonald's!" The humorous shared code serves to authorize the practice of stopping the teacher's teaching, and the teacher's affirming reaction shows the practice to be a valued one that earns kudos for the child rather than a frown or a veiled accusation of inadequacy.

31. STUDENT-GENERATED QUESTIONS

Lang (2016a) gives another vehicle for student choice: *student-generated test questions.* "Traditional exams represent one of those moments in a course in which students seem to lose all control," says Lang (para. 11). In an issue of *The Marshall Memo* (April 25, 2016), Marshall summarizes: "To counteract that, he suggests having students work in groups for 30–45 minutes coming up with test questions that might be used (or reworded) in the actual exam. This is a twofer, says Lang: it not only gives students a sense of control over their learning but also serves as an effective review session."

32. NEGOTIATING THE RULES OF THE CLASSROOM GAME

Negotiating the rules of the classroom game means involving students in creating the routines and procedures of classroom discourse and class business. These rules are different from the rules of behavior that teachers and students commonly work out at the beginning of the year. The rules we are talking about here are usually tacit, underground, and unstated. They pertain to teacher-student and student-student interaction around such issues as questions and answers, class dialogue, and procedures and protocols for taking turns. Recitation lessons of teacher questions and student answers do indeed often turn out to be a game, where students try to win by getting the right answers and avoid losing by shrinking into invisibility when they don't know the answers.

Once in one of our courses, Dick Adams, a housemaster at Newton North High School, in Newton, Massachusetts, asked his students if he had ever played Guess What's on the Teacher's Mind with them. The concept had come up when we studied questioning techniques under clarity. Recall that teachers who play Guess What's on the Teacher's Mind ask inexplicit questions when they have a particular answer in mind but the way they ask the question allows for a universe of possible answers. "I don't ever do that, do I?" asked Dick. A number of slow, knowing, affirmative nods came back at him from the students. "No . . . really? Give me some examples."

They did. And from that opening there proceeded a class discussion of how to conduct class discourse in such a way as to eliminate student pet peeves and increase productive participation. For example, they decided together that a student who couldn't answer a question could refer it to another student whom he or she named. If three students in a row couldn't answer the question, Dick would conclude he had asked a bad question. Then he had to ask it in a different way or ask students where the gap was.

His students became so excited over the way the class was going that they asked me to videotape it. We realized that the students were not just happy over the new dynamics and improved clarity of class discussions, but elated over having been a force that influenced the shape of the class itself. Students had changed the rules of the classroom game in collaboration with their teacher and emerged from the traditional nether region of passive ciphers to active and authorized players.

The point of this story is to raise the question: What opportunities do students have to influence the rules of the classroom game, to shape the form and dynamics of interaction and operation? How can teachers give them ownership of these rules?

33. TEACHING STUDENTS THE PRINCIPLES OF LEARNING

A third way to give students influence in classroom life is to share with them teaching and learning strategies we use ourselves. By including them in the secret knowledge of teaching and learning strategies, we give students choices, power, and license to control their learning.

Principles of learning should be explicitly taught to students so they can use them to be more powerful learners. This is a good moment to reflect on such principles to decide which ones you think would be most beneficial to turn over to your students as tools for learning. The more we are interested in empowering students and giving them choices, the more we will explicitly put learning at their disposal and urge them to use them autonomously.

Here are some of our nominees for principles and tools to teach to students from Saphier, Haley-Speca, and Gower, 2017:

- *Sequence.* Students can use this principle to sequence their own lists when studying vocabulary words (or anything else that is sequential in nature) so the items hardest for them are in the optimal first and last positions.
- *Practice.* Students can use knowledge of this principle to optimize their personal practice schedules.
- *Goal setting.* Students can use this principle to set realistic academic and behavioral targets for improvement and make effective plans of action to meet them.
- *Explanatory devices.* Visual imagery and especially graphic organizers can become regular tools for students. Imagery can be used to pause during study and construct meaning in a visual way. Graphic organizers can become a habit as a note-taking technology through which students assimilate information as they read, hear, or see it. Teachers can integrate the use of these devices into assignments and work toward having students choose when and how to use them.

While passing these strategies on to students, teachers who are aware of attribution theory and are committed to conveying the three expectations messages—this is important, you can do it, and I won't give up on you—will see they have a special opening. They will seize frequent opportunities to connect the use of these strategies with student success rather than let students attribute successful performance to intelligence. "Well, José, did you use any graphic organizers when you reviewed that chapter? No? Well, look—you're a strong visual learner. You and I both know that. Let's go over how to use that strategy with material like this. I know you can make it work for you!"

Yvette Jackson (2011) recommends a step beyond: inviting students to professional development sessions for teachers on instructional topics. What an inclusive way to make students co-learners in the path of empowering everyone's learning!

34. LEARNING STYLE

Students gain a sense of empowerment when we urge them to use knowledge about their own learning styles to choose learning activities or selection of performances to show what they know.

Learning style has diminished credibility as a variable we should pay much attention to in designing instruction to improve student achievement (Hattie, 2009). But putting students in charge of influencing lesson design by using knowledge of their supposed "learning style" is something quite different. It's about agency, about control, about voice, about being allowed to participate in shaping the learning experiences, not an application of unsubstantiated cognitive science.

Students using knowledge of learning style means teachers are not just using their knowledge of learning style to adapt lessons for the styles of their students; they are teaching the students about their own learning styles and the implications of those styles for what kinds of assignments will be difficult and what will be easier. Furthermore, they encourage students to use knowledge of their own styles to guide their study routines and even to ask for modifications in assignments that allow them to use their strengths. These steps set the stage for a more complex level of empowerment: giving students explicit choices over assignments, forms of tests, and forms of projects.

Many teachers have been to a workshop on learning style, and some may be trained in one or more of the learning style frameworks. These frameworks help them understand the similarities and differences in the ways humans take in, process, and express their learning. These frameworks also help in understanding the features of the learning environment and the different kinds of activities that work best for individuals. For example, some people learn best when they can talk and interact with others as they deal with new concepts. Others like to read, listen, view, and assimilate alone before interacting with others. This body of knowledge about learning style preferences can be a powerful vehicle for giving students ownership in classroom life.

Helping students understand their own learning style sets the stage for some important forms of empowerment. First, students can predict (and teachers can help them predict and prepare for) the difficulty of certain assignments or tasks that do not match their preferred learning style. If teachers have set the stage properly and taught about learning style, the value system associated with learning style frameworks enables students to see their difficulty in certain tasks as attributable to differences, not deficiencies. Second, the predilection for predicting learning style match or mismatch to tasks enables students to mobilize extra effort and seek help when appropriate. It should not be used as an excuse to sidestep an important learning experience. When teachers encourage students to use knowledge of their own learning style to do either of these two things, they are empowering them in significant ways.

The simplest place to start teaching students about learning style is with modality preference: visual, auditory, kinesthetic, or combinations of them. Simple modality preference tests (see Barbe & Milone, 1980) can be used to have students identify their preferences. Then teachers must look for (and share out loud with students that they are looking for) ways to vary their teaching to address different modalities.

Another framework for learning style differences that students can use in the same way is the left brain–right brain or global-analytical framework. Dunn and Honigsfeld (2009) provide another useful set for students to know about and for them to use to empower their learning effectiveness. Gregorc's (1985) framework provides a fourth and more complicated but highly useful take on style difference. McCarthy's (2005) 4MAT System is a fifth, and Gardner's (2006) multiple intelligences framework a sixth. Finally, the sophisticated Myers-Briggs provides a seventh.

All of these frameworks are worthy of investigation, and we believe they are a part of teachers' professional knowledge. But for the sake of classroom climate and this particular dimension of influence, the point is to choose one of them and work on giving the framework to students, that is, teaching them to use it not to label themselves but to modulate their effort, seek help when appropriate, and sometimes take the initiative to alter assignments based on their self-knowledge from a learning style perspective. Giving students license and encouragement to speak up in this way to ask for modifications of assignments brings us to the topic of choices. What kinds of choices do students get to make about their academic work, and how do they do it?

Carolyn Mamchur (1990) writes: "Giving students choices may seem like a complex issue. But actually, it is dead simple. The rule is this: whenever you can give a student a choice of any kind, do it" (p. 636).

35. NON-REPORTS AND STUDENT EXPERTS

A non-report, an idea we found some years ago in a *Mindsight* newsletter, is a good example of students' influencing assignments and the shape of products. There is nothing particularly unique about non-reports. They are simply outside assignments—but with several major differences.

A non-report is anything that does not fall into the category of straight written information. The task is to convince students accustomed to the way school is supposed to be that their teacher will accept and value their ideas. Their first question is usually, "What do you want?" since they know that pleasing the teacher is the quickest way to a good grade. Here is how a non-report works:

1. Impress on students that a standard written report will receive no credit, since it does not meet the requirements of the assignment.

2. Make the assignment worth enough points so that not doing it will result in a substantial drop in grade. At first, there is a great risk in doing something not completely spelled out, so the risk of losing credit must be greater.

(Continued)

(Continued)

3. Create a grading scale that gives equal merit to content and to creativity (more loosely, to the effort the student has to make to personalize the knowledge he or she conveys).

4. Keep the topic very general, giving the students ample opportunity to select from among a wide variety of ideas. For example, if you are studying a unit on measurement, allow them to select anything at all dealing with measurement. Point out to them that there are few occupations (or hobbies, sports, etc.) that do not contain measurement of some kind. Give them examples. Challenge them to name something that apparently has nothing to do with measurement—but be quick enough on your feet to find the measurement involved.

5. If they insist, and they may at first, give them a couple of examples of Non-report type formats (they are endless and limited only by imagination). For example, they could create a game, write a song, role-play a game show, do a slide or tape presentation, make a scrapbook, or build a model. But warn them that they will receive more credit for doing something you haven't thought of than copying something you have. And stick by that statement!

6. Perhaps most important, don't do this assignment unless you are willing to truly value the students' ideas. If you can't suspend your own idea of what is right or good and try to see the product from their point of view, they will never believe you again. But neither should you give credit for hastily conceived and executed junk. I once received a shoebox with a hole punched in one end that was labeled "Working model of a black hole." Hah!

I have found that giving 10 points for the idea, 10 points for the execution, and 10 points for the content, plus 5 for effort, works out well—a total of 35 points. The effort points come in when a person has had three weeks to do a project that might be reasonably well done but obviously took only 15 minutes compared to someone else who spent several hours. You can tell by looking.

The first time you do this, you will probably receive the usual assortment of collages, collections, and posters copied from books. But when these students see the more adventurous, creative, and "fun" projects getting all the praise, they will be more willing to let go a little the next time.

By the end of the first year that I had students do these projects, I turned them loose on a topic we had not covered in class: solar energy. They researched the topic, did their Non-reports—including a working parabolic solar cooker and a miniature solar greenhouse complete with Trombe walls made of plastic soft drink bottles—and presented them to the class, thus covering almost all the important aspects of solar energy—with no effort on the part of the teacher. One of the most rewarding aspects of these assignments is that, frequently, the students who usually get C's or D's in regular assignments really come into their own on Non-reports.

Non-reports allow students to plan, research, and execute. It evokes their creative potential and forces interaction with the content. Many students sought "experts" to help them and learned the intricacies of carpentry, photography, sound and art—because they wanted to. And it is tremendously exciting to see projects come into the classroom that are far beyond anything the teacher would have assigned or expected.

Source: Non-reports. (1989).

We would add specific criteria for success that make it clear to students exactly what the attributes of quality work in the non-report will be. For example, in the non-report on solar energy, the criteria could be (1) explains three different ways of converting solar energy, (2) discusses costs and efficiencies of various forms of solar energy, and (3) uses data to compare the efficiency of solar, fossil fuel, and nuclear energy. Students using these criteria could create dozens of different kinds of products to represent their learning, from radio shows to models to video productions.

Randolph and Evertson (1995) give a simple example of student choice that suggests how plentiful the opportunities are for giving them:

Ms. Cooper often delegated tasks that would typically be assigned [by her] to students. We have already described students as providing the text for writing class through Sharing Models/ Generating Characteristics. In this activity, students also took on the task of controlling the floor, which would traditionally be a teacher task. Areas of student control include deciding how to participate, getting the class's attention and leading the discussion by calling on peers. . . . Student readers usually stood in the front of the room, but Ms. Cooper gave students the option of reading from their desks. Students were given the same choice when they shared their rough drafts with the class. The fact that Ms. Cooper did not define this aspect of appropriate participation gave students choice in how to manage this aspect of controlling the floor. (p. 22)

The ability of students to make choices and control the activity flow and the discourse within the group is partially responsible for the success of cooperative learning. In all cooperative learning models, students work in groups in which they control the dialogue, who speaks, when, and for how long.

Chapters 6 and 7 of *Learning to Choose, Choosing to Learn* (Anderson, 2016) provide some good nuts and bolts for facilitating students making good choices.

The following sections address using students and their communities as sources of knowledge. This aspect of choice and voice is about reaching out to and respecting what students bring to the classroom, their experience, and their questions.

36. CULTURALLY RELEVANT TEACHING

As we look around us and see that over half of all children in the United States are people of color, it is especially important to be creating schools that acknowledge and value the cultures of all students. Excluding these children's cultures from school artifacts, customs, arts, and curriculum not only demotivates but alienates significant numbers of students (Cummins, 1986). Ladson-Billings (2009) brings this argument into the more immediate domain of curriculum by pointing out that using the community as a source of curriculum experiences makes learning meaningful and active and also culturally relevant. Zaretta Hammond (2015) adds a powerful brain-based slant to culturally proficient teaching and gives the rationale and the science for why culturally relevant teaching frees the brain for learning.

Class Experts

Early in the school year, one teacher asked the students to identify one area in which they believed they had expertise. She then compiled a list of "classroom experts" for distribution to the class. Later, she developed a calendar and asked students to select a date that they would like to make a presentation in their area of expertise. When students made their presentations, their knowledge and expertise was a given. Their classmates were expected to be an attentive audience and to take seriously the knowledge that was being shared by taking notes and/or asking relevant questions. The variety of topics the students offered included rap music, basketball, gospel singing, cooking, hair braiding, and babysitting. Other students listed more school-like areas of expertise, such as reading, writing, and mathematics. However, all students were required to share their expertise (Ladson-Billings, 1995, p. 481).

Some may wonder how such open-ended assignments can be congruent with a school curriculum that contains specific skills the students are supposed to be mastering. By using such practices, teachers can weave skill objectives for research, organization, and reading, writing, and speaking skills (or any other skills that are in the curriculum) into the criteria for good presentations by student experts. The point that Ladson-Billings makes is that the students own the knowledge they present, and the knowledge is acknowledged to have value. The "classroom experts" assignment is a practice that is congruent with augmenting student owner-ship and influence because the knowledge of students and the culture from which that knowledge comes—the students' own culture—is explicitly validated by a school learning activity.

Culturally relevant teaching does not mean teaching about other cul-tures, though that can have value. It means validating students' cultures by including in school learning experiences, topics, scenes, and knowledge that derive from those cultures. It looks not only to individual students but also to the community from which the students come as a source of cur-riculum experiences:

> One teacher used the community as a basis of her curriculum. Her students searched the county historical archives, interviewed long-term residents, constructed and administered surveys and a ques-tionnaire, and invited and listened to guest speakers to get a sense of the historical development of their community. Their ultimate goal was to develop a land use proposal for an abandoned shop-ping center that was a magnet for illegal drug use and other dan-gerous activities. The project ended with the students making a presentation before the city council and Urban Planning Commission. One of the students remarked to me, "This [commu-nity] is not such a bad place. There are a lot of good things that happened here, and some of that is still going on." The teacher told me that she was concerned that too many of the students believed that the only option for success involved moving out of the com-munity, rather than participating in its reclamation. (Ladson Billings, 1995, p. 479)

Constructivist Teaching

Constructivist pedagogy brings student influence to the intellectual life of the classroom and may be the most advanced level of student ownership. It is also the most complex and requires the largest paradigm shift for teachers; most of us, after all, were educated in schools where other peo-ple's constructions of knowledge were handed to us for consumption and digestion. Brooks and Brooks (1993, p. 33) provide five overarching prin-ciples of constructivist pedagogy:

1. Posing problems of emerging relevance to learners

2. Structuring learning around "big ideas" or primary concepts

3. Seeking and valuing students' points of view

4. Adapting curriculum to address students' suppositions

5. Assessing student learning in the context of teaching

There is still a place in good education for *active reception learning*, as Ausubel (1963) puts it. But there is also a large place for carefully designed teaching that allows students to construct meaning for themselves.

Randolph and Evertson (1995), in their analysis of interactive discourse in a writing class, describe this kind of pedagogy:

> The construction of knowledge, which takes place through negotiation, depends on the redistribution of power from teachers to students. The fact that knowledge is presumed to come from students defines students as knowledge-holders, an identity usually retained by the teacher. (p. 24)

Constructivist teaching puts students in the legitimate role of knowledge generators and knowledge editors, whether in science, social studies, language arts, or any other academic discipline (Brooks & Brooks, 1993). The examples in the Randolph and Evertson (1995) study describe a series of lessons on literary genre. They show how teachers' conscious regulation of dialogue and interaction with students can make students genuinely empowered knowledge generators. For example, one teacher, Ms. Cooper, asked students to bring in examples of fables to share and discuss in class so they could extract the characteristics of fables from analyzing these examples. At one point, she asked the class to look for generalizations they could make about the morals of fables:

Teacher: What can we say about the characteristics of morals? [Students offer some suggestions.] Maybe we need to explain what a lesson or moral is—how to be a better person. I'm going to put that up, unless you have objections.

Laurie: They're trying to prevent you from making mistakes. [Teacher writes, "Stories are used to help you become a better person and not make mistakes."]

Tim: I disagree. Sometimes some of the things are wrong.

Hillary: Can be. [Teacher changes "are" to "can be" in the sentence on the board: "Stories can be used to help you become a better person and not make mistakes."]

Onika: But everybody makes mistakes.

Teacher: You're right [Adds to the sentence on the board: "or learn from characters' mistakes in the story"], but the purpose of the fable is to help you not make so many mistakes.

In analyzing this episode, Randolph and Evertson (1995) comment:

The discussion begins with Ms. Cooper's question. The answers she receives do not give her the information she wants, so Ms. Cooper supplies her own answer: a moral teaches how to be a better person. In stating her answer, Ms. Cooper clarifies her question: she is asking about the purpose of a moral. With this new information, Laurie is able to supply a response that Ms. Cooper validates by incorporating it into the characteristic she is writing on the chalkboard. So far Ms. Cooper is in the position of authority in the classroom: she initiates the topic, students respond with possible answers, and she evaluates them, rejecting all responses until she hears one that fits her expectations.

The nature of the interaction changes, however, as Tim questions the characteristic that is the joint construction of Ms. Cooper and Laurie. In effect, Tim takes on the role of evaluator of the response, moving Ms. Cooper into the role of co-collaborator with Laurie. Ms. Cooper's response is thus demonstrated to be as open to evaluation as any other participant's response.

Onika and Susan then join the deliberation, questioning the need for morals as they have defined them in class more than they are questioning the definition itself. Why, they argue, should morals try to keep you from making mistakes, when you're going to make them anyway, and they help you learn? These contributions are initiations of a new topic, which Ms. Cooper responds to and evaluates by treating them as negotiations of meaning, signaling her acceptance by incorporating the new contribution into the statement on the board. Thus, the characteristic as it is finally stated is the joint construction of Ms. Cooper, Laurie, Tim, Hillary, Onika, and Susan. (pp. 23–24)

Similar scenarios can be found in the literature for helping students construct knowledge in science and mathematics. This kind of teaching requires a role shift for some teachers of significant proportions away from being dispensers of knowledge to facilitating negotiation of meaning by students.

The role of the teacher in constructivist science teaching is often to involve students in predicting phenomena, then reacting to observed phenomena and constructing hypotheses, which they then test to account for their observations. For example, most students predict that heavy objects fall faster than lighter ones—which is incorrect. The hypothesis making and dialogue about subsequent experiments and explanations that constructivist teachers facilitate have similar qualities to the dialogue in the Randolph and Evertson (1995) example.

The changes that take place when teachers move to include more constructivist teaching in their repertoire are subtle but significant. The classroom does not look any different, and the assignments and topics may not seem much different. Where the changes show up is in dialogue with students and in the roles teachers and students are playing in the conversations they have in class. Though surface changes may appear small, the role shift is large, and the evidence strong that the effect is large in student motivation, effort, and understanding (Newmann & Wehlage, 1995).

37. STUDENT-LED PARENT CONFERENCES

A final arena for developing student choice and voice is in student-led parent conferences. Berger, Rugen, and Wooden (2015), Stiggins and Chappius (2011), and Jackson (2011) have wonderful sections on how to structure these conferences and prepare students to lead them. Such conferences, properly structured, are powerful structures for generating student agency and responsibility for their learning. Given their full treatment of the how-tos on this topic, we refer readers to these works.

REFERENCES AND RESOURCES

Anderson, M. (2016). *Learning to choose, choosing to learn*. Alexandria, VA: Association for Supervision and Curriculum Development.

Ausubel, D. P. (1963). *The psychology of meaningful verbal learning*. New York, NY: Grune & Stratton.

Barbe, W. B., & Milone, M. N., Jr. (1980, January). Modality. *Instructor, 89*(6), 44–47.

Berger, R., Rugen, L., & Wooden, L. (2015). *Leaders of their own learning*. San Francisco, CA: Jossey-Bass.

Brooks, J. G., & Brooks, M. G. (1993). *The case for constructivist classrooms*. Alexandria, VA: Association for Supervision and Curriculum Development.

Cummins, J. (1986). Empowering minority students: A framework for intervention. *Harvard Educational Review, 56*, 18–36.

Dodd, A. W. (1995, September). Engaging students: What I learned along the way. *Educational Leadership*, pp. 65–67.

Dunn, R., & Honigsfeld, A. (2009). *Differentiating instruction for at-risk students: What to do and how to do it*. Lanham, MD: Rowman & Littlefield.

Gardner, H. (2006). *Multiple intelligences: New horizons*. New York, NY: Basic Books.

Gould, S. J. (1981). *The mismeasure of man*. New York, NY: W. W. Norton.

Gregorc, A. F. (1984). *The Gregorc style delineator*. Columbia, CT: Gregorc Associates.

Gregorc, A. F. (1985). *Inside styles: Beyond the basics*. Maynard, MA: Gabriel Systems.

Hammond, Z. (2015). *Culturally responsive teaching and the brain*. Thousand Oaks, CA: Corwin.

Harrison, A. F., & Bramson, R. M. (1982). *The art of thinking*. New York, NY: Berkeley Books.

Hattie, J. (2009). *Visible learning*. New York, NY: Routledge.

Jackson, Y. (2011). *The pedagogy of confidence*. New York, NY: Teachers College Press.

Ladson-Billings, G. (1995). Toward a theory of culturally relevant pedagogy. *American Educational Research Journal, 32,* 465–491.

Ladson-Billings, G. (2009). *Dreamkeepers.* San Francisco, CA: Wiley.

Lang, J. (2016a). Small changes in teaching: Giving them a say. *Chronicle of Higher Education, 62*(32). Retrieved from http://chronicle.com

Lang, J. (2016b). *Small teaching: Everyday lessons from the science of learning.* San Francisco, CA: Jossey-Bass.

Mamchur, C. (1990). But . . . the curriculum. *Phi Delta Kappan, 71,* 634–637.

McCarthy, B. (2005). *Teaching around the 4MAT cycle: Designing instruction for diverse learners with diverse learning styles.* Thousand Oaks, CA: Corwin.

Myers, L. B., & McCaulley, M. H. (1985). *Manual: A guide to the development and use of the Myers-Briggs Type Indicator.* Palo Alto, CA: Consulting Psychologists Press.

Newmann, F. M., & Wehlage, G. G. (1995). *Successful school restructuring.* Madison: University of Wisconsin.

Non-reports. (1989). *Mindsight.* New Lenox, IL.

Randolph, C. H., & Evertson, C. M. (1995). Managing for learning: Rules, roles, and meanings in a writing class. *Journal of Classroom Interaction, 30,* 17–25.

Saphier, J., Haley-Speca, M., & Gower, R. (2017). *The skillful teacher* (7th ed.). Acton, MA: Research for Better Teaching.

Stiggins, R. J., & Chappius, J. (2011). *An introduction to student-involved assessment for learning* (6th ed.). Hoboken, NJ: Pearson.

8

Schoolwide Policies and Procedures

The numbers in the list below are keyed to the section in the Introduction called "50 Ways to Get Students to Believe in Themselves."

38. Hiring teachers

39. Assignment of teachers

40. Personalizing knowledge of and contact with students

41. Scheduling

42. Grouping

43. Content-focused teams that examine student work in relation to their teaching

44. Reward system for academic effort and gains

45. Push, support, and tight safety net (hierarchy of intervention)

46. Quality afterschool programs and extracurricular activities

47. Building identity and pride in belonging to the school

48. Creating a vision of a better life attainable through learning the things school teaches

49. Forming an image of successful people who look like them and value education

50. Building relations with parents through home visits and focus on how to help

This chapter foreshadows another book to follow this one, because the topic of school policies and procedures implicates administrative decisions, education of school boards and policy makers, and revision of state regulations. Here we present a brief preview of the issues. The purpose is not to provide a comprehensive analysis of administrative supports that make high expectations teaching sustainable districtwide; it is to put down a placeholder for the systemic work that is necessary to scale up the work of this book from the classroom level to the system level.

Similarly, the schoolwide programs that enable students to value school and form a peer culture that supports academic effort are reserved for the book to follow and only previewed here.

It is within our grasp to make the whole environment of a school and all the student experiences provided by that environment include tacit messages to students that effort is what makes the difference and that we (the faculty and staff) believe in the capacity of each and every one of them. Where would those commitments show up?

38. HIRING TEACHERS

Screening of applicants would include an interview using the questions and follow-up skills of Martin Haberman's (2004) star teacher interview. Haberman's interview training focuses as much on follow-up questions as on the original scripted questions. The two-day training includes practice and role-playing. This protocol is geared toward identifying the candidates' beliefs about their responsibility to ensure student learning and to persevere with students who appear to have given up. "Do you believe it's your job to get students to believe in themselves . . . and to persevere if they don't?" We have to find that out.

We could also look for the behaviors in Chapter 3 of this book when candidates give demonstration lessons. What messages do they convey to students as they handle questions and answers, facilitate student work, and respond to requests for help?

39. ASSIGNMENT OF TEACHERS

In a school that authentically wishes to eliminate the achievement gap, the best teachers would be assigned to the lowest performing students. Making progress with underperforming students would carry high-recognition social rewards in the school, and gain scores would be as important as AP scores on a teacher's résumé. Demonstrated belief in the growth mindset would be a requirement for these positions, which would become coveted rather than reserved for the newest hires or the low-status teachers.

In recent years, Charlotte-Mecklenburg Schools, in North Carolina, implemented a countywide version of this approach that included assignment of high-performing principals as well as teachers. Ann Blakeney Clark's (2015) chapter in *Excellence Through Equity* is worth serious study for the details of making such a policy sustainable.

40. PERSONALIZING KNOWLEDGE OF AND CONTACT WITH STUDENTS

Beyond the classroom teacher, other teachers and administrators would be assigned to get to know each student personally and follow them through their years at the school. Thus every student, but particularly underperforming, low-confidence students, would have an adult or two who went out of their way to show interest and knowledge of the student's life and academic progress.

Some schools identify incoming students deemed at highest risk of failing or dropping out and implement the recommendations above only for those students. Others use data collected in the first six weeks of school to identify the students for whom this social safety net may be important.

Home visits should be on the agenda for families of students for many reasons, and not just for troubled students. Such visits are where we get to show family members that we are interested in their children and want them to succeed. But they are also where we get information about the students' culture and family values, information that is essential to developing culturally relevant lessons. See Margery Ginsberg's (2011) book *Transformative Professional Learning* for a thorough treatment of the rationale and practical how-tos for making home visits effective.

41. SCHEDULING

42. GROUPING

School schedules would be designed to maximize student focus, not adult convenience. Thus there would be periods available for extra help, peer tutoring, and also extension and advanced work for students who learn quickly. Grouping for re-teaching would be a guiding principle in the design of schedules. And collaborative planning time for teams of teachers would be a must.

43. CONTENT-FOCUSED TEAMS THAT EXAMINE STUDENT WORK IN RELATION TO THEIR TEACHING

Error analysis of recent work and the design of re-teaching for small groups would be a regular and frequent activity in professional learning communities (PLCs). We define a PLC here as a group of teachers who teach the same content in middle school or high school or a grade-level team in elementary school. See the rating scale in Appendix B for evaluating the effectiveness of how these teacher teams would use their time.

In addition, principals and department chairs would visit these PLCs with an educated awareness of what productive use of this meeting time looks and sounds like. If the PLCs were not using their time productively, the principals or department chairs would intervene or provide help so the teams went to greater depth in analyzing student work and responding to patterns they found.

We have long advocated that supervisors of principals use school visits to investigate the level of supervision and support principals give to PLCs who share content. They could visit them with the instrument in Appendix B and assess how effective they are. For details of how supervisors of principals can do this work, see Saphier and Durkin (2011).

44. REWARD SYSTEM FOR ACADEMIC EFFORT AND GAINS

Every school has reward systems for students (and informally for adults too). One can tell what the reward system values by what the trophies in the trophy case are for, by who is honored at school assemblies, by whom newspaper articles feature, and by certificates and prizes that are distributed.

More informally, certain students have status among their peers for their accomplishments, determined by what the students have picked up in the culture that communicates what is valued. So who are the stars on campus?

- Football players?
- Science Olympiad winners?
- Scholarship awardees?
- Recipients of good citizen or kindness awards?
- Students with high gain or improvement scores?

The point is that we shape these reward systems by what we pay attention to. In a high expectations school, rewards would be associated with effective effort and progress.

45. PUSH, SUPPORT, AND TIGHT SAFETY NET (HIERARCHY OF INTERVENTION)

It always seemed to me that the "hierarchy of responses" that Rick DuFour (DuFour, Eaker, Karhanek, & DuFour, 2004) put together for Stevenson High School 25 years ago was the tight structural safety net our lowest performing, lowest confidence students need. Marry that structure with consistent messages to students about effort-based ability and our caring and belief in them, and a school has a winning formula. Appendix C spells out the sequence of these responses in detail. It's a pivotal text for any district that is serious about eliminating the achievement gap.

The following is a brief summary of its principles.

Principle 1. When students don't learn the first time around, every school needs to have a progressive hierarchy of academic interventions planned and ready to go.

Principle 2. This series of interventions needs to be activated quickly when students are failing or academically at risk.

Principle 3. These interventions must be timely, flexible, and required. There are no options for students to skip, avoid, or sidestep learning what is in the curriculum. There are also no options for students not to participate.

Principle 4. The interventions are escalating but nonpunitive. They are also prompt and focused on academics.

A main point for leaders is that this kind of intervention structure springs from a deep and abiding commitment to preventing students from falling through the cracks. The staff must be united behind the commitment to get *all* students to proficiency and take responsibility for doing so. Then the structures available to fulfill this task get amazing results.

46. QUALITY AFTERSCHOOL PROGRAMS AND EXTRACURRICULAR ACTIVITIES

Afterschool programs became more and more widespread in the United States as multiple family members joined the workforce. Originally needed for child care, they have grown in their role. The best offer rich educational opportunities for children in the arts, sports, and academics. This benefits all children, but for the underperforming, low-confidence children who are the subjects of this book, afterschool programs provide other vital supports. They provide opportunities for enrichment and recreation that might not otherwise be available to them. The best programs provide healthy fun, academic support, exposure to the arts, community connections, and social-emotional learning of life skills like persistence, self-control, goal setting, and planning. While documentation of their effectiveness is in its early stages, there is already firm evidence of positive impact on student attendance rates (Browne, 2015).

What will be interesting in the future is to see what effects can be achieved by marrying quality afterschool programs with regular school programs that teach effective effort and the growth mindset.

47. BUILDING IDENTITY AND PRIDE IN BELONGING TO THE SCHOOL

48. CREATING A VISION OF A BETTER LIFE ATTAINABLE THROUGH LEARNING THE THINGS SCHOOL TEACHES

49. FORMING AN IMAGE OF SUCCESSFUL PEOPLE WHO LOOK LIKE THEM AND VALUE EDUCATION

We learned a great deal about these forms of outreach to the community in the 1997–2005 period, when we worked with Steve Leonard and the faculty of Burke High School, in Dorchester, Massachusetts. Five of us were there in various capacities weekly for those years and saw a high school rise from being so dysfunctional that it had lost its accreditation to a pinnacle where every graduating senior, 220 students, was accepted to college.

The more disadvantaged the neighborhood, the more necessary it is to get these three engines of motivation pulling in our direction. Together with school- and districtwide policies and practices, discussed earlier in the chapter, these forms of community connection will fill out the picture in the companion volume to follow.

50. BUILDING RELATIONS WITH PARENTS THROUGH HOME VISITS AND FOCUS ON HOW TO HELP

There is an extensive literature on the importance of family relationships in successful schooling (Epstein, 2016). What I hope to add to that in the future is material on how family members could help with homework and speak to their children about effort and struggle if they were coming from a growth mindset. This material will have language samples and scenarios much as Chapter 3 did for teachers who respond to student requests for help and other common situations. Having family members as partners in teaching students how to exert effective effort would be an unbeatable combination for students of all ages.

We encourage readers to imagine now, however, how these thoughts might influence their conversations with families at back-to-school events and student conferences.

REFERENCES AND RESOURCES

Browne, D. (2015). *Growing together, learning together.* New York, NY: Wallace Foundation.

Clark, A. B. (2015). Human capital as a lever for districtwide change. In A. M. Blankstein & P. Noguera (Eds.), *Excellence through equity: Five principles of courageous leadership to guide achievement for every student* (pp. 127–133). Thousand Oaks, CA: Corwin.

DuFour, R., Eaker, R., Karhanek, G., & DuFour, R. (2004). *Whatever it takes: How professional learning communities respond when kids don't learn.* Bloomington, IN: Solution Tree.

Epstein, J. L. (2016). *School, family, and community partnerships.* Boulder, CO: Westview Press.

Ginsberg, M. B. (2011). *Transformative professional learning: A system to enhance teacher and student motivation.* Thousand Oaks, CA: Corwin.

Haberman, M. (2004). *Star teachers: The ideology and best practice of effective teachers of diverse children and youth in poverty.* Chicago, IL: Haberman Foundation.

Saphier, J., & Durkin, P. (2011). *Supervising principals: How central office administrators can improve teaching and learning in the classroom.* Retrieved from http://rbteach.com/sites/default/files/supervising_and_coaching_principals_saphier.pdf

9

Conclusion

This book proposes some significant challenges: changing our language, adding a number of student agency structures and procedures, implementing new school policies. But this is certainly not mission impossible. Virtually any teacher can learn the skills illustrated in this book. And any school can build itself into a reliable engine of student success based on effort-based ability. The problem is sustainability, scale, and leadership.

WHAT LEADERS DO

Leaders who want their teachers to learn and practice the skills in this book must say so. The formula I have always found relevant for moving people toward cultural changes (and acting from a belief in effort-based ability is surely a culture change in American education) is this:

- Say it.
- Organize for it.
- Model it.
- Protect it.
- Reward it.

Say it. Say at every possible opportunity, both ceremonial (opening of the school year speech) and mundane (the header of the meeting's agenda) that one values and wants the change.

Organize for it. Support the classroom structural changes and the school policies and procedures profiled above.

7

Choices That Generate Agency

Voice, Ownership, and Influence

> **The numbers in the list below are keyed to the section in the Introduction called "50 Ways to Get Students to Believe in Themselves."**
>
> 30. Stop my teaching
>
> 31. Student-generated questions
>
> 32. Negotiating the rules of the classroom game
>
> 33. Teaching students the principles of learning
>
> 34. Learning style
>
> 35. Non-reports and student experts
>
> 36. Culturally relevant teaching
>
> 37. Student-led parent conferences

A primary concern of this book is mobilizing every strategy we can muster to get students to be active agents in their learning. All of the structures in Chapter 5 and the teaching of effective effort in Chapter 6 aim

Model it. This means, for example, partnering with teachers in implementing attribution retraining case studies with underperforming students, being the caring adult who connects regularly with an at-risk student, giving workshops for parents on how to help with homework from a growth mindset point of view.

Protect it. Defend teachers who experiment with growth mindset practices like encouraging retakes of quizzes and giving the highest grade a student gets.

Reward it. Give opportunities for conference participation and other perks to those teachers who are on board with effort-based ability.

Finally, leaders bring the same growth mindset we want to display to students to their supervision and evaluation of teachers. Teachers are evaluated on their implementation of behavior in the arenas of classroom life presented in Chapters 3 and 4. "If your beliefs haven't changed, act as if they had. We can act our way to new beliefs." And evidence of student progress beyond what one thought possible will be the best convincer.

We also want our teachers to believe in themselves, believe in their efficacy in changing students' mindsets and in their students' capacity to outperform their own stereotypes of themselves. Therefore, all the language forms we studied in Chapter 2 will start to enter our verbal interactions with our teachers too.

TEACHER PREPARATION

Some teaching skills are best learned when one has a class of students to actually teach, and other skills can be learned in college settings because they are more "head work," that is, theoretical in nature. A topic related to the latter set of skills is the growth mindset and the research that has supported the idea of brain plasticity in recent decades. All teacher prep programs should contain a module of some sort of this topic.

Similarly, the history of the concept of intelligence we laid out in Chapter 1 could be part of teacher preparation prior to one's first job. Anything we do to set up beginning teachers for committing themselves to effort-based ability will be a strong contribution.

OBSTACLES

If a group of teachers, a whole school, or even a whole district chooses to take on the challenges of this book, they risk doing so alone. This is because our society as a whole has not really reconceptualized the achievement gap as an opportunity gap. The opportunity gap for students of poverty and students of color can be reduced significantly only by investing in a high-expertise teacher workforce. This investment must come from political and policy groups whose commitments are elsewhere now (e.g., competing with the public school system, doing more teacher evaluation, implementing high-stakes testing as an accountability device).

Making "smart is something you can get" an organizing principle in each school is a foundational element of school improvement, but it cannot be dependent on putting in place inspired and skillful principals one finds ready-formed. The personnel pipeline for principals does not have at any point the development and certification of culture-building skills as a benchmark, nor the study of how to bring effort-based ability alive in the school.

A new slant on the supervision and evaluation of principals would require that those supervising and evaluating them know what to look for and how to coach principals to get better at growing a culture of effort-based ability.

Looming over all these issues, however, is the elephant in the room: Three power constituencies—policy makers at all levels of government, state and federal legislators, and the voting public—are not aware of or motivated to respond to the need to create a true, knowledge-based teaching profession (Saphier, 1994). As long as these three constituencies continue to believe that teaching is easier work than it actually is, requiring only good management and motivated employees rather than requiring high expertise of both teachers and leaders, there will not be sufficient resources available to elevate the performance of all our schools systemically. Nor will there be a focus of national and state leadership on the "right stuff." Policy makers need to understand (1) the range and complexity of teaching knowledge and skill that our children need and (2) the working conditions that support deep collaborative work. For decades, literally dozens of organizations producing piles of well-written and well-documented reports annually, and hundreds of scholars and practitioners individually have been speaking and writing forcefully for this agenda all the time. I have been one of them for 30 years. And we are talking to ourselves.

Identifying the right problem is the first axiom in problem-solving lore. The problem is not uncovering the knowledge for teaching from the growth mindset, and it is not revealing the components of a knowledge-based profession. *The problem here is a political one—how to mobilize collective action of those to whom the power constituencies listen.* Educators, researchers, and teacher educators can, of course, focus on educating the three power constituencies at assemblies and convocations where these people go (e.g., Aspen Institute, Gates Foundation forums and those of other large players in the funding world, Council of Chief State School Officers, annual conventions of legislative Education Committee chairs from the 50 states). That would be a good start. But the issue is fundamentally a political one. Groups that the power constituencies listen to must be mobilized—grassroots voter organizations, big-audience media outlets, billionaire donors like the Koch Brothers and George Soros. (Imagine those two in the same camp!)

The problem is also a moral and philosophical one. To the degree that individualism and not-in-my-backyard, it's-not-my-responsibility thinking dominate political decision making throughout the United States, the chances for change are slim. To the degree that the social contract and the interest of the common good captivate public imagination, we have a chance to make our educational system the envy of the world, as it once was. The noblest aspirations of our public education system have always enshrined a guarantee of a fair chance at a good life through education. Overcoming the "separate but equal" doctrine (via *Brown vs. Board of Education*, 1954) brought us somewhat closer. But we are still a long distance from honoring that promise.

The issues of institutional racism, income inequality, unequal access to health care, and unequal access to fair treatment in the criminal justice system have the same roots as our unequal public education system—an erosion of commitment that the government should serve the common good.

With all these other issues of equity roiling in our society, it seems that equity in educational opportunities is a way off, but the commitment to get it underlies all the changes reformers have been proposing for decades.

CODA

This book has been about a pivotal aspect of school improvement—convincing students to believe that they can grow their ability and motivating them to want to.

This commitment is, indeed, a sine qua non for empowering schools to raise achievement for disadvantaged students. It provides the energy for deep collaboration and constant learning about high-expertise teaching. But effort-based ability is not the only element on which to focus. There must be accessible outside sources from which to acquire some of the knowledge and skills of high-expertise teaching, which includes some skills that are absent from teacher education and usually missing from professional development.

Likewise, it is necessary to have a data flow to teachers (and students) that continually illuminates which students have mastered what. The data flow comes when there is common curriculum as well as common quizzes and interim assessments created by teachers for analysis in high-functioning professional learning communities. But neither outside professional development nor a data flow from interim assessments is enough without the fire and fertility of strong beliefs and a commitment to success for all our students, not just some.

I wish to close on an optimistic note and with a call to action. Building a strong culture around the growth mindset is the foundation for closing the opportunity gap, and individual schools right now can use the rich 40-year history of research and practitioner invention to transform their schools. Right now, whole school districts with stable and committed leadership could use the information in this book to guide the professional development of leaders and secure long-term support through education of their school boards. But the frustrating experience of ups and downs that so many of us have witnessed, the every-decade issue of *Time* magazine about our "failing schools" (the first in my collection goes back to the 60s), and the continued low quality of education for our most needy students will continue until we as educators enter the political arena.

Avante!

REFERENCES AND RESOURCES

Brown, P. L. (2016, February 7). #blackmindsmatter. *New York Times.*

Saphier, J. (1994). *Bonfires and magic bullets.* Retrieved from http://rbteach.com/sites/default/files/bonfires_and_magic_bullets_2.pdf

Appendix A

Case Studies in High Expectations Teaching and Attribution Retraining

This appendix contains two sets of case studies. The first were carried out by teachers in our courses on high expectations teaching. Each teacher picked an underperforming, low-confidence student and put to work all the tools the teacher could muster to get that student to change his or her stereotype of self as a student who was "too dumb" to learn.

The second set were carried out by administrators who picked a teacher to work with and coached that teacher to do a case study like the first set. Many of the administrators built themselves into the case study by having regular interactions with the selected student. The potency of this set of case studies is that in many cases the teacher did not think the student could actually improve. So the administrators had to change both the teacher's mind and the student's attributions. These are success stories, and they shine a bright light on the possibilities for courageous and committed supervisors.

First read Case Study 1. Then read a case study for the grade you interact with most and then comment on what was significant about it. What could you transfer from this case into your own practice?

TEACHER CASE STUDIES

Teacher Case Study 1—Eighth Grade

It was already mid-September, and I was sorry I ever told my principal that I wanted a change and a challenge in my teaching assignment. After teaching sixth-grade English for years, I was assigned two classes of eighth graders who seemed destined to fail the Maryland Writing Test (an assessment of functional writing skills, the passing of which is a requirement for graduation in Maryland). I had until November to prepare these eighth graders for the test. By the end of the first day of class, I knew that the task was going to be a greater challenge than I had anticipated. The students in my two writing classes took one look at each other and knew immediately that the class was a remedial class for *dummies*. How could I convince these kids that they were capable of passing the test? I had the perfect situation for my Expectations Case Study.

Although I could easily have chosen any student from either of my classes as a subject for the case study, I picked K from seventh period. Her informal reading assessments from the spring semester showed K reading at a fifth-grade level. Her criterion-referenced test scores from the spring for reading/language arts indicated that her performance was slightly below standard. (I had not given any other tests to assess students' current levels of writing proficiency.)

K had been turning in very little work in the Test Prep class, and what she did turn in was of low quality. She came late to class and looked for ways to escape. She wouldn't bring the materials she needed for class, wouldn't stay in her seat, and wouldn't stay on task—all behaviors that would indicate K had very little self-confidence in her ability as a learner. K often created situations that ensured that I would have to focus on her poor behavior rather than her academic performance. She would occasionally produce work when she was sent to the in-school-suspension room, but there seemed to be no way to get her to make much effort in class.

I knew enough about K's history to recognize that both her academic performance and behavior were in sharp decline. As a sixth grader, she had been eager to participate in all learning activities, especially enjoying those of a cooperative nature. She'd had a sunny temperament and was willing to try new things to please her teachers. I remembered reading about students who stop liking school and begin avoiding academic challenges after reaching middle school and wondered if K was a case in point. I felt that unless I could reach this student, she would surely fail the Maryland Writing Test as well as the Test Prep class and seem to tune out of school.

Experiment 1: Communicating an Essential Belief

Since the students in my Test Prep classes believed that they were placed in my class because they had little ability, I had to evaluate what I believed about these students. If I thought they had little chance to pass the Maryland Writing Test, the class was doomed. So I actively read the chapter on expectations from *The Skillful Teacher* (Saphier, Haley-Speca, & Gower, 2008). I thought about the essential points and interesting details. I really did believe that all the students in my class could pass the writing test if only I could get them to work at it. I decided to test whether I had clearly communicated a "you can do it!" attitude to my students. The following day, in place of the regular warm-up activity, I asked my class to write down what they thought my expectations were for them and what they thought it would take to pass the Maryland Writing Test. The results were a real eye-opener.

Reflection on Case Study Student

To the first question, K responded, "I think you expect [sic] us to act dumb because you don't think we know how to write." To the second she replied, "I could pass the test if they ask me to write about something I know or if we have practised [sic] writing the prompt in class."

These responses were similar to those given by others in the class. Most thought I believed them to be incapable of becoming good writers. Like K, a few who thought they had a chance to pass the writing test attributed passing to luck. Most believed they could never pass it. I was appalled by the responses and at the beginning of the next class spent 20 minutes focusing on the positive—all the good writing skills the group already possessed. I told them that there was plenty of time for them to acquire the skills they still needed to pass the test. All they needed to do was put forth a little effort. "I know you can all do it!" was repeated again and again. That day, we accomplished more in the class than on any previous day, even though the first 20 minutes of class was spent in discussion. Even K turned in a couple of paragraphs at the end of the class!

Experiment 2: Setting Goals

I was pleased with my initial efforts at more clearly communicating the "you can do it!" message to students and didn't want to lose momentum. I would take the written work that students had turned in the previous class and use that as a baseline assessment from which students could set specific learning goals for themselves. I constructed a series of posters that outlined specific skills students needed to pass the test. I then marked the class papers identifying which skills individuals showed mastery of and which they still needed to practice. I also developed a chart that students could use to list the skills they had already mastered and to keep track of the ones they needed to work on.

Reflection on Case Study Student

At the beginning of the next class, I had students list the skills they had already mastered on one side of their charts and pick just one skill that they would like to master next. Students were comparing lists with one another and boasting about the skills they had already mastered. Better yet, I heard the beginnings of cooperation among the students. I overheard one student saying to K, "Oh, that's easy. I can show you how to do that." K had chosen to work on the skill of writing an introduction that incorporates words directly from the prompt. Although she wasn't willing to let me work with her, K did allow the student who had said she could show K how to write an introduction to sit with her. Together the girls wrote introductions to three different prompts. When I spoke to K near the end of class, she seemed pleased with her own work. She told me that is was easier to work on getting one thing right than to try to keep "everything I'm supposed to do right in my mind." I'd say that the strategy of having K focus on one small but attainable goal was a good match between learner and strategy.

Experiment 3: Proving Detailed Feedback

I no longer dread seventh period. I think that after saying, "You can do it!" so many times to my class, I now truly believe it too! Yet of all the students in the class, I feel I've made the least progress with K, who is still reluctant to let me work with her. Since building a personal relationship with some students is a long process, I tried not to give up on K. Instead I began to work on the type of feedback I give to my students, making the feedback more detailed and having it focus on skills performed well, in addition to providing specific guidelines on how to improve those areas where further efforts were still needed. Also, rather than just handing back papers with feedback to students, I decided to set up in-class appointments with students to discuss their efforts.

Reflection on Case Study Student

Two weeks ago, in-class conferences would have been impossible because much of my time was spent dealing with inappropriate behaviors and complaining students. Now during seventh period, students are on task *most* of the time—they are still eighth graders after all—but the class climate seems much more positive. Students know that when they sit down with me they will hear about what they have done right as well as what they still need to work on. K still needs to be redirected more often than others, but she is producing more work, and that work is of a higher quality. She now allows me to sit down next to her and discuss her work, and for the first time she is coming over to ask me a question about her work. K has added writing introductions to her list of mastered skills and is now working on supporting her opinions with details and examples.

Final Reflection

Although for the purpose of this assignment I focused on the performance of one student, K, I knew I needed help with the whole class. Because all of the students in my Test Prep class were low-confidence learners, the strategies I selected were chosen to benefit all the class, not just K.

I know that when (not if!) I teach this class again, I will begin with a baseline assessment of my students' writing skills, which I will use to help them set small, attainable goals for their own learning. Once I did that with my seventh period, students began to see the task of passing the Maryland Writing Test as achievable. I felt that students responded well to more direct feedback from me and that I would continue to discuss that feedback personally with them. I sensed that students began to perceive me as more of a guide than "the enemy" when my feedback included positive comments as well as specific steps they could take to improve the skills they were trying to hone. Finally, I hope never again to have to ask students to write down what they think my expectations are for them and what they think it would take to pass the Maryland Writing Test. I hope to communicate my expectations for them so clearly and so frequently that that particular experiment would never have to be repeated. I believe that the mistake I made with my Test Prep classes was in communicating the *importance* of passing the test without clearly communicating that I thought they were all *capable* of passing it. And to make matters worse, I realized until I broke the tasks down into different skills that they were able to master one at a time, passing the writing test must have seemed like a hopeless task to them.

Although K has not become a model student, I have not once had to refer her to the office for poor behavior since our experiments began. I now keep supplies in class for when K doesn't bring her own, and I'm employing the sort of "persevere and return" tenacity that is necessary to motivate K to make more of an effort in class. My tenacity has paid off to the extent that K seems much less defensive now about her writing and is beginning to accept help from me and other students in the class. I will continue to wear down K's resistance with repeated "I won't give up on you!" messages. In November, when the test is given, I'll see how successful my experiments have been.

Teacher Case Study 2—Fifth Grade

Amhad is a fifth-grade male student who is attending Maple Avenue as his fourth elementary school. Recently, I have noticed that Amhad is spending most of his academic and recess time in the office working alone—if you can call it working. He travels with a large group of boys, all of whom have difficulty with English. They are often seen in the hallways at inappropriate times, coming out of the bathrooms together and causing a variety of problems for lunchroom and playground aides. When these students are asked about the incidents they cause, the blame consistently comes back to Amhad. I am a new teacher to the district and am working hard to learn objectives, outcomes, and standards. I am involved in planning for instruction and consider specific behaviors important to classroom management. I believe in class meetings and give student feedback, especially when there is a change in performance. I admit that I find Amhad unmanageable and feel he should be accomplishing more both in and outside the classroom after 3 months of school. The principal and his parents and I are all concerned about him and want to look at underlying causes for his inappropriate behaviors and relationships with peers.

Amhad is clearly not meeting school discipline standards, evidenced by behaviors such as throwing food in the cafeteria, talking back to the teachers, not handing in assignments, failing tests given as review in spelling and mathematics, and fighting in class. The standards of behavior, classroom and schoolwide, have been discussed with Amhad and his parents (brought in for support), and Amhad is able to relate behaviors that he knows are inappropriate. However, he does not allow himself to take the blame. It is always someone else's fault, and his parents often back him up. He understands that cursing at teachers and fighting in the classroom are offenses that have resulted in him getting suspended from school; however, he continues to behave in this manner. One to one, Amhad is often a very verbal student, interested in a variety of topics that are beyond a fifth-grade understanding. He is often frustrated by assignments that involve writing and therefore does not hand in assignments. He does not participate during class discussions after silently reading a passage that he would otherwise be excited about. Considering his passion for talking and his interest in topics that are widely covered in Time for Kids (a *Time* magazine subscription service for youngsters), such as space exploration and underwater adventures, it is often a surprise that he is not attending in class or participating with a lot of teacher intervention.

Amhad seems to learn best in small-group settings where he can take on a leadership role. He often is more comfortable when an adult is present and seems to be more participatory when my focus is directed at him. He is attentive for long periods of time when passages are read to him, rather than when reading himself, and is often more successful when given opportunities to self-direct his study methods. Options such as dramatizing, listening to tapes, and drawing often give Amhad more successful scores on classroom tests and keep his behavior in check for longer periods of time.

Amhad is a very loving, caring individual who is extremely compassionate and is often the leader of the school's service corps, which assists our special education students. He is truthful and righteous and is a born leader. His strengths far outweigh his faults/weaknesses in terms of affect, and he seems to draw others in with his sense of humor and friendly attitude. Unfortunately for Amhad, when trouble finds him, his friends run for the hills. He is motivated by kind words and adult praise.

Amhad exhibits many behaviors that indicate his own feelings of inadequacies and low confidence as a learner. He does not participate in school discussions; he is constantly putting himself down as stupid, dumb, and a loser. He attributes his failures to the teacher, his parents, himself at times, and even the other students. He often curses at the teachers and other students when he is lost or misunderstands directions, and often I am frustrated and impatient with him as well. This turns Amhad off to any interaction that would assist him in feeling successful. Amhad has become the class clown, which is often indicative of feelings of inadequacy. When other students laugh at inappropriate comments, he feels a part of the group without having to spend any extra effort. This behavior has become automatic and is causing him to react more frequently to his poor performance in academic areas.

Journal Entry 1

Amhad will often answer a question with a silly answer or in some way try to take my focus away from the question and redirect it onto his behavior. Often, I would leave him, ignoring the behavior, and move on to another student, expressing nonverbally my dissatisfaction with Amhad's behavior. The first strategy I explored to focus on the attribution retraining efforts was to stick with the student. I did not move on when he deliberately tried to shift direction from my question to his inappropriate behavior. I expressed to him that I was willing to wait for him to attend to my question and that I would help him participate appropriately. I encouraged him to think aloud and often modeled think-alouds for all students. Amhad seemed a bit surprised by my confidence in his ability to answer, and the students seemed to play along, noting that I was not going to move on until progress was made with the specific question asked. Therefore, it helped the situation if the students did not laugh at Amhad, and when he realized he did not have an audience, he seemed to focus on coming up with an answer that the rest of his class could discuss.

Journal Entry 2

To assist Amhad in learning how to use his leadership skills to help himself through lunch and recess, I gave him a role to play in helping younger students. He was motivated by the fact that because I told the class that I was choosing students based on their "people skills" to help others, Amhad was immediately seen as superior! He was unbelievably excited by the prospect that I thought he was capable of being responsible for other students, and it was easy to note that this was an immediate confidence builder. The message that I gave him was that I had positive expectations for him and that he was capable of following through on his job.

Journal Entry 3

Amhad was constantly feeling the pressure of having the lowest score on all his tests. Most of his tests in fifth grade were written evaluations, and Amhad had extreme difficulty staying focused long enough to complete this task. I decided to assess Amhad through verbal evaluations and rubrics so that he would know exactly what he needed to say in order to successfully complete the test. Using the rubric gave Amhad the specific parameters of what he must do to earn an acceptable score. For the first week, Amhad and I designed the rubrics together so that he would feel a sense of ownership of his success. Once the written piece was eliminated, I was surprised to find out how much this student knew. By communicating expectations and standards for the tests and evaluations, Amhad had an opportunity to use his strengths to indicate his knowledge.

Final Reflection

This experience has helped me focus on individualized instruction as it was meant to be. Rather than teach five different levels, I began to think about individualizing in terms of what each student learns and how I need to develop the lessons so that each student has the possibility and probability of success. In 25 years of teaching, how often have I heard "That test was too hard!" Often, I questioned the test itself but did not always recognize that it was the child's belief about his or her own learning that I was missing.

The study of attribution theory and how it relates to a teacher's own repertoire of strategies for teaching is vital to the success of students in our classrooms. Through the experiment with Amhad, my own views of his behaviors and why he does what he does have changed. Rather than attributing his inappropriate behavior and low grades to his constant moving around or language barriers, I began to look at how he was expected to learn. Amhad's learning style depended on multiple intelligence opportunities. His biggest weakness was writing, and that was what most teachers expected from him for evaluative purposes. He could not help but fail. By assisting Amhad with appropriate learning tools to fit his learning style and by sticking with him and not using the ignoring strategy, I enabled him to participate more fully in instructional lessons and actually go to recess occasionally. Some aides were not expecting his behavior to improve and did not alter their own behavior to accommodate Amhad's. It became evident that their expectations were exactly the level at which he performed. I always felt sad when I would see him in the office because of discipline issue in the cafeteria. He was out of control when the adult in charge did not focus on his ability to lead and rather gave him lots of opportunities to fail.

I am amazed at the improvements this student made in a very short period of time. We have developed a good relationship as evidenced by the absence of cursing and limited statements of "I'm stupid" or "I can't do it." His peer relationships have been developing, and I have noticed that he is taking the blame more frequently when deserved. Amhad still continues to have issues when reading silently and is not learning the prereading strategies as we had hoped. We have decided that he should be screened for specific learning disabilities and perhaps work in small groups with the resource teacher when using prereading strategies.

Teacher Case Study 3—Kindergarten

As I administered the writing vocabulary assessment to Sean, his first words were, "I don't like to write. I can read, but can't write very well." This sounded familiar. The year before I'd had Sean's older brother in my third-grade class. Sean's brother was also an above-average reader with messy handwriting and an aversion to written tasks. When I asked Sean to write all the words he knew, he could barely write his name. This was a child who had a high level of vocabulary and could read on a first-grade level. He exhibited poor fine motor control. This was also evident during other tasks like cutting, coloring, and gluing. I noticed that he would avoid all fine motor tasks by going to the bathroom or transitioning to another area of the classroom. I had to determine how to best encourage Sean. If I put pressure on him to finish a difficult task, he would often break down. From my experiences with his older brother, I knew that if not carefully guided Sean could experience confidence issues similar to his older brother. I had to develop ways to boost his confidence while maintaining the high standards of the curriculum.

Experiment 1: Help Beginning a Task (Personal Contact and Expectancy)

I noticed Sean would often wander from a task that involved lots of fine motor work. He tended to give up. I experimented with giving him a lot of personal contact in the beginning of a task, and I could also assess any material modifications that would increase his success. I would be sure to take advantage of teachable moments during and after the task to help Sean realize that effort yields success. I would not allow Sean to simply not finish a difficult task, but help guide him through it.

Reflection on Case Study Student

During one session, I helped the class make "color books." They needed to cut up yellow pieces of paper and glue them onto an outline of a pear. Sean began saying, "I can't do this." I said, "Sure you can. Let me show you all a couple of different ways to make little yellow pieces. You can cut them or tear them like so." He decided to tear them and successfully completed the task. When he finished the pear, I came by to recognize that he had really worked hard and had a beautiful product. He eagerly began the next page of his book. An important part for Sean was catching him before he became discouraged. Letting him know I thought he could do it and sharing several strategies really worked for him. I addressed his table when offering strategies and that seemed not to isolate his weaknesses. I have tried this approach in the past, and it has yielded success. I need to continue using it. I also have to be aware of some potential pitfalls like dependence. I feel he needs this much support right now, and I will gradually release it as he becomes more comfortable.

Experiment 2: Recognizing Superior Performance

One way to boost his confidence was to recognize the things he did really well, like reading and using computers. This may present an opportunity to talk about how effort yields success. I began by selecting a picture book to read about students in a primary class who each could do one thing really well. At the end of the story the main character discovers that he can use chopsticks better than the others because his family uses them daily. He begins to teach others.

Reflection on Case Study Student

Later, when Sean was frustrated with a coloring task, I referenced the idea that time was needed for skills to develop. He still remained frustrated because he wanted his project to look just like my example and the work of the student next to him. I understood that it was natural to compare yourself with others. I realize that I will need to show Sean how he is improving. I want to explore the ideas of portfolios. During computer lab, I asked Sean to help a student with the computer. I explained to Sean that this student was not very comfortable with the computer yet, but since Sean had a lot of experience he could help out. Sean brimmed with confidence as he helped another.

Experiment 3: Positive Expectancy

I had to be clear what my expectations were for Sean's writing this year. I expect all students to write their names "the kindergarten way" by the end of the year, with a capital letter at the beginning and lower case letters following. I also expect them to attempt writing each other's names and simple words. How could I modify this for Sean? I planned to talk to his occupational therapist to get some ideas for how to accommodate him. I need to keep expectations high and not lower standards. Sean's occupational therapist suggested that he use a smaller pencil to help his grip and that the process of learning to write his name should be a progression of small successes.

Reflection on Case Study Student

I shared with the class how by the end of the year I expected all kids to write their name "the kindergarten way." When Sean finished a paper, I asked him to write just the first letter of his name using the modified pencil. I know writing is hard for him, but I will work with him to learn his name one letter at a time. I told the class they had the whole year to work on it. He agreed to write his first initial after I modeled it for him. When asked later in the week, he knew how to write the first letter in his name. He wanted me to write the rest. I took the pressure of time off of him and set a clear expectation for the end of the year. I'm eager to see him write his name by next June.

Final Reflection

I learned a lot about myself as a teacher in doing this project. Early on, I found myself falling into the habit of making suggestions that made things easier for the student. When working with Sean directly, I tended to lower my expectations so he could feel successful and also selfishly so we could move on. I needed to remind myself that it didn't matter if he missed one of his centers that day. In fact, he needed time to complete the project, and my expectations had to remain high. I found that Sean became more willing to participate if I anticipated some of his frustrations and supplied strategies to modify others. He had high standards too, and as teachers we would have to help him reach those goals. I would also need to help him see his own growth and the results of his effort. I will need to continue with the experiments I have tried. I will also need to have the goal in mind of gradual release of responsibility. In addition, I learned that students' confidence can begin to lower as early as kindergarten. Sean and others are already learning avoidance and giving up on certain tasks. It's never too early for attribution training or retraining. I learned that I need to examine my own belief system about what makes students smart. It's difficult to share some of the realizations I've made about high expectations and standards if I haven't made the journey myself. I realize every teacher needs to examine his or her own beliefs and expectations. As a classroom teacher I recognize the value of talking with another professional about your expectations for a child. Oftentimes I have been pointed in the right direction by another teacher who has listened to my frustrations. The most important thing for me to do is actively listen. This will help me understand and expand my repertoire of communication of "What we're doing is important. You can do it. I won't give up on you."

Teacher Case Study 4—Fourth Grade

I have chosen this student, named B, for several reasons. Primarily, he has not been achieving in the classroom to the level of which I believe he is capable. He seldom finishes his work, even when given many different cues to get back on task. He demonstrates many task avoidance behaviors, such as misplacing papers, asking to use the bathroom, volunteering for any activity that would allow him to leave the room, and "performing" for his classmates. I believe he is capable of a higher level of achievement because he will engage in conversations that show he is learning, he will dictate high-level responses to comprehension questions, and he enjoys coming to school. B learns best when he is standing, allowed to move about the room, and working one on one with an adult (ideally an adult who accepts his learning style).

His confidence level is low. This is evident by conversations he has during group activities. Rather than take a risk at being a leader or contributor, B will clown around, often sabotaging the group's progress. He easily accepts this role, because it is his belief that everyone is smarter than him, so why would they value what he has to say? Conversations he has had with a variety of adults in the school also demonstrate this low confidence concern. He frequently minimizes his achievements and will occasionally say, "I'm not smart," or will withdraw and not speak at all when asked if he needs help or simply wants to chat.

B will do anything for anybody. He is an excellent friend and gets along very well with adults. He is willing to do any organizational task (e.g., clean out the teacher's closet) and this is often used as a motivational tool.

The three areas that I felt needed immediate attention for B were low self-esteem, motivation, and underachieving. I conducted the following experiments to address these areas.

Experiment 1: Messages in Everyday
Verbal Interactions to Increase B's Self-Esteem

B's normal response to the statement "I know you can do it" would be to put his head down and respond that he can't. For 1 week I made greater effort to preface an assignment or task with "I know you are able to do this. I look forward to seeing your results" or "Look this over and see what areas you feel you will be successful in completing." When going over completed assignments, a similar interaction took place with any specific response that was completed: "This is a wonderful response," "I knew this was an area you would enjoy completing," or "What do you think of this response?"

Reflection on Case Study Student

Initially, B accepted his encouragement with a blush, still with his head down. Toward the middle of the week, he showed more of a response by having his work on his desk before being asked to take it out. On the last day of the observation, B presented the work to me for evaluation before being asked for it! I believe with this continued encouragement B will eventually be self-motivated. I am concerned B might regress if this is not continued and also concerned about whether this constant reassurance is reasonable for a teacher in a class of 28 students.

Experiment 2: Attribution Retraining for Motivation

B believes that everyone is smarter than he is and that's just the way things are. He doesn't believe that working hard and putting out effort will help this situation. Acceptance by his peers would go a long way to improve his motivation. I created with B a Group Work Contract with the following goals:

- I will listen to others' opinions.
- I will tell and explain my opinions.
- I will accept when someone disagrees with me.
- I will write my opinion of my participation in the group.

Reflection on Case Study Student

B's use of the contract became a focus in his group. He suggested that everyone in the group complete the same contract, and everyone agreed. In doing this, the others in the group encouraged each other to speak. At first B was more concerned with completing the contract than doing the group activity. I suggested that he glance over the goals at the beginning of the activity and review them again at the end of the activity. This shifted his focus, and he became a more active member of the group. His opinions were accepted, and the group members listened to his ideas. Part of the reason for this was that they wanted to be successful when evaluating the goals. But for whatever reason, B became much more comfortable and willing to participate.

Experiment 3: B's Lack of Focus and Difficulty With Fine Motor Skills

B has so much difficulty getting his thoughts and ideas down on paper that he associates this with being "stupid" and not as smart as everyone else. The use of an Alpha Smart, a portable keyboard that can be used at the desk and then hooked up to a printer, provided B with the opportunity to present his thoughts and ideas.

Reflection on Case Study Student

At first the Alpha Smart served as a toy for B, and there always seemed to be an issue that caused him not to be able to use the tool (it wouldn't print, what was typed got erased, etc.). Little reaction by me to these distractions allowed B to realize that this was his responsibility and that he would have no one else to blame if he wasn't able to use the Alpha Smart correctly (he had been trained on how to use the tool). By midweek he was asking permission to use the Alpha Smart in more and more classroom activities. One of the students in his group asked permission to use the tool, and B became his trainer. At the end of the week the class was given a writing assignment. I observed that B took out the Alpha Smart, created an appropriate outline, printed the outline, and turned it in. The outline was clear, was well thought out, and contained information from an expository reading that the class shared during the week. This outline represented B's ability, without the barrier of having to write. His focus shifted from frustration with the fine motor skills to focusing on using the Alpha Smart appropriately.

Final Reflection

I originally incorrectly interpreted B's classroom performance as being combative and resistant. For the first month of school he was underachieving and unhappy, causing a lot of others in the classroom to be unhappy because of his disruptive behavior. Taking the time to focus and being able to really observe B's actions, temperament, body language, and approaches to a task gave me an opportunity to better understand his limitations. I feel that the experiments conducted allowed B to perform better in the classroom, thereby raising his self-confidence and making him an active participant. I am concerned that because of the large class size B will eventually slip by and revert back to his old habits next year.

Teacher Case Study 5—Ninth Grade

Juan is a Hispanic ninth grader in honors U.S. History. His grade for the first marking period was an E. Repeated attempts to contact his parents throughout the marking period were not successful. The interim mailed home halfway through the marking period was not returned with acknowledgment of receipt. He received interim warnings in other academic courses as well.

Juan's counselor has no specific information on either Juan or the family situation. A review of his file indicates a criterion-referenced test score of 538 in middle school, which is below the county average. He earned Cs in middle school in honors World Studies and also received multiple interims in middle school in several courses, including World Studies, but generally managed to pull his grades into the C range for each report card. I had had contact with Juan in the summer Freshman Orientation class; he had attended the class and did the minimal amount of work, which resulted in a passing grade of C.

Juan is not meeting the classroom standards in multiple ways: He does not complete most of the work either in class or for homework; he does not volunteer or contribute in class; he does not ask for help or acknowledge that he needs it when asked as part of the whole class or individually.

In the summer course, Juan was strongest at objective-type assignments and assessments—multiple choice versus writing. Strategies that have had little or no impact include moving his seat from between two talkative girls to a desk surrounded by hardworking, motivated students. He has repeatedly declined my offers of help.

Juan is polite and pleasant. He is respectful and courteous when spoken to.

Journal Entry 1

Because Juan appears reluctant to ask for help or acknowledge needing any help, attribution retraining seems appropriate. Juan does not seem to have a strong positive sense of himself as a capable, accomplished student. I was able to address unmet expectations when Juan received a unit test with the grade of E. As Juan left class after the tests had been returned and discussed, I spoke to him privately. I began by connecting to our summer work together in the Freshman Orientation class. Although he had not been a stellar student in the summer class, he had had some success. I reminded Juan that he had been successful in the summer course and told him that I knew he was capable of more and better quality work than he was currently producing.

I reminded Juan that he had chosen not to complete the 3 x 5 note cards that each student was expected to prepare as a test review strategy. I expressed disappointment in this choice and stated that for the next unit test I expected Juan to bring in his note cards prior to the class due date during a lunch period so we could look them over.

I told Juan I was confident that he could create the note cards and that I would help him when we met if he had any questions or concerns about them. I stressed that I wanted him to make the effort to complete the note cards and that they did not have to be "perfect" or even the same as other students' cards but, more importantly, be useful to him. I also told Juan that I believed using the note cards as a study aid would ensure the kind of grades I believed he was capable of receiving on assessments. Juan agreed to meet with me and bring his note cards prior to the next review session. He appeared somewhat flattered by the personal attention and the repeated references to his potential ability.

The results of this attribution retraining appear positive. Juan has agreed to come in for help at lunch—a big step forward. He also has responded favorably, nonverbally, to the description of his past successes and to the belief that he will and can succeed in the future. This interaction could and probably should have taken place earlier in the year. The one-on-one pep talk seems to have stimulated a response where nothing else did.

Journal Entry 2

Now that Juan appears more amenable to my intervention, I have decided to tackle his writing skills. He tends to answer any essay questions with one or two sentences. He rarely uses supporting details or examples. This, of course, contributes to his low grades on many assignments.

I decided to try the concept of a graphic organizer to help Juan (and other students) identify the details and examples needed to write a coherent, detailed essay. As class work, the students had been given a one-page handout of letters written to a newspaper during World War I by blacks discussing the rumor of job openings in the North. The students were asked to read the three letters and then respond to the following question in an essay format: "How do the letters reflect the dissatisfaction of blacks with life in the South and their hopes for a better future?"

When I read the responses, I found that some students, Juan included, had either misread the questions or had written very brief, unsupported statements for an answer. I returned the assignments to the class without having graded them. I then reviewed the essay questions with the class and asked for their input in creating a graphic organizer for possible answers. As the students brainstormed and contributed, I created a simple organizer on the board using their ideas. Once the students understood what I was doing, some of them offered suggestions for additional categories and details. I specifically asked Juan for a corroboration of another student's answer and was pleased to see that he responded (correctly).

I then asked each student to copy down the organizer that had been jointly created and look at his or her own answer to the essay question. Had the answer included some or all of the main points for the organizer? Students had the opportunity to rewrite the essay using the organizer as a guideline. The majority of the students, Juan included, chose to rewrite the assignment, which was subsequently graded.

I think my effort at providing the graphic organizer as a tool for eliciting details and support for essay writing was successful. It appears that students like Juan may have some good ideas but do not know how to organize them or group them for inclusion in an essay. Overall, the strategy was received positively; I plan to use it again but as a prewriting tool.

Journal Entry 3

The next strategy I employed in an attempt to increase Juan's success in the class was the introduction of a mental imagery lesson. This was a departure from anything I had ever used before, but I was willing to try anything that might engage Juan in the learning process. I was preparing the introduction to a lesson on life in the city from newly arrived immigrants' viewpoint. Using the *Skillful Teacher* (Saphier, Haley-Speca, & Gower, 2008) as a guideline, I created a descriptive passage to share with my students. I then set the stage for the mental imagery exercise and presented it.

At the end of my description, I gave the students a few minutes to individually jot down ideas/images that had come to mind. I then assigned the students to groups of four and had them discuss with each other what they had envisioned. I reminded them that there were no right or wrong answers. While walking around the room, I was pleased to see that Juan was interacting with his group and contributing some of his ideas. As Juan left class at the end of the period, I quietly praised him for his active participation.

The mental imagery exercise appeared successful in engaging Juan in the introduction to the unit. It also gave him an opportunity to interact with his peers in a nonthreatening environment.

Final Reflection

A student like Juan is a challenge—not much background information or parental support and a repeated pattern of failure on assessments. My ability to intervene on a personal, private level with Juan and provide him with attribution retraining to support his need for encouragement made all the difference. He gained the confidence he needed to attempt the course work and then was given specific strategies (the 3 x 5 note cards, the graphic organizer, and the mental imagery activity) to allow him to be successful.

I believe that as Juan continues to experience success in the U.S. History class, he will become more confident in his own abilities and will be more willing to take risks (for example, answering a question in class on his own initiative). Overall, I believe I was successful in making a difference in Juan's perception of himself and in his level of success at schoolwork.

ADMINISTRATOR CASE STUDIES

Administrator Case Study 1—Sixth Grade, Special Education

For the purpose of this case study I have selected a sixth-grade special education student who will be called Tamika.

Tamika visits a resource room for both reading and mathematics. I chose Tamika because while working with her teacher I heard her describe a student in her class as a "nonreader"; that student was Tamika. While working with Tamika's teacher and visiting the classroom frequently to observe, I started noticing how Tamika, the nonreader, was demonstrating some higher level cognitive ability. This was demonstrated in her responses to different questions her teacher asked after reading and discussing various literatures. Tamika's teacher is working on several areas of her instructional practice, but the one that inhibits Tamika's academic and cognitive development is her underlying belief that Tamika is not capable of handling higher level material. Here the teacher has predetermined that Tamika cannot function in a level much higher than first grade, yet my experiences and observations of Tamika's responses demonstrate a student who is quite capable of interpreting and formulating meaningful responses to various types of questions.

In this case, Tamika is not meeting my standards because although she is *not* a nonreader, she is reading four levels below her grade level. Her reading level was assessed using a developmental reading assessment that indicated Grade 1 to be her independent reading level and Grade 2 her highest instructional reading level. Observation of her reading behaviors indicate that Tamika is still a "whisper" reader and still needs to track her reading with her finger. She demonstrates awareness of reading for meaning by self-correcting frequently as she reads. Tamika makes various attempts in reading unknown words by identifying beginning and ending sounds and some clusters. In addition, she uses picture and context clues to assist her in word analysis and meaning.

One of Tamika's greatest assets is her attentiveness and hard work. This is a student who works hard and feels comfortable enough to take some risks. You can tell after a few minutes of visiting the classroom that Tamika also enjoys the relationship she has with her teacher. There is a sense of trust and safety as the children in this classroom, including Tamika, take risks by responding to questions even when uncertain. This is the culture that the teacher has developed in her classroom. Part of that is because the teacher shares a lot of her personal life and experiences with them and relates those experiences to course work and events that the children are reading/studying. What fails in this approach is that the teacher occasionally asks questions and then doesn't take a long enough time to pause so that students can respond. It becomes a story time for the teacher to share her life and childhood. The result is that the teacher ends up answering her own questions or sharing her own experiences without listening to the responses of her students. So part of my work with this teacher is to get her to listen more to her students and to change her belief that her students, including with Tamika, can achieve at high levels even though they are special education students.

Tamika learns best when working in a small group. The class size in this classroom is approximately 15 students at any one time; this is a resource room where enrollment changes based on student individualized educational program requirements. Tamika's small group consists of her and two other students. To observe the personal dynamics of this group is amazing. Tamika remains relatively quiet but is not afraid to speak up by sharing her viewpoint or to ask clarifying questions. The other two members of this group are totally different from Tamika. There is another girl who is the "recognized" leader because of her personality. When the group is given an assignment, the other group members look at her for clarification of the assignment and for any other questions they may have. Tamika has a good relationship with this student, and you can see that they feel comfortable working together and that they are accepting of each other's strengths and weaknesses. The final member is a boy who for the most part is easily distracted and off task most of the time. When the group is given an assignment, this student usually is still daydreaming. After realizing that everyone is working, he turns to ask the girls about the assignment. In this group, everyone has adapted and has accepted the differences in each other's learning style.

Tamika works very hard in the classroom but seems to lack confidence in her ability. I believe that this has developed over time because of her educational placement and her past teachers' perception of her capabilities. Tamika has become comfortable with just getting by and has lost the "love" of learning. This behavior has created a student who has lost confidence in her ability and has become satisfied with just the basics. It's time to shake things up and demonstrate for the teacher just what Tamika can do!

Journal Entry 1

The first attribution retraining effort we were to demonstrate for this teacher was wait time. It became very clear from the start that if I were to help Tamika, I also had to address the teacher's belief about Tamika's capability. The way I did that was to have a direct conversation with the teacher about Tamika, my observations, and then a challenge. That challenge involved Tamika and my belief that she has the ability to respond to higher level questions. I spoke to the teacher about her wait time, and she was quite surprised by my comment. She really wasn't aware that she was cutting off the comments of the students and not allowing them to respond to her questions. So the first thing I set out to do was to demonstrate for her proper wait time while questioning.

I planned to come into class and demonstrate a guided reading lesson with Tamika's group. During the lesson, I asked the teacher to record my questions and make note of the wait time used. Before beginning our story, I began to tap the students' prior knowledge and to set a purpose for reading. As we began to discuss the theme of the story, one of the group members started sharing an experience she had that related to the story theme. Tamika perked up and started to connect her real-life experiences that were similar to the character's experience based on her story prediction. It was a wonderful experience watching Tamika and the other members of her group interact and connect to the story. This happened because I remained quiet and allowed them time to connect. After reading we talked about the character traits of the main character and connected them to people we have experienced in our own life. Tamika began the discussion, and she was eager to share with her friends stories about family members who reminded her of the character in the story.

After the lesson the teacher and I planned to get together to talk about what she just observed.

Journal Entry 2

I met with Tamika's teacher during lunch the next day. She told me she was really surprised to see how Tamika responded to my questions and then discounted the event by saying that the subject was something Tamika connected to and that was why she was so engaged. I directed the conversation back to her observations of my wait time use, and she noted that she felt that I asked fewer questions than she usually asks and that I listened more to student responses than spoke. The data helped to support what I wanted the teacher to see. We decided that I would now come in and observe her teaching, and this time I would record her questions and the student responses. But wait time wasn't the cure for what was going on in this classroom, and with this teacher and student we had to have another difficult conversation.

I spoke with the teacher about the comments she made about Tamika being a nonreader and how that belief affected how the teacher responded to her and perhaps other students in the classroom. We talked about the lessons that I observed and comments that the teacher made as I shared my literal notes with her. I think that the reason this conversation went as well as it did was because the teacher and I have developed a trust over the last few months. I have been visiting her for a while and have helped her through some difficult instructional situations. She was grateful that I was so direct, and we had further conversations on how she could improve her teaching.

Journal Entry 3

This time it was my turn to observe the teacher, her exchange with Tamika, and her group. The teacher has learned to be more of a facilitator than the one in control of the conversation. All of the children have benefited from my demonstration and from me having a very direct and to-the-point conversation with this teacher.

Final Reflection

One of the things that I realized from working on this case study is the importance of having those uncomfortable conversations with teachers, getting right to the point instead of dancing around a problem. In order for me to help Tamika, I had to change the teacher's perception of Tamika's ability, and there wasn't enough time to hope that the teacher would eventually get it. Tamika is a spirited child who in many conversations with me revealed a life with much turmoil. She is a survivor who has learned to adapt and push through many unhappy situations in her life. The spirit that drives Tamika is the spirit that we saw when she joined in conversations about her life experiences while connecting them to her learning. This ability to connect real-life experiences to her learning allowed her to begin to scaffold information into her metacognition. Tamika began thinking about her own thinking. She demonstrated the ability to monitor her own knowledge base and the factors that influenced her thinking.

I continue visiting the classroom and working on projects with them. Tamika has become one of the leaders in the classroom, something that has had a tremendous impact on her self-confidence. She is starting to see herself differently as a reader, and so has her teacher. Tamika now takes an active role in her learning.

In this case study, in order to help Tamika we had to first cure the ailment of a teacher who didn't have high expectations for Tamika and her other special education students. I continue to have conversations with the teacher reflecting on her lessons and planning for upcoming activities. Tamika is still two grade levels behind in reading but now looks at herself *as a reader*. We all have confidence in Tamika, and what is more wonderful, Tamika now has confidence in herself!

Administrator Case Study 2—Fourth Grade

I selected a fourth-grade boy for this case study. He will be referenced as T.

I chose T before I met him! T was referred to the Child Study Team to determine whether he needed to be assessed for a disability. The instructional associate, the classroom teacher, the special educator, the principal, and Ms. D, the ESOL teacher, spent about 45 minutes explaining to me why T could not succeed. Most of these reasons were rooted in his family, who apparently are a cold, miserable, uncaring, uneducated group of people. T does not speak English as a first language. T is unmotivated. (I said, "Well, everyone is motivated by something. Can you push yourself to think more about this?" The ESOL teacher replied, "Nothing motivates him.") T does not "know how to act." After listening for a good time, I challenged the team to think about what we could control, rather than what we could not. This did not go over very well! They began to tell me the sordid details of his family. Ms. D, the ESOL teacher, has known the family for years, as she instructed T's older brothers. I stopped her. "I don't want to know," I stated. Ms. D was surprised and frankly annoyed. She asked why and I told her that I wanted to be sure that I could expect the best of T before I even met him. I didn't know it at that moment, but my expectations case study had begun. The interesting thing here is that Ms. D cares deeply for T. She is nearly obsessed with his home life. She allows him to eat lunch with her daily. The underlying adaptive work is getting Ms. D to believe that what she does as a teacher (specifically around expectations) will actually impact T's performance!

T is not meeting standards in any way that is traditionally measured. His report card grades are unsatisfactory for quarters 1–3 in language arts and quarters 1 and 2 in math. T earned an S (satisfactory) in math for quarter 3! It is interesting to note that T has an I (incomplete) in ESOL for quarter 1 and no recorded grades for quarters 2 and 3. Although T has told me that he loves art, he has unsatisfactory scores in this area as well. Ms. D comments, "T is such a sweet child and he wants to learn; however, he has very low skills and seems to be getting frustrated." I think that frustration is understandable! She has also said, "T is having a hard time grasping fourth-grade concepts. He will need more time at this level." Interventions listed include only "afterschool academy offered but T did not attend" and "Ms. M's class for reading." Ms. M is a third-grade teacher. T does not meet school discipline standards as evidenced by behaviors such as leaving the classroom, wearing a hat in school constantly, not completing work, and roughhousing. However, he is rarely held accountable for these inappropriate behaviors. Most adults are hesitant to discipline T because everyone "feels so sorry for him."

Ms. D and I have been focusing on spelling for T and have been keeping consistent data in this area. Coaching Ms. D was challenging; I soon discovered that I needed to narrow our instructional focus to one area to ensure small early victories. The data are as follows as measured by weekly spelling tests:

Week	Score
1	25
2	5
3	0
4	0
5	0
6	10
7	0
8	0
9	0
10	23
11	20
12	10
13	30
14	50
15	0
16	50
17	45
18	45
*19 Case study begins	**50**

Week	Score
20	70
21	50 (100 on retest!)
22	70
23	70
24	100

T, like most students, learns best when there is a clear objective. He enjoys adult attention and seems to learn better in a small-group setting. T has lots of energy that is best utilized in shorter lessons with lots of participation. T also likes to respond with art.

T is cheerful and has a pleasant disposition. He is easy to encourage and responds extremely well to praise. As mentioned, T gains the affection of adults quickly. He expresses himself well through art. He earned a passing score in math in quarter 3, the first all year. He attends school on time and daily.

Behavior that has led me to infer that T has low confidence as a learner is that he hesitant to participate in class and rarely does. He does not attempt most assignments and is often out of the classroom. He depends on Ms. D to assist him with most work. (I know this is her responsibility to address.) T leaves the classroom frequently and often mutters that he "can't do it." He does not complete home assignments and did not attend the offered afterschool intervention because "it won't make no difference."

I do need to clarify, though, that T's own behaviors led me to believe that he has low confidence as a learner. They have been overshadowed by adult statements, particularly Ms. D's, that he is unable to achieve. Although masked by pity for T, Ms. D did not expect T to learn. These beliefs shaped her actions. As a principal, I want to coach teachers to recognize the power of expectations, rather than coach the students myself. This case study morphed into a study of Ms. D rather than T!

Experiment 1: Attribution Retraining

T often eats lunch with Ms. D. I lunched with them one day, mentioning to Ms. D that I would facilitate a discussion about effort and expectation. I asked Ms. D to explain to T what behaviors she saw from him. She mentioned, "It seems like you don't try." T responded, quite honestly, that he doesn't. Ms. D seemed surprised that he stated this so bluntly. She asked him why and he responded that it was because he didn't care. Ms. D seemed unsure how to respond. I told T that I care and that Ms. D cares too. He smiled at this. Ms. D eventually told T that she thought he didn't try because he didn't think he could do it. T looked skeptical and sucked his teeth. Ms. D asked T what he liked best and he answered spelling. "Great!" Ms. D told him. (This is how Ms. D and I came to narrow our focus.) "You can get better at spelling and I can help you." I told T that spelling was an area where the harder you work, the better you get. "Other kids are smarter and can spell better," he replied. Ms. D told him that other kids in the class study spelling words every night for a week, but that T didn't study at all. T looked thoughtful and surprised. T and Ms. D decided to study spelling words at lunch every day.

Reflection on Case Study Student and Teacher

I was actually rather impressed with Ms. D during this conversation. Our brief conversation seemed to really impact her and get her thinking. T and Ms. D did study together that week, and he passed his weekly spelling test. His classroom teacher was late one morning the next week and I held his class for a few minutes. There were no lesson plans available, so I held an informal spelling bee! T perked right up when I announced this, and he took his turn. He hid a smile when I announced that he was correct.

Ms. D and I had a conversation after the weekly spelling test that I was disappointed by. She mentioned that she helped him on the test and that she was happy she could support her ESOL students so much. I asked her to explain, and she stated that she helped T sound out words during the tests. "Ms. D," I asked, "don't we want to know what T can do on his own?" She responded with the litany of excuses mentioned earlier, mainly involving his family. "Our students don't need us to cheat for them," I eventually said firmly. Ms. D looked surprised. I asked her what she thought this "help" communicated to T, and she thought for a while. "I just want him to be successful." I explained that I wanted the same and that we needed to, again, maintain high expectations and communicate to him that his effort will make him successful. When I asked her if she thought T could pass without this help, she looked unsure. I gave her a big pep talk about his potential. She agreed to try again and not overdo the "help."

I felt terrible about this! I praised T so much for his passing test score, but it wasn't really his own work. I also thought Ms. D had understood, but changing beliefs takes time, so I continued to work.

Experiment 2: Providing Specific Feedback

A week passed, during which Ms. D met with T at lunch to work on the spelling words. She reminded T, as did I, that the harder he worked, the better he would do. T took the weekly test. We were all a little taken aback that he scored only a 50. Ms. D and I discussed it before T heard the news. We were kind of panicked, both really believing that all this studying would result in a passing score! We decided that Ms. D would review the test with T and give him feedback. Our mistake, in retrospect, was that it was too late. We should have given him an informal quiz and given immediate feedback before the class test. We planned this conversation with T carefully. Ms. D wanted to facilitate, which I was happy about. It showed me that she was starting to "get it."

T and I waited in Ms. D's office the next Monday. She burst in, holding T's test. "T!" she exclaimed, "I found something out! You were so close on all these words but didn't change the *y* to *i* before adding *s*!" T looked at Ms. D like she was crazy, and so did I. She quickly reviewed the rule with T, who was interested by her enthusiasm. They practiced a few words together and then Ms. D gave him the test again. He scored 100. Clearly, the feedback made a big difference in his performance. Ms. D mentioned that she never thought to look that carefully at a student's errors and that she never thought about telling T specifically what to correct because she didn't want to make him feel bad about his work. T scored a 70 on the next week's test!

Reflection on Case Study Student and Teacher

I can't believe what a difference it made to help Ms. D give T specific feedback on his work. It was the most powerful of the experiments. Ms. D clearly communicated that she believed in T when she took the time to look at his work and tell him how to make it perfect. T seemed surprised and pleased that he scored perfectly. My regret here is that we waited until after the assessment to give him the feedback. After this, Ms. D gave T a quiz on Wednesday, 2 days before the classroom test. They worked together to find patterns of error. When I spoke to both about this, they lit up. It was like a fun little mystery for them to solve together.

Experiment 3: Modeling "Sticking With T"

I observed Ms. D teach a small group that included T and noticed that when T did not immediately respond to an oral question, she did one of two things:

- Move on to another student: Ms. D often asked students who seemed unsure to call on another student to answer for them. T used this privilege freely and three times in one 45- minute lesson.
- Give the answer: Ms. D gave the correct answer to T and other students if they did not quickly respond.

I shared this with Ms. D in a post-observation conference and she was not surprised. She stated that she was never sure what to do when students did not give a correct answer. She said she worried about embarrassing students and felt a little embarrassed herself when she was being observed and students seemed unsure. I praised her for her reflection and she perked up even more. We briefly discussed wait time, follow-up questions, acknowledgment, restating in fuller language, asking students to elaborate, and praise. She identified allowing wait time as an area of growth. I agreed to model a lesson with a small group. She would observe and then apply what she learned in her own lesson. I would observe that lesson and we would debrief.

Reflection on Case Study Student and Teacher

Ms. D's implementation of wait time was moderately successful. It was interesting that students were uncomfortable with it. We ended up taking time from the lesson to talk with students about how important it is to stop and think. T became impatient and uncomfortable. Ms. D and I decided to continue to try to implement more time to think. We came up with a few cues to give students, like "No hands up until everyone has a chance to think" and "This will be a hard question or word, so let's all slow down a bit."

I observed T during spelling instruction the next day. He answered questions correctly when Ms. D gave him wait time, but scoffed at other students when they did not immediately answer. Ms. D noticed this and promised to talk to him. T passed the weekly spelling test with a 70. We were pleased when T said, "I passed, but I'll do even better next week."

Final Reflection

Ms. D, T, and I celebrated every test with a "Lunchable" for each of us. (Clearly, this was T's choice of lunch!) Although T has grown and understands that effort yields achievement, I am most proud of Ms. D. She has begun to understand that her expectations of students are fulfilled, so they need to be high. She has begun to understand that pity does not yield success.

This case study was challenging for me. It was difficult to coach a teacher who used her caring as a defense. She could respond to many of my questions with "I just love T. His family is such a mess." I need to hone my skills in coaching a teacher like this. However, once Ms. D and I saw T succeed, our relationship strengthened, and it became more comfortable to have these difficult conversations. Furthermore, Ms. D was able to see her own efficacy. When she worked harder with T to encourage him to work harder, they were both successful. When I expected Ms. D to show me improved academic performance and set explicit goals with her, she rose to my expectations. It makes me wonder about how many teachers have failed to succeed because no one expected anything else from them. Clear and high expectations will impact an entire school. I must clearly communicate my high expectations to students, staff, and teachers. If I do so, I am confident they will meet them. This is the most important lesson of all. After all, T scored a 100 on this week's spelling test.

Administrator Case Study 3—Seventh Grade

For my case study, I chose a student who had a unique situation. Joe is a seventh-grade scholar who entered the Academy at the beginning of the school year. Since most of the scholars at the Academy enter in the sixth grade, they are indoctrinated into a setting of high expectations before they enter the seventh grade. Due to low performance, Joe's previous school was closed over the summer and he was placed at the Academy without prior notice or preparation. Therefore, he had never experienced such an academically rigorous environment.

At his previous school, Joe was accustomed to success with mediocre work. Though he quickly became familiar with the school culture, he began to align himself with the underperforming scholars because they made him feel comfortable. There were occasions when he showed interest in class but became intimidated when other scholars understood concepts at a faster pace.

I had a discussion with Joe about his low mathematics grades. He averaged approximately 67% in the first three terms and scored at Level 2 (below proficiency) on the Citywide Mathematics Practice exam. Prior to my residence, I was the mathematics teacher at the school, so I knew all of the scholars. Since he was new to the school, I made sure that I extended my hand to him so that he would become familiar with the entire faculty.

I questioned him on his grades and his feelings about the Academy. Joe explained that he felt most comfortable in language arts but had difficulty comprehending and remembering the formulas and the rules in math. During testing, he would forget what he had been taught. Consequently, he stopped studying because, he said, "It was a waste of time." Joe also confessed that he did not participate in class because he thought that the other students knew more than he did. His lack of consistency significantly affected his grades.

The grading policy at the Academy consists of four equally weighted components: tests/quizzes, class work (including do-now assignments), projects, and homework. Joe was not meeting the standards because of incomplete assignments and failing test scores. Due to the upcoming standardized tests in mathematics, monthly assignments had been given, and the results were dismal.

After observing Joe in numerous classes, I found that he learns best with really animated teachers. He responds to teachers constantly moving while using various pictures, stories, and jokes to convey the lesson. He also becomes active with group work. Though he may not be the first to offer a suggestion, he does become an active participant. He is very articulate when he has confidence that he is correct, but he becomes withdrawn when the aim of the lesson is difficult to grasp. Lately, I have observed Joe becoming more withdrawn in mathematics class.

Journal Entry 1

Ms. F is the seventh-grade mathematics teacher. When I began writing the journal for this case study, she had begun teaching New York City Mathematics Performance Standard M6, which is mathematical skills and tools. By definition, it is using equations, formulas, and simple algebraic notation appropriately. I knew this might be an area of difficulty for Joe because it required memorizing and retaining various formulas.

I discussed Joe's performance with Ms. F, and she was also concerned by Joe's lack of success in her class. She described Joe as a child who was only interested in activities and never participated in class even when questions were directed at him. We decided to develop some methods to get Joe more involved in her class. Ms. F was already a lively, energetic teacher who was open to new ideas, so we worked together to create a new environment for Joe.

I focused on giving Ms. F the language to inspire and to motivate Joe. I instructed her to use the three following messages:

1. This is important.

2. You can do it.

3. I won't give up on you.

Along with these phrases, I introduced her to scripts from *The Skillful Teacher* (Saphier, Haley-Speca, & Gower, 2008) that showed how a teacher can respond to students who say "I can't do it" when responding to a question. We also discussed the use of wait time. At first, Ms. F was reluctant to use wait time because she said that it made the children feel like they were "on the spot." We focused on developing different methods of wait time so Joe would not feel pressured to "catch on" quickly. I directed Ms. F to devise a wait time system that would empower Joe and make both parties feel comfortable.

Journal Entry 2

Ms. F began to use various wait time techniques with the scholars and saw a significant change in many of the children. After observing how wait time affected Joe, Ms. F began using a wonderful technique she calls Helping Hands. When she asked a scholar a question, the entire class knew to put their hands down and remain quiet once someone was chosen. If the scholar she selected did not know the answer, it was his or her duty to ask for a Helping Hand. The student then had the opportunity to ask another student the same question. The scholar had to listen to the answer given, rephrase the answer, and ask for verification of whether the interpretation was correct. This minimized the pressure of seeing dozens of hands waving in the air.

Ms. F was very excited about the change in Joe's response. It was a good idea to give Ms. F some directions, but it was also good to give her the ability to test and to plan her own strategy. By this point we were very much on the same page, so Ms. F was open to continuing to use new strategies with Joe.

Journal Entry 3

I asked Ms. F to have a meeting with Joe to discuss his performance. During their discussion, she told him that she was available after school for assistance. She also explained to Joe that she would not accept "less than the best" from him. During their conversation, she also realized that Joe was lacking study skills. Since Joe had not entered the school in the sixth grade, he had missed out on the first unit of a class called Whole Life Management, which focused on successful study habits. He didn't know how to study. Ms. F gave Joe the textbook for the class and promised to explain how to use it at a later date. After the conversation, Joe seemed even more motivated.

Journal Entry 4

My next objective with Ms. F was more physical. I discussed the use of eye contact and nonverbal communication. This would let Joe know that she was there for him. In class, Ms. F would make sure he was on task by lightly tapping his desk when he was not taking notes. She would also give him a thumbs-up signal when he answered a question correctly on his paper. Another technique she would use would be to touch his shoulder to make him aware that she would be calling on him soon. I loved her rapport with Joe so much that I invited other teachers to observe their interactions and to use some of the techniques in their own classrooms.

Final Reflection

What I have noticed about all children is the fact that they want to learn. Though some may have given up on the possibility to learn certain information, they all desire to have extensive knowledge about various subjects. The problem is that school creates an environment that forces children to learn at a prescribed pace and creates a pressure-filled environment. As educators, we have the daunting task of using one prescription to cure many ailments. This is difficult, but it is not impossible.

One of the first statements made by doctors is "Tell me where it hurts." If we take this approach, we can learn some important information about our students. Once they trust that we know where the "pain" is, they may be more receptive to our cure. They can believe us when we say, "This is important. You can do it. And I won't give up on you."

Administrator Case Study 4—Ninth Grade

I worked on this case study with Mr. S, the same teacher with whom I did the mastery case study. Mr. S is in his second year of teaching, and his job is split between teaching math and technology. He and I co-taught a class last spring, and in many ways he sees me as a mentor.

For this project Mr. S selected J, a student in his second-year math class. J is a female ninth grader in a predominantly 10th-grade curriculum. At times, Mr. S has wondered if she is misplaced, but her previous performance in math—both on test scores and on report cards—indicates she is not. Her lack of belief in herself has held her back, and he thinks that she might develop more math esteem in the easier first-year curriculum. While that might be true, I worked to persuade Mr. S that J was where she should be and it was up to us to help her grow accordingly. Other teachers have also struggled with J, and in one case the teacher has essentially given up on her, resulting in J quitting the class in return. On several occasions, she's been sent to the office for "sleeping" in this teacher's class, which I interpret to be her defense mechanism against the teacher's treatment. Mr. S remains committed to helping her succeed.

My observation of J in class confirmed the traits Mr. S described in our pre-observation meeting. She spent the warm-up part of the class fixing her hair and preening in a mirror. Then, during guided work, she raised her hand incessantly. By my calculations, Mr. S spent 6 of his 20 minutes in this part of the period tending to J, which left the other 20 students minimal access to him. Her ability to rope him into helping her was masterful. Her normal move of calling his name while raising her hand was standard. Her ability to engage him from across the room, however, was impressive. In my post-observation meeting with Mr. S, I shared my view of J's behavior. He had no idea she was monopolizing his time that much, and he was clearly concerned. But he also felt that he allowed such indulgences because he wants J to know that he cares, and he doesn't want to send signals that he's given up on her. We agreed that the two aren't mutually exclusive and that there were some next steps he could take. I also gave him three chapters from Fred Jones's *Tools for Teaching* (2007) to read. They focus on weaning the hand-raisers and providing audio and visual cues to help scaffold students' learning.

First Phase

Mr. S and I discussed how he could approach the situation with J in their next class. First, I recommended that he be over-the-top positive in his interactions with her. By using the mantra "This is important. You can do it. I won't give up on you," he could help her get at her lack of math esteem. He was already living the mantra; now it was time to verbalize it to her.

Second, we discussed Jones's chapters and identified strategies from them to help wean J of her hand-raising addiction. Mr. S felt that he could do a better job of only providing J with cues to the next step of a math problem, instead of getting suckered into completing the problem for her. He was most concerned with how she would react to him refusing to help her when she had a question. We discussed at great length the best strategy for a transition. Fearing that she would shut down if it just happened all of a sudden, we added an element to his overall plan. Students were going to be working in groups on a particularly challenging word problem. In order to direct the focus on having them help each other, he was going to announce that each group would only get two consultations, one written and one spoken. Additionally, he decided to rearrange J's group so that she had more collaborative partners. In this way, she wouldn't be able to rely on Mr. S in a way that didn't isolate her.

Second Phase

In our next meeting, Mr. S reported that J had done well, though the class hadn't followed his script as he'd hoped. The do-now activity ended up taking more time than anticipated, so the group component was reconfigured to be an individual task. Students were asked to read through the problem and write down conceptually the steps they would need to take without plugging in numbers. J was one of the first to raise her hand, and Mr. S said he made a conscious effort to provide her with only the essential information. He felt that it had worked well and was encouraged.

We discussed additional steps that could be taken. In looking over the homework he was going to assign, he noted that in the sample problem he had included each step, as suggested in Jones's book. When I asked him if J would understand it all, he admitted that he didn't think so. We then talked about what additional information she would need and agreed that annotating the steps would help considerably. He also planned to continue the group work problem and would institute the "consultation" rule.

Third Phase

We met again after the next class. Mr. S was excited to report that the group work had gone well. J had followed directions and had worked especially well with her team. In one instance, she started asking Mr. S a question, and he asked the group if it was their official consultation. They quickly said no and returned to the work at hand. Also, she had gotten a 4 out of 5 on her homework.

I asked him how he was doing with the mantra. Interestingly, his answer launched us into a complex discussion about classroom management and Mr. S's relationship with his students. He feels that kids like him because he's young and fun and he makes math enjoyable. But he is also frustrated that they take advantage of his kindness. In this instance, he was disappointed that J's friends didn't take the mantra more seriously. Instead, they tried to use it as a chance to get him off topic and engage in lengthy philosophical discussions. They asked questions such as "Why is this important, Mr. S?" and "So if you won't give up on me, does that mean you won't fail me in the class?"

He took the bait and responded with long, careful answers. Ten minutes later, he found himself talking in circles with only a few kids, while the others dozed off or did other homework. I promised him that he could find the balance between making math fun and still running a tight ship, but that it was hard work and he would have to be willing to make changes, in both his curriculum development and his personal demeanor. We agreed to return to this topic early and often, and I let him borrow my copy of *Tools for Teaching*.

As far as J was concerned, we agreed that the next step was for him to discuss the situation with her directly. At this session he would need to be supportive but honest. First, he would need to convey the mantra in his own words, while providing examples from the year to remind her that she really could do it. He would then need to share with her the 6-out-of-20-minute data point and use that as an example of a broader dependence. Finally, he would identify the most recent group work as an example of her ability to not rely on Mr. S for all the answers.

Final Reflection

This was a fantastic project. At first I was concerned that it would be far too time-consuming and possibly too limited in scope to help on a broad enough scale. I was wrong on both counts. First, the time commitment was minimal. Mr. S and I had six conversations about J, one of which lasted only 5 minutes. The long ones were excellent discussions about broader pedagogical issues and I think helped Mr. S grow as a practitioner. Others were quick updates that included facts about what happened with J and idea-swapping about next steps. Second, our discussions about J were certainly about her, but her issues pertained to other students as well. Furthermore, by searching for solutions to help J, Mr. S was adding to his toolkit a host of strategies for helping all his students.

Of course, I also felt limitations. Isolating J's situation from the rest of the class was difficult to do. Getting her fully weaned from unnecessary hand-raising is a tremendous challenge, since it's a behavior she's developed through years of training. On its own, perhaps the problem could be addressed more directly. However, in a classroom where another 10 students have different issues of similar impact, Mr. S must pick and choose his battles. Additionally, since attribution retraining takes time, it's still uncertain how J will turn out.

Regardless of J, though, Mr. S benefited tremendously from this project. He is a better teacher as a result, and I am a better supervisor. I will most certainly use this strategy again. It focused my efforts with Mr. S so that he and I both were thinking in small incremental steps while still making large gains in his ability. It also kept our energies centered on what was best for J, which is a powerful way of connecting teacher development to student achievement.

Administrator Case Study 5—Tenth Grade

I have been working with Mr. T for the entire year, coaching him while he adjusted to his new school. We have worked together on numerous components of teaching, especially classroom management, attempting to grow him into the best practitioner he could be. He has been an excellent study, truly listening to my recommendations and actually attempting to implement them. I commend his efforts; Mr. T sincerely wants to improve his teaching and classroom performance. He realizes there is ample room for improvement and is eager to please. For these reasons, I would choose no other individual but Mr. T for this assignment.

Mr. T is an 11-year veteran of the district, but a first-year teacher at our school. His previous appointments have been at institutions that were extremely challenging and had very low academic expectations. Mr. T primarily teaches geometry but is also capable of instructing other areas and/or levels. He is very rich in content knowledge but requires some refinement in delivery and implementation. His work ethic is commendable, as is his sincere desire to master his craft.

For the student aspect of the assignment, we chose to work with a young lady we will refer to as KC. She is a 15-year-old 10th grader. KC could be described as a disruptive student who sometimes creates problems for staff and students. However, KC has some great attributes. Once you get to know her, you find her very personable and respectful. But to have the privilege to be exposed to this side, you first must earn KC's admiration. Once you are "in," you will see an entirely different side to her. We selected KC mainly due to the relationship I have with her and especially because of the difficulties she gives Mr. T.

In Mr. T's geometry class, KC was extremely disruptive, completed minimal work, and exhibited an "I don't care" attitude. Mr. T and I decided that we would attack these three issues independently and consecutively. We did not want to further alienate KC by "jumping down her throat" for everything. We realized that one step at a time would probably be the right move. We also felt that coming at her from different directions would help.

The first initiative was to get the behavior under control. Mr. T had tried numerous times and various strategies but to no avail. I told Mr. T to write a "pink slip" the next time she acted out and to send it with her to me. He followed my directions explicitly. Two days later, KC came to my office with the pink slip in hand. As always, she was polite and respectful, even after I began my anticipated lecture. After that formality, she and I got down to business. Where was she going to go from here? She gave no response. As planned, I informed her that Mr. T had requested that I not suspend her because he wanted to find a more productive consequence. Upon hearing that news, she perked up and was more attentive, saying, "What do you mean he doesn't want me suspended?" I restated what I had just said, but under the agreement that the three of us meet to discuss a new course of behavior. Still floored by Mr. T's request, she graciously agreed. KC and I continued to talk, as I set the stage for our conference. I shared my perspective of Mr. T, emphasizing his dedication and sincerity. I could see KC beginning to see him in a new light.

Class ended, and it was time for our conference. Mr. T and KC both had the same lunch period, so we were going to have a lunch conference. As devised, we had ordered lunch, a pizza, telling KC she could share with us. She was taken aback that we would share with her. Everything was going too well; I expected the whole thing to blow up shortly. Pleasantly, I was wrong. The KC I knew showed up in full force. Mr. T even joked, later, about whether it was the same girl. He asked what I did.

We began the conference, talking to KC about her behavior and how it disrupted not only the class's learning but also hers. We began exploring her actions, but more importantly the root causes. First, KC acknowledged her disruptive behavior. She even highlighted the causes. She went into detail about how her assigned seat had her sitting back-to-back with a young man she continually argued with. She went on, saying that she had nothing else to do but to play around. Usually, she argues with that boy, as he constantly annoys her. As usual, she gets caught and he gets away. This leads to further frustration and contempt for Mr. T as he "always corrects me and not him." Mr. T quickly interjected, explaining that unfortunately he does not see the other individual, but rather catches her reaction. After additional explanation, KC reluctantly saw our perspective.

So with some clarity on the behavior issue, we now moved on to discuss the minimal work. KC was right on target with the reasons. She said that when she falls behinds or has difficulty understanding, she just gives up. She then gets in trouble and gets removed from class, enabling her to further avoid the material. Also, due to her number of suspensions, she misses days of school. So she does the minimal because that is all she can do. She felt she would do more if she knew how. We explained to KC that she was allowing her behavior to interfere with her progress. We continued by highlighting that running away from a problem doesn't address the problem. She took some offense, like we were calling her a coward, but I did some tap dancing around it to sensitively show her what we meant. We began to discuss the importance of asking for help and seeking additional explanation when needed.

Finally, we addressed our last concern, the "I don't care" attitude. When we asked what that was about, she proclaimed it didn't matter what she did because she was being "thrown out" at the end of the year. This question was all mine. I quickly explained that students are only asked to leave if they are not living up to the expectations for choosing to come to a magnet school. I expanded that only students who are not positively contributing are asked to leave. I wanted her to understand that it had taken time to get her to this place, and it would take time to get her out. Furthermore, I pointed out that no decisions are made until the end of the year, and if there is no reason then she cannot be forced to leave. However, the ball was in her court now. She had to decide to play ball or throw in the towel. Mr. T and I both committed to help her succeed if she chose to play. KC decided she wanted to fight to stay. We said that Mr. T's geometry class was the place to start. She said okay. I felt this was the turnaround. There was hope in her eyes, and determination.

Mr. T and I concluded that we were going to talk together to set up a plan for success in the class. We just needed KC to improve the three things we had discussed. We were going to discuss strategies to help her get there. KC left in a good mood, even apologizing to Mr. T for previous actions and grief. Mr. T and I wasted no time; we began to establish our action plan.

To address the disruptive behavior, Mr. T agreed to move her seat, preferably closer to the front. He also agreed to circulate throughout the room more, keeping all students focused and on task. But we agreed that checking in on KC with words of encouragement more frequently was a must. We did not want her to sink back into her old ways. Next, Mr. T agreed to sit her next to a peer who was on the ball. Hopefully, some peer modeling would prove beneficial. More importantly, Mr. T extended an opportunity for KC to come to their common lunchtime for help. (Little did he expect what he got!) Finally, we thought routine feedback would validate her efforts and eliminate the "I don't care" attitude. Mr. T would do it daily with one positive remark about class, while I would do it periodically when our paths crossed. We had a plan, and we were off.

About 2 weeks had passed, and I decided to check in with both Mr. T and KC for an update.

I strolled over to Mr. T's room at lunchtime, only to be greeted by KC doing some of her work. Not only was she there, but also she had brought a friend who is in the same geometry class. Both were completing extra work and having the time of their lives. Privately, Mr. T explained that it was like night and day. There had been no problems, she was completing her assignments, and she came to his room every day regardless of any difficulties. I then went in to congratulate KC, but she boldly beat me to the point. She was so excited to tell me how great she was doing. She proclaimed she had not gotten into any trouble, and she received an 86 on a test. I then asked how things with Mr. T were. Was she giving him any problems? She quickly responded, "No, Mr. T and I are cool." Indeed they were! There had not been anything but positive remarks from Mr. T. Not only was she behaving, she was making sure other students were behaving. A successful story!

Final Reflection

This was an enjoyable assignment, an opportunity to help a struggling student and teacher make a situation more productive. The surprising component was the little amount of time and effort necessary to make a drastic impact. Too often, the biggest complaint from teachers is that they don't have enough time. As seen with Mr. T and KC, time often isn't the problem. It is typically the willingness and expectations of those individuals. I have to commend the efforts of both Mr. T and KC, because they were the decisive factor that ensured success. Mr. T's caring manner and desire to improve laid the foundation to build upon. KC's ability and insight to see the error of her ways was monumental. But the willingness of both to adapt and change, to make accommodations, was pivotal. It was the expectations of each individual that made a difference. Mr. T's ability to help KC raise her personal expectations is what improved their relationship and each other's situation. As KC improved, Mr. T's life became a little easier. It goes to show you what a little love and care can do. In this situation, it made the difference for a teacher and his student. Hopefully, neither individual will stop here. There are many more opportunities. Seize the moment!

Administrator Case Study 6—11th Grade

River West, my internship school, was within a hair's breadth of being assigned to the SURR list (Schools Under Registration Review) due to low performance on math and English Regents exams when I began this project. Because most of my experience is in literacy, I wanted to work with math instructors to learn about math instruction. I was particularly interested in failing students, because for them math is the greatest obstacle to a high school diploma. All the students in the January Regents math preparation classes had either failed the test before or failed a prerequisite course and were slated to take the Regents in January. A minimum of 55% is required for a high school diploma.

Visits to the remedial classes (there were a total of five) filled me with dismay. The teachers seemed to go through the motions, expecting little response from the students, many of whom were doodling, socializing, or listening to music. When I talked with the teachers about student behavior, they all gave a variation on the same theme: "It's not fair to expect these kids to pass the Regents. It's too hard. This isn't Stuyvesant. They come here with a proficiency level of 1 or 2. They can't do it." The teachers seemed even more discouraged than the students.

After several visits to Mr. D's math classes, I decided to invite him to help me with my project on expectations. He shrugged his shoulders and told me that it is too late to help the students; preparation has to start in first grade, not 11th grade. Regardless, he was willing to do anything to try to help the students. I pointed out that despite the low class participation, class attendance was actually very good. Perhaps that is a sign that they are interested, but do not want to show it. "Maybe," he said.

We decided to focus attention on CW, who sits in the back paying little attention to the instruction. Radiating attitude, she is exactly the kind of student I am most resistant to approaching, which is precisely why I thought she would be a good candidate for our project. Mr. D agreed to speak with her about her lax attention and missing work to see if some individual attention would encourage her to focus on the work.

Experiment 1: Assessing CW's Beliefs

At the end of class, Mr. D asked CW to stay for a few minutes. She said, "Make it fast because I don't have time for this." He asked her why she was taking the class and she said that she had failed the Regents twice so "they" keep making her take it. He pointed out that she had good attendance but was not doing much math. He asked her if she wanted to work to pass the Regents so she could graduate. "Me and math don't get along," was the reply. Mr. D told her that if she did the work, she and math might get along better. CW said that she did not think so. Mr. D pointed out that the Regents exam was not designed for rocket scientists, but for high school students. Perhaps if she looked at it that way, she would see that she could do it. "I don't think so," she said.

Reflection on Case Study Student and Teacher

Although CW was dismissive, she was not as contemptuous as I had feared. She used evidence to explain her attitude: Because she had twice failed, any effort would be a bad investment on her part. I asked Mr. D what he thought about assessing her present strengths and weaknesses in the curriculum. He thought it did not matter because he planned to cover everything anyway. I suggested that if CW had a clearer picture of what she already knew, she might see passing as a realistic goal. I pointed out that we had a perfect tool, the June Regents on which CW had scored 43%. She had not done too badly on the Part I multiple-choice questions, but received almost no credit on the long-answer parts, which are mostly more elaborate versions of Part I. We decided to show CW her results as a tool to help her acknowledge her strengths and focus on the skills she needed to improve.

Experiment 2: Helping CW View Success as Achievable

After our first meeting with CW, she seemed to glance at the board occasionally. We told her we wanted to show her something after class. She gave us a "this better be good" look, but stayed. We explained that we had checked on her June exam and saw that she already knew about 70% of what she needed to pass the exam in January. This got her attention.

Mr. D suggested that instead of thinking about all the things that she had gotten wrong, it would be useful to look specifically at how many more problems she needed proficiency in to pass the exam. She recited the mantra: "But you never know what they will ask on the exam!" Mr. D explained that this is only partially true; we have a fairly good idea of the types of questions asked, and we can practice them. "If you had gotten 12 more points, you would not be in this predicament now." CW expressed interest in this view.

We explained that we wanted to do an experiment and handed her a question involving Venn diagrams that she had gotten wrong on the Regents. I had asked Mr. D not to jump in and help before she had a chance to wrestle with the problem. (All the math teachers seem unwilling to let students experiment with solutions and quickly rushed to the rescue.) CW drew the problem on the board and after a couple of minutes asked whether a number inscribed in two circles counted once or twice. "Once." After a few minutes, she said, "Oh, I get it." Mr. D told her that in less than 5 minutes she had learned enough to gain two additional points and, incidentally, understood something more clearly than she had before. He told her that if she put in the effort, he was confident that she could do far better than the minimum passing grade. "Oh," she said, "I gotta go. Thanks."

Reflection on Case Study Student and Teacher

I was fascinated by how analytical CW was. She had dismissed math on the evidence, but was willing to look at it afresh. It was no longer an all-or-nothing proposition, but a movement along a continuum that she was already on. Suddenly, passing seemed like an achievable goal. Based on my original impressions, I had expected much more defeatism and negativity. Her quick understanding of the Venn diagram problem surprised me because a student capable of that intense focus should not have failed in the first place. I was eager to see what she would do with her perspective.

Mr. D and I decided that he would give Regents-style questions on his tests so that the class would feel comfortable with the format and learn how to get partial credit for problems that they could not completely solve. We also debated the merits of letting students try to work things out for themselves before showing them the "right way."

Experiment 3: Encouraging CW to Think About Her Thinking

I showed Mr. D a chart I had made about categories of questions on the math Regents and asked if we could have the class fill them out. The chart asks students to rate their confidence and comfort level with questions ranging from trigonometry to graphing to solving quadratic equations. We asked CW to stay for a few minutes and told her about the upcoming exams and questionnaire. She looked at the form and said, "I don't know all this stuff," but quickly grasped that this was a general outline of the class curriculum and that we wanted her to think about the things she is learning and what she still needs to learn. We also suggested that when she is stuck on homework or a test problem, she try to diagnose the obstacle and what she needs to learn to overcome it. As practice, Mr. D put a list of locus of points questions on the board. After some dialogue, CW cleared up a point of confusion (the locus of points could be in a circle, not just a point).

Reflection on Case Study Student and Teacher

By this stage, CW was paying more attention in class. She even volunteered to put problems on the board and generally stopped wearing headphones. She was not, however, interested in coming to tutoring and resisted most efforts to get her to stay. Her tone became "I've got this under control, so don't hassle me about it." She asked clarifying questions but was not interested in a "most favored student" status and kept her distance. Interestingly, other students started getting more serious and asked for help after school. (Mr. D. was spreading the "you can do this" message fairly liberally.)

A few weeks before the Regents, I saw CW socializing in the hallway when she was supposed to be in math. She told me not to worry because she was going to pass. I wondered out loud why she was settling for "passing" when she could do very well. She shrugged.

On the day of the Regents, I checked and, sure enough, she scored 60%, enough to graduate. I was disappointed. When I saw her, she was relieved about passing but disappointed with herself. "I could have done much better."

Final Reflection

"Low expectations" has become the trite explanation for so many failures, but in the case of CW it was accurate. I was fortunate to pair with a very conscientious teacher who worked hard, graded and returned tests promptly, and was more than patient and willing to help students and me. Further, he was open-minded. About a month before the Regents he told me that he had never thought these students could do the work, but now he believed that they could. He said that his own expectations had been raised as a result of our project. On the first of several practice Regents, the highest score had been a 37%, but by January, almost half of the class was passing the practice tests. (Although this is still disappointing, these students were all designated failures at the beginning of the term. Their passing rate far exceeded the math department's expectations.)

Mr. D was energized by the thoughts of widespread success and pointed out to the class that their scores were going up with each practice. He put model answers on the overhead projector (which he purchased himself) to demonstrate how students gain partial credit on a question even if they could not finish it. He was reaching out to other students to come to tutoring, not just waiting for them to show up. He invited students to lunchtime tutoring during the week before the exam, and many came.

I had wanted to work with CW because her demeanor had signaled "challenge." However, she was far easier to engage on a rational level that I had expected, so some of the strategies that worked with her would need modification for another student. For example, the external motivation, a graduation requirement, was quite compelling. Learning a set of skills had a big payoff. CW had recognized the value, but not her own potential. Once she saw that she could pass, she became motivated. CW was mature enough to do her own cost-benefit analysis and commit to success. Still, without Mr. D showing her a valid reason for her own commitment, she might never have invested in studying.

As a result of our investment in CW, the whole class benefited, and that is probably the intended result. Thinking about helping one student makes us see things from his or her perspective, which in turn provides a road map to issues others may have. Raising one student's expectations for herself helped to raise the teacher's expectations for the whole class and increased his subsequent disappointment that they did not all "make it." When grades were posted, many "jaded" and "uninterested" students squealed with delight and did pirouettes down the hall to let everyone know they had passed. What affected me most was that several failing students told me they had been stupid not to take advantage of all the help Mr. D had offered them. "I saw other kids in the class who did the work and they passed. I want to pass, too. I know I am going to do better this time."

Mr. D said that he was happy that we worked on this project; his increased optimism about student potential made him more interested in student understanding rather than in just "covering the curriculum." We both agreed that the next time around we would try more classroom strategies to get an even better result.

REFERENCES AND RESOURCES

Jones, F. (2007). *Tools for teaching*. Santa Cruz, CA: Fredric H. Jones.
Saphier, J., Haley-Speca, M. A., & Gower, R. (2008). *The skillful teacher* (6th ed.). Acton, MA: Research for Better Teaching.

Appendix B

Levels of Sophistication of Common Planning Time (CPT) Activities

LEVEL 0

- CPT meetings are scheduled, but teachers do not always show up or show up on time.
- There are no written agendas, established group norms, or student work on the table for examination.
- Conversation is about children, upcoming events like field trips, testing, and so on, but rarely about the specifics of how to teach something or teach it better.
- There is occasional sharing of worksheets and activity ideas.

LEVEL 1

- Teachers meet consistently one to three times a week.
- There is a written agenda, and next steps are recorded after each CPT meeting.
- There are established CPT norms, but not necessarily close facilitation to ensure they are followed.
- Student work is sometimes on the table at meetings.
- There is discussion about student difficulties and what to do about them.
- There is sharing of activities, strategies, and worksheets.

LEVEL 2

- There is a written agenda, a facilitator, and next steps identified and recorded at each meeting.
- Group norms are honored and practiced.
- The team has created common assessments for major benchmarks and agrees on implementation and scoring processes. (These could be end-of-course tests, quarterly assessments, interim assessments, and so on.)
- The CPT team establishes SMART[1] goals for their students.
- Administrators occasionally attend.

LEVEL 3

- Team members make up common quizzes or formative assessments to find out how students are doing and to identify problems and gaps in student understanding. They bring these back, analyze results, and do error analysis together.
- Team members design units together.
- Team members establish reliability on scoring common assessments, regarding what to call a 1, 2, 3, or 4.
- The team revisits and decides to re-teach key concepts, inventing new re-teaching strategies developed in detail for concepts or skills students are struggling with.
- Team members disaggregate data on an assessment they gave in common and pool data on which students did well and which didn't. Then the team regroups students across sections to re-teach.
- Discourse is focused on evidence and teachers begin to question one another's ideas and practices.
- Team members practice actually doing the re-teaching strategies with one another.
- Team members decide in common which re-teaching strategies to try and compare results at the next meeting.
- Administrators attend on occasion and participate as peers.

LEVEL 4

(Levels 4 and 5 include all the positive elements of Level 3 and add the following.)

---

[1] **Specific:** Who? What? Where? **Measurable:** How will the goal be measured? **Attainable:** Is the goal realistic yet challenging? **Results-oriented:** Is the goal consistent with other goals established, and does it fit with your immediate and long-range plans? **Time-bound:** Is it trackable, and does it allow for monitoring of progress?

- Team members dig into concepts and subconcepts of what they are teaching to get clearer on the relationships of concepts and subconcepts and on what student confusions, misconceptions, and necessary prior knowledge might be.
- The group plans lessons together in *depth and detail*, including doing the activity they are asking students to do. All materials are brought to the meeting.
- Administrators attend regularly and assist in arranging intervisitations among teachers in the CPT group.

LEVEL 5

- Team members visit each other's classrooms regularly to do focused peer observation for one another. They collect data in service of a question one of them wants answered (evidence of student learning, etc.). There is skillful debriefing of the observation and planning of next steps.
- Teaching becomes public, with teachers visiting each other's classrooms regularly and providing critical feedback and suggestions.
- Teachers work collaboratively with administrators to develop individual and collective professional learning goals and design support for achieving them.

Appendix C

Hierarchy of Interventions

The phrase *hierarchy of interventions* is the organizer DuFour, Eaker, Karhanek, and DuFour (2004) use in their must-have book *Whatever It Takes*. No others have, to our knowledge, implemented such a thorough and successful design for preventing student failure. Also called the *pyramid of interventions,* it is an escalating series of moves with low-performing or failing students that surrounds them with caring, support, and no-option structures that dramatically raise their chances for academic success. Below is a summary of the steps DuFour implemented at Adlai Stevenson High School.

1. Placement Test

A locally developed criterion-referenced eighth-grade test is used to identify proficiency that represents what graduating eighth graders are supposed to know and be able to do to be considered proficient in reading, writing, mathematics, and foreign languages. Results are used for ninth-grade placement in Honors, College Prep, and Modified Program. Students entering the Modified Program will receive accelerated, not remedial, instruction and be expected to take only college prep or honors courses from the beginning of 11th grade. The Modified Program ceases to exist as a level after 10th grade.

2. Counselor Watch

Each January high school counselors ask middle school principals to complete Counselor Watch Referral Sheets on any eighth grader with poor academic progress, personal or family problems, poor attendance, peer relationship issues, low self-esteem, or chronic underachievement. In April the high school counselors visit every middle school to review with the principal, counselor, and social worker the referral sheets that have been written for every eighth grader. The meeting clarifies concerns of the middle school staff and identifies interventions and support the student will require upon entering high school.

3. Proactive Student Registration

Each February, high school counselors travel to the middle schools to meet with each individual eighth grader. Counselors use this opportunity to foster an expectation of participation and achievement at the high school. All students are asked to identify three goals they hope to achieve during their freshman year as well as three co-curricular activities they may want to do.

4. Summer Study Skills Course

Survival Skills for High School teaches how to take notes, annotate reading, use a planner to organize time and materials, read for comprehension, set goals, and communicate effectively. The course is taught by a high-performing teacher who has talent with and interest in working with students who have a history of achieving below their potential. The course lasts four hours each day for four weeks.

See pp. 53–54 of *Whatever It Takes* (DuFour et al., 2004) for how the high school staff makes this course popular with 80% of incoming freshmen and not associated with remediation.

5. Freshman Orientation Day

One day earlier than the formal beginning of school, all freshmen get tours of the building to find out how to find their way around by going to each class with their actual teachers on an abbreviated version of their own schedule.

6. Freshman Advisory Program

For 25 minutes four days each week, all freshmen are with a faculty advisor who creates an environment where students relax, get to know one another, and have their questions answered. There are 25 freshmen in each group. Because all students assigned to an advisor have the same counselor, the counselor attends Advisory period once a week.

7. Freshman Mentor Program

Assisting each faculty advisor are five upperclass mentors who meet with their 25 freshmen during Advisory period. The mentor's job is to do whatever is necessary to help his or her 5 students be successful at the high school. Within the first week of school, all freshmen are required to pass a test on the school rulebook; mentors tutor them on the rules until each freshman is able to pass.

8. Co-curricular Activities

A co-curricular fair is scheduled (and a co-curricular handbook is developed and given to each freshman) to provide information on every program and answer any questions students or parents might have about the programs. Students who indicate interest in a program are sent a letter by the sponsor urging them to join.

When students meet with counselors during course registration in April the previous year, they also have the opportunity to register for co-curricular activities.

9. Progress Reports

All students receive a progress report at the midpoint of each 6-week grading period (that there is a six-week grading period instead of the traditional nine-week period is a change in itself). This means each student has a report on his or her learning every three weeks.

Steps 1–9 are implemented universally for all incoming eighth graders. Steps 10–15 are an escalating series of steps implemented with students as needed.

10. The Good Friend Program

The Counselor Watch process may result in a student being recommended for the Good Friend Program. Prior to the first day of school, counselors link a student with an individual teacher who pledges to take a special interest in the student.

11. Counselor Check-In Program

Students identified for this program are scheduled to meet with their counselors individually on a weekly basis for at least the first six weeks of school.

12. Early Expression of Concern—Quadruple Teaming

When students' reports show they are in danger of failing, they experience a cadre of adults expressing concern. (a) The advisor suggests the tutoring center. (b) The advisor assigns the upperclass mentor to work on homework with the student every day. (c) The counselor stops by during Advisory period, expresses concern, and asks what the student is doing. (d) The parents receive a copy of the progress report.

13. Mandatory Tutoring

If students get a D or F at the six-week mark, they are assigned to mandatory tutoring for two days a week. Teachers send materials for the students directly to the tutors with assignment sheets and upcoming due dates. Progress is monitored weekly.

14. Guided Study Program

If students fail to improve, the three people on the Student Support Team (SST) for that student (teacher, counselor, and advisor) recommend the student go to the Guided Study Program. The Guided Study Teacher has no more than 10 students during what would otherwise be a study period each day. The SST meets with student and parents to clarify goals and expectations, and to develop a contract. The Guided Study Teacher works with the students on study skills such as using an assignment notebook, creating a schedule to ensure timely completion of work, and developing test prep strategies. She or he also contacts classroom teachers and is the principle liaison between students, staff, and parents on a weekly basis.

15. The Mentor Program

This is two periods of support each day in a small group of 10 students. The first period is similar to Guided Study above. The second period is quasi-therapeutic, the guided study teacher working in close alliance with the social worker. Students with specific problems that are interfering with academic success—substance abuse, anger management, grief, and so on—are also enrolled in student support groups. The mentor and the social worker reserve one evening a month to meet with parents in support groups designed to help parents acquire skills that will make them effective partners in the effort to help their student achieve success.

REFERENCE

DuFour, R., Eaker, R., Karhanek, G., & DuFour, R. (2004). *Whatever it takes: How professional learning communities respond when kids don't learn*. Bloomington, IN: Solution Tree.

Appendix D

Goal-Setting Experiments

GRADES 3–5

I attempted to implement goal setting in the classroom so that it could touch as many students as possible. Below is the form I presented to the students. I tried to set some manageable and clear limits for them so that goal setting would be a positive experience and one they would want to try again. The goal had to be either classroom work or a specific mutually agreed-upon skill. The time frame could be more than a week.

After consulting with me, the children put their goal sheets up on a public sharing board (bulletin board).

There was some resistance initially. When children realized that goal setting was solely up to them and that they owned the goal, the response was very positive. Students focused on a wide variety of work and skills, and about 90% accomplished their goals. Goal setting is now a part of the classroom.

I learned that (a) children often focus on work about which they are insecure or lacking in skills; (b) goal setting gives both student and teacher an opportunity to relate in a positive, supportive context; and (c) goal setting can be motivating proof that students have power and control where they once felt they had none.

Goal Setting

I want to work on _____ (work or skill).

I will accomplish this by _____ (one week or less, day and date).

I realize that this is something I really want to work on and that it is my own decision.

_____

Student's signature

How it went. Did I accomplish my goal?

Student: _____

Teacher: _____

GRADES 3–5

I try always to be very specific with students about long- and short-term goals for them. They always know, for example, what is going to happen in any given class period and why I think it's important. At the beginning of each new unit, and at several points along the way, I speak about the long-term benefits I hope they will realize. During the writing unit, I did a great deal of work with individual students on setting goals for their writing. I had not, however, asked students to set goals for themselves (without my input), and I thought it might be useful for them and instructive for me to see what goals they might choose.

I began with an inventory of writing skills—both technical and stylistic—which I asked students to think about. Most were able to check a number of areas in which they felt they had achieved mastery. The second step was to look at the items they had not checked and think about which ones they might be able to make progress on in the weeks remaining. I asked them to list four or five of these and to devise a strategy they could use to achieve progress.

Students seemed to have a very clear idea of their own strengths and weaknesses as writers. In almost every case, I was impressed with how forthright students were in assessing their needs and how reasonable their plans for addressing them were. Here are some examples:

Goal: to be less shy in class about reading my work

Strategy: try to get more confidence in myself and volunteer to read before my mind changes

Goal: I need to work on cutting parts that don't relate to what my piece is about. When I write something, I'm not too crazy about taking it out when someone says I don't need it.

Strategy: I have to learn to accept advice without taking it personally. Criticism isn't easy to take, but it is helpful.

Goal: I need to work harder in class every day.

Strategy: I usually need to write in a totally silent place, like a library or my room. I'll try harder to concentrate in class or find a quiet corner to work in.

We discussed our ideas in class, and then students put their inventories and goal-setting sheets in their folders. It's been very helpful since then to have these documents handy for checking in on how things are going.

This strategy will become a permanent part of my writing unit. I think it helped reinforce the implicit (and explicit) goal of the process approach to writing that students take responsibility for their own growth as writers. I also can see applications of these ideas in any number of other situations in an English class. Next year, for example, I think I will have students complete such a survey before they begin working in their reading logs.

GRADES 3–5

I'm interested in working goal setting into my daily interactions with kids.

Initially, I thought I should set up some system or other that worked on a regular basis with all the students. Perhaps I still "should," but what is happening at present is that I am trying goal setting with individuals, as it pops to mind as a possible method of coping.

For example, with a child who is loud, scattered, and tends to be up and away creating turmoil as he tries to establish friendships, I said (in place of my usual exasperated remarks), "Let's see what you've done so far. OK. What would you like to have finished by meeting time in 20 minutes?" To my considerable surprise he knew just how much he wanted to get done and explained his plan and his reasons for it. For the next 20 minutes he concentrated well (for him), showing me occasionally how far he was getting, and most important getting help when he needed it. He did indeed accomplish his goal by meeting time.

What's striking to me is that as I try this with individual kids, I feel as though I'm accomplishing something for once . . . because in fact *they* are.

With another child who is very productive, capable, cheery, and disorganized, I said (instead of feeling simply that I'm not providing adequately for him), "That's a great idea. Now what do you need to finish up before you start on this, and how about deciding to get it all finished by the end of this week?" He was enthusiastic, and I felt much more focused on him, rather than trailing in his wake.

GRADES 3–5

The principle of learning I chose to introduce to my classes over the last couple of weeks was goal setting. It tied in well with the beginning of the New Year.

A discussion of why people make New Year's resolutions led to our program of goal setting. Through a brainstorming activity we listed sensible, realistic goals each of them could work toward weekly.

After the class discussion, each student was handed a form—a bell or a snowman. They recorded the date and their goal for the week. A bulletin board was created using these forms.

In the beginning of each class, I asked each student to repeat his or her chosen goal. On Wednesday, I gave the children a few minutes to discuss their goal with another student. On the last day of the week we congratulated each other on reaching our goal or offered encouragement for the following week.

A pleasant surprise happened in my class. Setting their own goals appeared to make students more responsible in following through with assignments, and the quality of their work greatly improved.

Also, the children experienced a sense of satisfaction, and I reinforced the fact that they were responsible for this wonderful feeling of accomplishment. The second week the children wrote a new goal. Their enthusiasm was refreshing. At this time, we set up a buddy system. Each child chose a friend to help him or her accomplish their goal.

This simple activity was very worthwhile.

GRADES 9–12

The chapter "Principles of Learning" in *The Skillful Teacher* (Saphier, Haley-Speca, & Gower, 2008) is relevant to everything we do. Interestingly, as I was thinking of an experiment, one of my calculus students came to me concerned that she did not understand summation notation. While she could have gotten by without understanding it, she knew she would benefit from a better grasp. Thus, the perfect opportunity was presented to use goal setting.

Debbie and I talked for quite a while, and she decided to set a goal of understanding the material. I assigned her some reading and spent some time going through the process with her. In my work with her, she began to understand the material better when I started from the end and worked backward (thereby creating a more appropriate sequence of learning). After spending 3 days practicing her new skill, Debbie took a quiz on sigma notation and did very well. In the time since, the concept has come up on a test and in class. In both instances, Debbie has demonstrated a firm understanding of the concept; in fact, in class she readily volunteers to explain problems involving this concept.

Obviously, Debbie benefited from this goal-setting experience. She set the goal (understanding sigma notation) and sought to accomplish it in a short period of time (3 days). She was held responsible for it through the quiz and has had it reinforced regularly.

Since this time, I have sat down with a number of students who have had similar difficulties with other concepts. In most cases, I have tried to set up a similar experiment. Not surprisingly, I have found that most students fare better when they isolate their problems, set goals around them, and are held accountable. I suspect that the added one-to-one contact with the teacher is also helpful. The kids know the teacher cares.

REFERENCE

Saphier, J., Haley-Speca, M. A., & Gower, R. (2008). *The skillful teacher* (6th ed.). Acton, MA: Research for Better Teaching.

Appendix E

Kristin Allison's Log

I have divided Kristin's log into sections. Section 1 is about explicitly presenting the growth mindset to students and parents, and getting the students to make growth mindset attributions in everyday class life. Section 2 is about her application of the verbal behaviors so that they convey embedded messages of belief and confidence to students. Section 3 is about explicitly teaching students learning strategies. Section 4 is about teaching students to use growth mindset language. Section 5 is about teaching students what effective effort is.

SECTION 1: PRESENTING THE GROWTH MINDSET

Explicitly Teach the Growth Mindset and Brain Malleability to Students

9/14/15 and ongoing throughout school year: Whole-body listening

This is one of the first lessons in the Social Thinking Program by Michelle Garcia Winner that we do in junior kindergarten and kindergarten (JK/K). It establishes the expectations for listening to others in our community. We use the book *Whole Body Listening Larry at School!* (Wilson & Sautter, 2011) and other visual aids to remind children to listen with their eyes, ears, brain, heart, body, feet, hands, and mouth. This is a great launch for the growth mindset and learning from others.

11/4/15 Establishing a growth mindset: Parent and family workshop

I am a member of the Morse Math Advisory Group. At the beginning of the school year, we noted that many of the staff were using the language of growth mindset, but often parents were questioning this term, what it meant, and how to use this belief. As a result of this concern, we collaborated with the Literacy Team to plan and facilitate an Introduction to Growth Mindset Workshop for families in our school.

> The rationale and presentation of the Introduction to Growth Mindset Workshop are found in the links below.
>
> http://morse.cpsd.us/cms/One.aspx?portalId=3044391&pageId=11794794
>
> http://morse.cpsd.us/UserFiles/Servers/Server_3044307/File/news/Growth_Mindset_Workshop%20.pdf

11/5/15 *The Little Engine That Could*

This book was read aloud to the JK/K class. It is a classic story of perseverance and working hard to accomplish a task. The catchphrase "I think I can. I think I can." was contagious among the children. Soon after we discussed the book, children were heard saying this mantra on the playground, during center activities, and when getting outdoor clothing on in the winter months.

11/9, 11/20, 3/15 and throughout school year: Morning meeting

Each morning we have the Person of the Day do specific jobs (calendar, weather, tell about the daily schedule, poem, etc.). A highlight for children is asking the Question of the Day. This ritual allows the Person of the Day to generate a question for his or her classmates and teachers to answer. It helps us all practice whole-body listening, gives everyone the opportunity to speak, and we can learn from others. The ritual includes "passing the eagle." The eagle is our school mascot, and we have a small stuffed eagle that is passed around our circle. The eagle is used as a visual reminder that the person with the eagle has a turn to speak and others should be thinking about what he or she is saying.

Here is a sample of questions asked by students: How are you feeling? What did you do over the weekend? What is your favorite song, color, food, animal, season, sport, book, and so on? What do you like to do at school? Have you ever been on an airplane? Do you like to go bowling?

11/9/15: After a recent talk about trying and learning new things, K asked, "What are you trying to get better at?" The answers were an amazing reflection of what is important to the children and how we all are learning new things.

11/20/15: A asked a question that led L to ask, "What do you want to be when you grow up?" The feeling in the class had shifted to a can-do attitude and goal-setting environment. I was pleased at how well children were listening to and commenting on others' answers.

3/15/16: E asked, "What is your favorite part of your body?" The paraprofessional and I exchanged glances of wonder at where this is going to lead. Each child's answer was appropriate, with statements such as "My brain because it helps me to have a growth mindset," "My heart because it shows that I care what others are saying," "My eyes so I can learn from others," and so on.

1/25/16: As a JK/K cluster, teachers decided to explicitly teach the growth mindset in the whole-class setting. Since I was the only one that had taken Research for Better Teaching's course Studying Skillful Teaching, I had resources to share with the four other teachers. Some questions surfaced from this idea: Will we observe children using a growth mindset during play? What are the challenges and success stories to supporting children's growth mindset during play?

2/8/16: I composed an email blast to families telling them we had been focusing on a growth mindset in our classroom and included links to the parent workshop and "Power of Yet" video.

2/10/16–2/12/16: Several parents commented at dropoff about how their family discussions had started to include phrases like "The Power of Yet" and having a "growth mindset or a fixed mindset." Many families found the resources helpful when encouraging their children to try new things or set goals.

2/25/16: Trying a new snack

B was a picky eater and would often not even attempt to try new food items during snack or lunch. On this day, he was refusing to try grapes. He told me, "I don't like grapes." I asked him when had he tried grapes and if it had been a while since he last tried them. He told me, "They were green and I did not like them." I explained to B that these were purple/red grapes and some people think they have a different taste than green grapes. He said, "Okay, I will have a growth mindset and try something new!" B ate all the grapes with a smile on his face and when asked if he was glad he tried something new, he said, "Yes!" The next day, his mother was so excited to share that he had told her all about the grapes at home the night before. She thought "Power of Yet" video helped change his thinking about trying new foods and hoped he would continue to try new things at school and home.

2/29/16: Blocks

Two children were playing in the block area. The blocks were all over the rug, and there was a small structure in the middle. When I asked them to tell me about their structure, one replied, "We are not ready yet. Come back in a few minutes." When I returned to the pair, I noticed how some of the blocks had been put on the shelf in the correct manner. I again asked them to tell me about their structure, which had grown larger. The children explained that they had needed to clean up the extra blocks so I could see their castle. They told me, "We used a growth mindset to make it look better."

3/29/16: *Making a Splash: A Growth Mindset Children's Book*

I had noticed children talking about swimming lessons in our class. I chose to read this book so students could connect having a growth mindset with activities in and out of school. Children really focused on the characters in the book and whether they were using a growth or fixed mindset. Students were able to comment on how you can "stretch your brain" when you challenge yourself to learn something that is not easy to learn. After the reading, we all were able to express something we were going to try to accomplish during the spring. This book was a great reminder about goal setting and challenging oneself.

SECTION 2: VERBAL BEHAVIORS THAT CONVEY EMBEDDED MESSAGES OF BELIEF AND CONFIDENCE (REFERS TO CHAPTERS 3 AND 4 OF THIS BOOK)

Communicating High Expectations in Your Teaching

Responding to Students' Answers (Oral)

10/22/15 and ongoing throughout the school year: Wait time

As a personal goal, I wanted to really work on giving kids more time to answer questions. I knew I needed to slow down to stick with the student if he or she was taking time to recall an answer. This is often hard in the beginning of the school year, when many JK/K students are calling out or interrupting their peers. The act of turn-taking and learning social graces develops at various rates among 4- and 5-year-olds. Part of our Social Thinking curriculum includes lessons about being a "thinking about you kid" or a "just me kid." After a few of these lessons, we talked about how interrupting friends or calling out when someone is thinking are "just me kid" behaviors. The number of interruptions decreased after these discussions. We all continue to work on being a "thinking about you kid" and letting friends have time to think and speak. I have noticed children are more considerate of their peers, and this allows me time to stick with a student.

Responding to Students' Performance

10/15/15: Science Observation—J

During our first Tree Study observation outside, students were asked to describe a fall tree near our playground. For most students it was easy to give explanations about a fall tree, but when asked to sketch the particular tree, one child became very hesitant. He said, "I can't draw that tree. It is too big. I am not good at drawing trees." This was met with a lot of encouragement from the teacher ("You told me about the tree and I believe you can use your words to draw the tree") and some more coaching ("We are all learning to draw; please just try your best"). This climate of risk taking turned into a success! As we packed up our supplies to return to school, J's final remark was, "I surprised myself!" and the smile on his face was just as telling.

3/28/16: Tangrams—C: feedback with encouragement

After reading the book *Grandfather Tang's Story* (Tompert & Parker, 1990), students were working at a math station to complete tangram puzzles. Christian remarked, "The puzzles with the lines are easy for me so I am going to challenge myself and use the puzzles with no lines." After watching C struggle to complete some puzzles, I asked, "How do you feel about the challenge you gave yourself?" He told me he would like to keep working on the tangram puzzles without the lines during the next math workshop. I was able to celebrate his growth mindset, tell him that he was stretching his brain by using the puzzles without the lines, and note that if he kept trying he would complete all the puzzles soon.

Changing Attitudes Toward Errors

9/29/15: *Beautiful Oops*

This book was a big hit and continues to be a resource for many children in our class! The story shows how everyone makes mistakes or has an accident, and you can turn these circumstances into an opportunity. Instead of starting over or feeling frustrated with an oops, we can change it into something else. The message of creativity and discovery coupled with changing emotions (from disappointment to joy) was a great way to help young storytellers, writers, and artists.

9/30/15: Coloring/drawing during Choice Time

Child A was upset when her picture did not look the way she wanted it to and began to crumple her paper up. Child B said, "Hey, you can turn it into a beautiful oops!" Child A was seen using the backside of the paper to practice drawing her rabbit.

10/1/15: Writers workshop (storytelling, drawing, and writing)

A child was working on her story drawing and didn't like the way her person was positioned on her paper. Her partner said, "You can just turn it into something else and put your person in a different spot." The child turned the "mistake" person into a flower and continued drawing her picture.

SECTION 3: EXPLICITLY TEACHING STUDENTS LEARNING STRATEGIES

Frame Strategies in the Context of Effective Effort to Accomplish Tasks/Connect How Students Use Tools and Show Effort

Name _____

Apples

Arpitha had 5 apples on the table. She ate 2 apples. How many apples are on the table now?

Whole	
Part	Part

Write an equation.

Show your work

Solution

There are _____ apples.

9/14/15 and ongoing throughout school year: Whole-body listening

3/14/16 and ongoing throughout school year: Whole, part, part—Visual aid

Students use this graphic organizer when solving math problems. The model helps children organize their thinking when completing the problems. Moving through the concrete-pictorial-abstract, this method lays the foundation for young mathematicians to persevere in solving mathematical problems. The Whole, Part, Part aid is a precursor to the MESS (model, equation, solution, sentence) graphic organizer used by our school in Grades 1–5. Beginning with teacher support and following a gradual release of responsibility, children are able to evaluate their work and effort with this tool to complete problem-solving activities.

SECTION 4: USE AND TEACH STUDENTS TO USE GROWTH MINDSET LANGUAGE AND AVOID FIXED MINDSET LANGUAGE

2/1/16: Establishing a growth mindset with "The Power of Yet" video

Students were engaged with the catchy song but did not seem to grasp the meaning of the word *yet*. Despite some clarification and discussion of the fact that we all are trying to get better at something, some students' egos were not ready to comprehend the message.

2/2/16: Re-teaching the word *yet*

We had more class discussion on how you might not know how to do something or do it well, but you can if you have the right mindset. There was also more discussion on the word *yet*, and we watched the video for the second time.

2/5/16: Fourth- and fifth-grade Variety Show

After we attended the show, we discussed all of the students' talents and how they must have worked hard to be able to perform their talents. JK/K students connected with the growth mindset of needing to practice before you are ready to show others and with the fact that you can also improve your talent/act.

2/22/16

After a lesson on George Washington, there was much classroom discussion on presidents of the past, present, and future. A child remarked, "There is no girl president." I replied, "Yes, E, there hasn't been a woman president yet." Another student stated, "Hey, Ms. Allison, that shows you have a growth mindset!"

SECTION 5: EXPLICITLY TEACH STUDENTS WHAT IT MEANS TO PUT FORTH EFFECTIVE EFFORT

9/21/15: *Three Little Pigs and the Big Bad Wolf* (Rounds, 1992)

During this story, students were introduced to the vocabulary word *slapdash*. This term is not often familiar to children but is used several times in the book. We discussed how the pigs who built their homes of sticks and straw did not spend a lot of time building their homes, and their careless, messy work created a problem for them. We then looked at how the pig who built his home with bricks took his time and made a sturdy and purposeful home.

The term *slapdash* continues to be a part of our classroom repertoire. Children know that when they notice slapdash in their printing, math, drawing, coloring, and other products, they are not putting forth their best effort. Often children are heard to say:

Student:　I took my time, so it is not slapdash.

Student:　My letter A looks just like the book. I slowed down so I didn't do slapdash.

Student:　Do you think this is slapdash?

Teacher:　What do you think?

Student:　I tried my best.

Teacher:　Then it is not slapdash.

10/26/15: *The Tortoise and the Hare*

Using this fable, students were explicitly taught perseverance. Students were asked, "How did the tortoise show a growth mindset?" Classroom discussion included the statements: "He did not give up. He tried his best. Slow and steady won the race. He worked hard."

Teaching Attribution Theory to Students

3/8/16: *The Fantastic Elastic Brain*

I read this book aloud to the JK/K students in my class. We talked about how everyone is born smart and you need to exercise your brain just as you exercise your muscles. This book helped students learn that you can stretch and shape your brain in positive ways. Through practice and perseverance, we can grow our brains. Children then went to Choice Time, and afterward we reflected on ways we stretched our brains. Comments included the following:

- We had to keep moving the blocks to make our structure stronger to stay up.
- I had to stretch my brain to use the Lincoln Logs to make a house and get the pieces to fit in the right spot.
- We made a booklet and used the names of our friends. We had to write the names with one uppercase letter and then the rest lowercase letters.

3/14/16: *The Fantastic Elastic Brain*

We revisited this story from the previous week, and I used a technique learned from a colleague in our Studying Skillful Teaching class. I showed the children a ball of rubber bands and let a few students demonstrate how rubber bands can be stretched. I then showed them a rock. We discussed how the rock cannot be stretched, and it is hard. We talked about how the ball of elastic bands was like a growth mindset and how the rock was like a fixed mindset.

Providing Opportunities for Students to Self-Assess Their Products and Performances

3/9/16 and ongoing throughout school year:
Writers workshop graphic organizer

We used this poster to help our young writers add to their writing booklets. Students were taught to make their characters feel, talk, move, and think. The visual aid was helpful when students shared their work with the class and assessed their own stories before moving to their next booklet. Children were asked, "Do the words and pictures in your stories show the characters moving, feeling, thinking, and speaking?"

Highlighting and Teaching Examples of the Growth Mindset

2/24/16: *Whistle for Willie*

When introducing the title of the book, I asked students to listen and look to see if Willie was a character that had a growth mindset or a fixed mindset. After this read-aloud, a student commented on how he thought

Willie had a growth mindset. When asked to explain his thinking, he made the connection that Willie did not give up on trying to learn to whistle. He said, "It was not working at first but he kept on trying and then it worked!"

SUMMARY

During the months of September–November, teachers are charged with establishing the rules and routines of school. I feel in JK/K we talk a lot at children, and everything is new and needs explaining in order to establish the classroom and school culture. It can be a time of exhaustion and saturation for both adults and children.

I noticed this year it was hard to talk about the growth mindset in the beginning of the school year along with Social Thinking lessons and our Morse Code/PBIS (Postive Behavior Intervention and Supports) system. In January, there was more consistency in the school calendar (fewer holidays, early release days, etc.) and the school expectations had been taught, practiced, and learned. This allowed more time to focus directly on teaching a growth mindset. The wonderful part was that it wove so nicely and easily into the other components of our classroom and school environment.

It is rewarding to hear children talk about challenging themselves in math, jumping rope, using lowercase letters, and so on. I have noticed when doing a read-aloud book that many students often make the connection that a character is displaying a growth mindset or a fixed mindset. Children like to explain to classmates how a character could change his or her thinking. The anecdotes described earlier allowed us to celebrate when students were seen using a growth mindset and provided the feedback to show we were on the right path for developing a growth mindset.

I also feel proud when parents or caregivers tell me their children are talking about having a growth mindset at home. I have worked hard to incorporate families into the growth mindset education, and it makes me happy to see the effort has worked. A parent recently said, "I gave my child a pair of roller skates and he told me he will need a growth mindset to learn how to use them!"

FINAL REFLECTION

At the beginning of the school year, I did not see students taking many risks, and a lot of students were hesitant to try new things. I have noticed that students are now more likely to try new things and not worry if they have setbacks. The concept of challenging oneself has become part of our class culture.

Recently, a child mentioned that he felt the growth mindset should become part of our Morse Code/PBIS system. I thought, "Aha! Perfect and initiated by a student." As a class we discussed how this would fit well with our Active Learner category on the grid. We planned to write a letter to the principal expressing the thought and reasons for the idea.

I continue to be aware of giving students wait time and providing feedback that is effort based. I believe these arenas have contributed to more students participating in class discussions, answering questions, and understanding that we need to exercise our brains just like our bodies.

Our JK/K team's goal, to support children's growth mindset during play, was empowering to teachers because it was our decision and not a mandate. As a group we felt that it fit in with what other staff were working on in the building, was supported by research, and complimented our Social Thinking Program and schoolwide PBIS initiative. Teachers believed it was not "one more thing to do" but something that could be worked into the natural elements of the school day.

I have enjoyed getting ideas about books and resources from my colleagues. It was nice to hear how a book worked to teach about the growth mindset or how some parts of the book needed to be skipped, reworked in child-friendly language, or were fine on their own to read. We have been able to share observations and conversations between children that used growth mindset language or behaviors.

When one teacher suggested we email special subject teachers about our initiative, I took on this task. The email included rationale (school initiative), our school-based goal (to teach and observe the growth mindset), and resources (books and "Power of Yet" video) we were using in our classrooms. The response from special subject teachers was that they were grateful for including them in our plan and how they were starting to support a growth mindset in their JK/K sessions. If you want to achieve a goal schoolwide, it's best to be inclusive and have good communication skills.

For an upcoming school assembly, each grade level has been asked to demonstrate how they have been learning about a growth mindset. The children will sing "The Power of Yet" song, and we will have a visual aid on the big screen showing all the books JK/K students read.

We have found that in developing students' growth mindsets, our resources work well with fostering a climate of respect and active learning. While we might not see strong examples in all students, we are confident that we have laid a solid foundation for children to establish a growth mindset that will carry them through their school career and life. We look forward to hearing success stories from our colleagues as the current JK/K students grow through their school years.

I plan to continue growth mindset instruction, and I am expecting, as is often the case with JK/K children, to see even more development in all areas of school during the spring. I know I will be able to send my students to their receiving teachers with a growth mindset and to have more social and academic confidence during their kindergarten or first grade school year.

The paraprofessional and I have discussed collecting evidence of children using a growth mindset and putting these notes, pictures, work, and other items on a bulletin board in our classroom. This would *make the learning visible* to all who enter our classroom. We think parents and other staff will have an appreciation for student work and play that is showcased in a different manner than through paper-and-pencil tasks.

As JK/K staff, we already decided to use our growth mindset Books Banner (used in the school assembly) for a September bulletin board. "Welcome back to school! Did you bring a growth mindset?" I would like to organize some growth mindset lessons in a logical manner for the next school year. I never know if I will have more junior kindergarten or kindergarten students or the exact demographics until September, but these lessons might help me introduce the learning earlier in the school year and fine-tune the pace of establishing a growth mindset. Thankfully, my JK/K colleagues are interested in fine-tuning our approach to a growth mindset, and I look forward to collaborating more with them.

REFERENCES AND RESOURCES

Rounds, G. (1992). *Three little pigs and the big bad wolf.* New York, NY: Holiday House.

Tompert, A., & Parker, R. A. (1990). *Grandfather Tang's story.* New York, NY: Crown.

Wilson, K., & Sautter, E. (2011). *Whole body listening Larry at school.* San Jose, CA: Social Thinking.

Appendix F

Effort Books

A Bibliography

This bibliography was originally compiled 10 years ago by Jackie Richardson, Library Media Specialist, Croton-Harmon School District. It has since been updated with contributions by various RBT con sultants and participants in our courses. We encourage readers to share with us additional contributions they recommend.

Title, author; illustrator
Publishing information
Description

K–3

Albie's First Word by Jacqueline Tourville; illustrated by Wynne Evans

New York, NY: Schwartz & Wade, 2014

This historical fiction picture book is about the early childhood of Albert Einstein, the world's most famous physicist. Three-year-old Albie has never said a single word. When his worried mother and father consult a doctor, he advises them to expose little Albie to new things: a trip to the orchestra, an astronomy lecture, a toy boat race in the park. Although Albie dances with excitement at each new experience, he remains silent. Finally, the thoughtful, quiet child witnesses something so incredible, he utters his very first word: "Why?"

Arthur's Christmas by Marc Brown

Boston, MA: Little, Brown, 1984

Arthur puts a lot of time, effort, and thought into his special present for Santa Claus.

Ballerina Rosie by Sarah Ferguson, Duchess of York; illustrated by Diane Goode

New York, NY: Simon & Schuster, 2012

Rosie wears her tutu everywhere and loves to listen to ballet stories. After enrolling in ballet class, she discovers that it is harder than she expected, making her look like a "wilted flower" instead of a prima ballerina. She almost gives up before her teacher shares with her a pair of red ballet shoes that bring her success. At first she attributes her dancing to the shoes, but her teacher points out that it came from her confidence within—and it was there all along.

A Barnyard Collection: Click, Clack, Moo and More by Doreen Cronin

New York, NY: Atheneum Books, 2000

Farmer Brown has a problem. His cows like to type. But Farmer Brown's problems *really* begin when his cows start leaving him notes.

Beautiful Oops by Barney Saltzberg

New York, NY: Workman, 2010

This interactive book shows children how every mistake is an opportunity to make something beautiful. Filled with pop-ups, flaps, holes, tears, and more, it encourages children to be creative without the fear of messing things up.

The Beetle Bush by Beverly Keller; illustrated by Marc Simont

New York, NY: Coward, McCann & Geoghegan, 1976

A little girl is convinced she is a failure at everything she tries until she begins a garden.

The Best Mistake Ever by Richard Scarry

New York, NY: Random House Books for Young Readers, 1984

Huckle Cat is sent to the grocery store but forgets the shopping list his mother gave him. His friend tries to help him, but they misremember the list and buy similar-sounding sweets instead.

The Boy Who Held Back the Sea adapted by Lenny Hort from Mary Mapes Dodge's *Hans Brinker, or the Silver Skates*; illustrated by Thomas Locker

New York, NY: Dial Books, 1987

By blocking a leaking hole in the dike, a young boy saves his town from destruction.

The Brain: All About Our Nervous System and More! by Seymour Simon

New York, NY: HarperCollins, 1997

Brave Irene by William Steig

New York, NY: Farrar, Straus & Giroux, 1986

Plucky Irene, a dressmaker's daughter, braves a fierce snowstorm to deliver a new gown to the duchess in time for the ball.

The Carrot Seed by Ruth Krauss; illustrated by Crockett Johnson

New York, NY: HarperCollins, 1973

Despite everyone's dire predictions, a little boy has faith in the carrot seed he plants.

Crow Boy by Taro Yashima

New York, NY: Viking Press, 1955

This is the story of a strange, shy little boy in a Japanese village school who was ignored by his classmates until suddenly, and almost too late, a new teacher showed them that Crow Boy had much to offer.

The Day That Henry Cleaned His Room by Sarah Wilson

New York, NY: Simon and Schuster Books for Young Readers, 1990

When Henry cleans his room, he attracts the attention of reporters, scientists, the army, and something long and green and scaly that lives under Henry's bed.

Do Not Open by Brinton Turkle

New York, NY: Dutton, 1981

Following a storm, Miss Moody and her cat find an intriguing bottle washed up on the beach. Should they ignore its "Do not open" warning?

The Dot by Peter Reynolds

Cambridge, MA: Candlewick Press, 2003

Vashti believes that she cannot draw, but her art teacher's encouragement leads her to change her mind.

The Enormous Carrot by Vladimir Vasilevich Vagin

New York, NY: Scholastic, 1998

A group learns the value of teamwork as one animal after another joins in the effort to pull a giant carrot out of the ground. Based on a Russian folktale.

Eyes of the Dragon by Margaret Leaf; illustrated by Ed Young

New York, NY: Lothrop, Lee & Shepard Books, 1987

An artist agrees to paint a dragon on the wall of a Chinese village, but the magistrate's insistence that he paint eyes on the dragon has amazing results.

The Garden of Happiness by Erika Tamar; illustrated by Barbara Lambase

San Diego, CA: Harcourt Brace, 1996

Marisol and her neighbors turn a vacant New York City lot into a lush community garden.

Giraffes Can't Dance by Giles Andreae. 2012

This book is a touching tale of Gerald the giraffe, who wants nothing more than to dance. With crooked knees and thin legs, it's harder for a giraffe than you would think. Gerald is finally able to dance to his own tune when he gets some encouraging words from an unlikely friend.

The Great Big Enormous Turnip by Alexei Tolstoy; illustrated by Helen Oxenbury

New York, NY: F. Watts, 1968

An old man plants a little turnip that grows and grows until it's so big that it takes everyone, including the mouse, to pull it.

Gumption! by Elise Broach

New York, NY: Atheneum Books for Young Readers, 2010

Peter goes on an expedition with his uncle Nigel in search of a rare African gorilla, but making it through the jungle involves lots of challenges. Nigel leads the way, surmounting each obstacle, from a dense thicket to a deep river, with cheerful encouragement ("All it takes is a bit of gumption").

Henry's Awful Mistake by Robert Quackenbush

New York, NY: Robert Quackenbush Studios, 2005

This story is about a disaster-prone duck named Henry who tries to rid his house of a pesky ant before his guest comes to supper.

The Hill and The Rock by David McKee

London, UK: Andersen Press, 2011

Mr. and Mrs. Quest lived in a little house on the top of a hill. The views were wonderful; they would have been perfect, had it not been for the rock. It would not budge.

How My Parents Learned to Eat by Ina R. Friedman; illustrated by Allen Say

Boston, MA: Houghton Mifflin, 1984

An American sailor courts a Japanese girl and each tries, in secret, to learn the other's way of eating.

Iggy Peck, Architect by Andrea Beaty

Harry Abrams, 2007

Iggy has one passion: building. His parents are proud of his fabulous creations, though they're sometimes surprised by his materials—who could forget the tower he built of dirty diapers? When his second-grade teacher declares her dislike of architecture, Iggy faces a challenge. He loves building too much to give it up!

Katy and the Big Snow by Virginia Lee Burton

Boston, MA: Houghton Mifflin, 1971

Katy is a crawler tractor who saves the city when it is snowed in by a blizzard.

Koala Lou by Mem Fox

Melbourne, Australia: Ian Drakeford, 1988

When Koala Lou's mother becomes so busy that she forgets to tell her firstborn how much she loves her, Koala Lou enters the Bush Olympics, intending to win an event and her mother's love all at one time.

Leo the Late Bloomer by Jose Aruego

New York, NY: Windmill, 1971

Leo, a young tiger, finally blooms under the anxious eyes of his parents.

The Little Engine That Could by Watty Piper; illustrated by George and Doris Hauman

New York, NY: Platt & Munk, 1990

A little blue engine comes to the rescue of a train that is loaded with toys, dolls, and good things to eat but cannot get over the mountains to deliver the cargo to waiting children.

Little Horse on His Own by Betsy Byars; illustrated by David McPhail

New York, NY: Henry Holt, 2004

Little Horse confronts lightning, fire, and dangerous animals in his effort to return home to his mother and the valley of the little horses.

The Little Red Hen Makes a Pizza retold by Philemon Sturges; illustrated by Amy Walrod

New York, NY: Dutton, 1999

In this version of the traditional tale, the duck, the dog, and the cat refuse to help the Little Red Hen make a pizza but do get to participate when the time comes to eat it.

Maggie and the Monster by Elizabeth Winthrop; illustrated by Tomie dePaola

New York, NY: Holiday House, 1987

Maggie wants to get rid of the monster that visits her room every night and accepts her mother's suggestion to simply ask the monster what it wants.

Mike Mulligan and His Steam Shovel by Virginia Lee Burton

Boston, MA: Houghton Mifflin, 1939

When Mike Mulligan and his steam shovel, Mary Ann, lose their jobs to the gasoline, electric, and diesel motor shovels, they go to a little country town where they find that one new job leads to another.

The Most Magnificent Thing by Ashley Spires

Tonawanda, NY: Kids Can Press, 2014

A little girl decides to make the most magnificent thing. She knows just how it will look. She knows just how it will work. All she has to do is make it, and she makes things all the time. "Easy-peasy!" But making her magnificent thing is anything but easy, and the girl tries and fails, repeatedly. Eventually, the girl gets really, really mad. She is so mad, in fact, that she quits. But after her dog convinces her to take a walk, she comes back to her project with renewed enthusiasm and manages to get it just right.

A New Coat for Anna by Harriet Ziefert; illustrated by Anita Lobel

New York, NY: Knopf, 1986

Even though there is no money, Anna's mother finds a way to make Anna a badly needed winter coat.

Now One Foot, Now the Other by Tomie de Paola

New York, NY: Putnam, 1981

When his grandfather suffers a stroke, Bobby teaches him to walk, just as his grandfather had once taught him.

Oh, the Places You'll Go by Dr. Seuss

New York, NY: Random House, 1990

This book offers advice in rhyme for proceeding in life; weathering fear, loneliness, and confusion; and being in charge of your actions.

The OK Book by Amy Rosenthal; illustrated by Tom Lichtenheld

New York, NY: HarperCollins, 2007

In this clever and literal play on words, OK is turned on its side, upside down, and right side up to show that being OK can really be quite great. Whether OK personifies an OK skipper, an OK climber, an OK lightning bug catcher, or an OK whatever there is to experience, OK is an OK place to be. And being OK just may lead to the discovery of what makes one great.

The Paperboy by Dav Pilkey

New York, NY: Orchard Books, 1996

A paperboy and his dog enjoy the quiet of the early morning as they go about their rounds.

Peep: A Little Book About Taking a Leap by Maria van Lieshout

New York, NY: Feiwel & Friends, 2009

Peep is a baby chick who follows his mother and sisters along the sidewalk, but when his sisters jump confidently off the edge, Peep hesitates. His reactions run the gamut from nervous to angry to terrified, and when he finally gulps and takes that leap, he's overjoyed at his own prowess. But new challenges always await; for Peep, it's the curb that he must climb next.

Someday by Ellen Spinelli; illustrated by Rosie Winstead

New York, NY: Dial Books for Young Readers, 2007

Goldie dreams of being a famous artist, an animal scientist, an archeologist, and much more. Each page alternates with "someday" and present day as she hones her skills she needs to make those goals happen.

Thank You, Mr. Falker by Patricia Polacco

New York, NY: Philomel Books, 1998

At first, Trisha loves school, but her difficulty learning to read makes her feel dumb, until, in the fifth grade, a new teacher helps her understand and overcome her problem.

The Very Busy Spider by Eric Carle

New York, NY: Philomel Books, 1984

The farm animals try to divert a busy little spider from spinning her web, but she persists and produces a thing of both beauty and usefulness. The pictures can be felt as well as seen.

The Very Quiet Cricket by Eric Carle

New York, NY: Philomel Books, 1990

A very quiet cricket who wants to rub his wings together and make a sound as do so many other animals finally achieves his wish. The cricket's sound is reproduced at the end of the book.

A Walk in the Rain With a Brain by Edward Hallowell; illustrated by Bill Mayer

New York, NY: HarperCollins, 2004

This story is about Lucy, a little girl who worries that she isn't smart enough, and a walking, talking cerebrum named Fred. When Lucy finds him, Fred is sitting forlornly in a puddle on a rainy day. He's lost, so Lucy decides to help him find his way back into his head. Along the way, the courtly cerebrum, who speaks in rhyming couplets, teaches and reassures Lucy that "everyone's smart/You just need to find out at what."

Wednesday Surprise by Eve Bunting; illustrated by Donald Carrick

New York, NY: Clarion Books, 1989

On Wednesday nights, when Grandma stays with Anna, everyone thinks she is teaching Anna to read.

What Do You Do With an Idea by Kobi Yamada

Seattle, WA: Compendium Kids, 2013

Whistle for Willie by Ezra Jack Keats

New York, NY: Viking Books for Young Readers, 1964

"Mr. Keats's illustrations boldly, colorfully capture the child, his city world, and the shimmering heat of a summer's day" (*New York Times*, 1964).

Young Frank, Architect by Frank Viva

New York, NY: Abrams Books for Young Readers, 2013

Frank lives with his grandfather and aspires to be an architect. His attempts to create a toilet-paper-roll chair and wiggly book skyscraper are initially dismissed by his grandfather, until the two visit the Museum of Modern Art and discover the creative aspects behind architecture and art. The message is that you can accomplish anything if you put your mind to it, whether conventional or creative.

Folktales and Fables

The Ant and the Grasshopper by Aesop

The Lion and the Mouse by Aesop

The Tortoise and the Hare by Aesop

The Little Red Hen

The Three Little Pigs

3–6

Amazing Grace by Mary Hoffman; illustrated by Caroline Binch

New York, NY: Dial Books for Young Readers, 1991

Although a classmate says that she cannot play Peter Pan in the school play because she is black, *Grace* discovers that she can do anything she sets her mind to.

Charlotte's Web by E. B. White; illustrated by Garth Williams

New York, NY: HarperCollins, 2006

Wilbur the pig is desolate when he discovers that he is destined to be the farmer's Christmas dinner, until his spider friend Charlotte decides to help him.

Dominic by William Steig

New York, NY: Farrar, Straus and Giroux, 1972

El Chino by Allen Say

Boston, MA: Houghton Mifflin, 1990

This is a biography of Bill Wong, a Chinese American who became a famous bullfighter in Spain.

Margaret's Moves by Berniece Rabe; illustrated by Julie Downing

New York, NY: Dutton, 1987

Nine-year-old Margaret, confined to a wheelchair by spina bifida, longs for a new, lightweight "sportsmodel" chair so that she can speed around as fast as the athletic brother with whom she has an ongoing rivalry.

Me and My Little Brain by John D. Fitzgerald; illustrated by Mercer Mayer

New York, NY: Dial Books for Young Readers, 1971

In the absence of his older brother, the Great Brain, J. D. finds that his own little elastic brain can accomplish feats on a somewhat lesser scale.

My Side of the Mountain by Jean Craighead George

New York, NY: E. P. Dutton, 1991

A city dweller learns to survive in the wilderness through determination, research, and effort.

On a Beam of Light by Jennifer Berne

San Francisco, CA: Chronicle Books, 2013

This is an accessible story about the life of Albert Einstein as a learner whose language was delayed and everyone feared he would never be able to learn. It highlights his different path to learning and his nature of always questioning along the way.

Stone Fox by John Reynolds Gardiner; illustrated by Marcia Sewall

New York, NY: Harper Trophy, 2003

Little Willie hopes to pay the back taxes on his grandfather's farm with the purse from a dog sled race he enters.

Thank You, Mr. Falker by Patricia Polacco

New York, NY: Philomel Books, 1998

At first, Trisha loves school, but her difficulty learning to read makes her feel dumb, until, in the fifth grade, a new teacher helps her understand and overcome her problem.

The Trumpet of the Swan by E. B. White

New York, NY: HarperCollins, 2000

The main character embodies all elements of effective effort.

Wilma Unlimited: How Wilma Rudolph Became the World's Fastest Woman by Kathleen Krull; illustrated by David Diaz

San Diego, CA: Harcourt Brace, 1996

This is a biography of the African American woman who overcame crippling polio as a child to become the first woman to win three gold medals in track in a single Olympics.

Your Fantastic Elastic Brain by JoAnn Deak; illustrated by Sarah Ackerley

Belvedere, CA: Little Pickle Press, 2010

This innovative book helps children understand how their brain is structured, what functions it performs, and then, most importantly, how they can stretch and grow their brains. The language is fun and easy enough for even young kids to follow along.

5–8

Athlete vs. Mathlete by W. C. Mack

New York, NY: Bloomsbury Children's Books, 2013

Owen Evans lights up the scoreboards. His brother, Russell, rocks the school boards. These twin brothers couldn't be more different. They've long kept the peace by going their separate ways, but all that is about to change. The new basketball coach recruits Russell for the seventh-grade team, and a jealous Owen has to fight to stay in the game. When someone tries to steal Russell's spot as captain of the mathlete team, will the two be able to put aside their differences in order to save his position? Or will they be sidelined?

Call It Courage by Armstrong Sperry

New York, NY: Aladdin Books, 1990

Mafatu, a young Polynesian boy whose name means Stout Heart, overcomes his terrible fear of the sea and proves his courage to himself and his people.

Dragonwings by Laurence Yep

Santa Barbara, CA: Cornerstone Books, 1975

In the early 20th century, a young Chinese boy joins his father in San Francisco and helps him realize his dream of making a flying machine.

Holes by Louis Sacher

New York, NY: Random House, 1998

Stanley Yelnats is under a curse, a curse that began with his no-good, dirty-rotten, pig-stealing great-great-grandfather and has since followed generations of Yelnatses. Now Stanley has been unjustly sent to a boys' detention center, Camp Green Lake, where the boys build character by spending all day, every day digging holes exactly five feet wide and five feet deep. There is no lake at Camp Green Lake. But there are an awful lot of holes.

Johnny Tremain by Esther Forbes; illustrated by Lynd Ward

New York, NY: Yearling Book, 2005

A young boy encounters many historical figures as he works as a horse boy for the local newspaper.

On the Frontier With Mr. Audubon by Barbara Brenner

New York, NY: Coward, McCann & Geoghegan, 1977

Audubon's young apprentice describes the experiences he shared with his master during their 18-month trip down the Mississippi studying and drawing the birds they found along the way.

Sasquatch in the Paint by Kareem Abdul-Jabbar

New York, NY: Disney-Hyperion Books, 2013

Theo Rollins had been one of the most inconspicuous members of his class until he experienced a six-inch growth spurt before the start of eighth grade. Now, Coach Mandrake wants to build his entire offense around him, much to the dismay of the other team members because Theo is a science geek who stinks at basketball. The first game he plays is a disaster, and, after a spectator makes a racist comment causing him to make a costly mistake, a classmate named Rain gives him the nickname "Sasquatch." Later, Theo discovers that there is more to Rain than meets the eye. Faced with dismissal from the "Brain Train," the school's Aca-lympic team, because of the time he spends on basketball, Theo must make an important decision about his future. This is a heart-warming story about growing up, facing down bullies, and learning what true friendship is all about.

The Sign of the Beaver by Elizabeth George Speare

New York, NY: Yearling Book, 2005

Left alone to guard the family's wilderness home in 18th-century Maine, a boy is hard-pressed to survive until local Indians teach him their skills.

The Story of Jackie Robinson, Bravest Man in Baseball by Margaret Davidson; illustrated by Floyd Cooper

New York, NY: Dell, 1988

This book examines the life of the talented black athlete who broke the color barrier in Major League Baseball by joining the Brooklyn Dodgers in 1947.

Walk Two Moons by Sharon Creech

New York, NY: HarperCollins, 1994

After her mother leaves home suddenly, 13-year-old Sal and her grand-parents take a car trip retracing her mother's route. Along the way, Sal recounts the story of her friend Phoebe, whose mother also left.

Where the Lilies Bloom by Vera and Bill Cleaver; illustrated by Jim Spanfeller

Philadelphia, PA: J. B. Lippincott, 1969

In the Great Smoky Mountains region, a 14-year-old girl struggles to keep her family together after their father dies.

Where the Red Fern Grows: The Story of Two Dogs and a Boy by Wilson Rawls

Austin, TX: Holt, Rinehart and Winston, 2000

A young boy living in the Ozarks achieves his heart's desire when he becomes the owner of two redbone hounds and teaches them to be champion hunters.

YOUNG ADULT AND ADULT

Angela's Ashes by Frank McCourt

New York, NY: Scribner, 1996

This is a memoir of the author's miserable childhood growing up in the perpetually damp country of Ireland, with the stereotypically long-suffering mother and drunken father who nurtures in his son an appetite for stories.

A Beautiful Mind by Sylvia Nasar

New York, NY: Faber and Faber, 1999

This biography chronicles the life of mathematician John Forbes Nash Jr. and discusses his contributions to the study of economics, his illegitimate child, his bouts with schizophrenia, and his Nobel Prize–winning theories.

Lost on a Mountain in Maine by Donn Fendler

New York, NY: HarperCollins Children's, 2013

This is a true story about 12-year-old Donn Fendler, who, when he gets tired of waiting for his father and brothers to join him on the summit of Maine's highest peak, decides to find his own way back to camp.

But Donn doesn't expect a fast-moving fog to obscure his path, knocking him completely off course. He doesn't count on falling down an embankment that hides him from sight. And he never could have imagined taking a wrong turn that leaves him alone to wander aimlessly for nearly 2 weeks in the empty mountain wilderness.

A Million Little Pieces by James Frey

New York, NY: N. A. Talese/Doubleday, 2003

This book presents the author's firsthand account of his recovery from drug and alcohol addiction, beginning with his enrollment in a Minnesota rehabilitation center after a 2-week blackout and ending with his rejection of all 12-step programs.

Three Letters From Teddy and Other Stories by Elizabeth Silance Ballard

Virginia Beach, VA: Eslyn, 2000

The title story is about the special relationship between a teacher and an underachieving fifth-grader.

In the Time of the Butterflies by Julia Alvarez

Chapel Hill, NC: Algonquin Books, 1994

This is a fictionalized account of four sisters in the Dominican Republic under the dictatorship of General Trujillo.

Index